REHANA ROSSOUW

PREDATOR POLITICS

Mabuza, Fred Daniel and the Great Land Scam

This book was made possible by a Henry Nxumalo Grant for Investigative Journalism, administered by WITS Journalism.

First published by Jacana Media (Pty) Ltd in 2020

10 Orange Street
Sunnyside
Auckland Park 2092
South Africa
+2711 628 3200
www.jacana.co.za

© Rehana Rossouw, 2020
Cover image: Gallo Images/Tebogo Letsie

All rights reserved.

ISBN 978-1-4314-3002-4

Cover design by publicide
Editing by Russell Martin
Proofreading by Lara Jacob
Indexing by Megan Mance
Layout by Aimèe Armstrong
Set in Janson Mt Std 12/14.5pt
Printed and bound by ABC Press, Cape Town
Job no. 003707

See a complete list of Jacana titles at www.jacana.co.za

REHANA ROSSOUW

PREDATOR POLITICS

Mabuza, Fred Daniel and the Great Land Scam

'Our experience had made us acutely aware of the possible dangers of a government that is neither transparent nor accountable. To this end our Constitution contains several mechanisms to ensure that government will not be part of the problem, but part of the solution…'

Nelson Mandela, speech at the African Regional Workshop of the International Ombudsman Institution, 1996

Contents

Preface   vii

1	Standing his ground	1
2	The library of nature	7
3	The race to the bottom	13
4	The Dolphin deal	21
5	In the lion's den	33
6	The One&Only deal	43
7	Hyenas gather	49
8	Blow the house down	59
9	Pariah town	71
10	The animals came in	77
11	A heist and a hijack	91
12	The gatekeeper	105
13	Fences and defences	117
14	Worlds apart	125
15	World-class corruption	143
16	The path to power	159
17	Take it to the president	169
18	You are not alone	183
19	Protection and retaliation	197

20	The land turns to dust	219
21	Time to say goodbye	227

Index 235

Preface

Picture a game reserve: a valley ablaze with late-summer grass bowed in homage to an approaching storm. A circle of mountains fades under heavy clouds pouring down into its amphitheatre. Herds of animals snort and shuffle as they test the wind.

Fred Daniel built the Nkomazi Wilderness Reserve with his dreams, commitment and sweat. He bought 89 farms between Badplaas and Barberton in southern Mpumalanga; some of them degraded by decades of asbestos mining and poor agricultural practices. He healed the land by clearing it and rehabilitating its ecosystems and habitats. Wild animals returned and restored it to the balance of nature. Foreign and local investors pledged to build luxury resorts on the reserve, one of them rating it as a 'unique location of outstanding natural beauty'.

The land has a spectacular geological heritage, drawing scientists from across the globe to study the first sparks of life on earth. The Barberton Mountains are the oldest chain on the planet. Its rocks preserve ancient biological fossils, including the last universal common ancestor of all living things. Fred built a project to host science conferences and school groups. He built a library of nature to teach people to preserve the environment for the benefit of all life.

Fred was appalled by the soaring levels of unemployment in the area. As farms withered to dust and mines closed, tens of thousands of people were thrust into poverty. His tourism enterprise had the potential to create hundreds of permanent jobs, many requiring training and skill. His neighbours were poor people, restored to their land with the government's assistance but given few resources to make a living.

Corruption is a cancer that destroys the lifeblood of taxpayer funds aimed at improving the lives of the poor. Fred learnt, the hard way, that graft is played on a killing field in Mpumalanga. He and his partners are suing the government for damages, claiming that a campaign of corruption-related retaliation was unleashed against them, his family and employees.

This story has largely been told – to audiences so bombarded by theft of public funds in South Africa that some scams have been forgotten. An estimated R1.5 trillion was lost to corruption during Jacob Zuma's second term as president, a tragedy reported by whistleblowers, journalists, auditors, forensic investigators, lawyers, judges and the public protector.

Former judge Willem Heath says Fred should be commended for standing up against 'a vulgar case of corruption'. His damages court case, initially scheduled to be heard in 2020, has huge potential to reveal how corrupt politicians abused public resources and their positions of trust and power.

Forensic investigator Paul O'Sullivan gathered evidence of systemic corruption in Mpumalanga, but to date no politicians have been successfully prosecuted. Business in Badplaas is 'severely obstructed by the cover-up of rampant corruption, cronyism and a dysfunctional government,' he says. 'Fred suffered immensely due to a sustained and well-orchestrated campaign of vilification, harassment, victimisation, violence, damage to property and death threats, all financed by the gross misappropriation of state resources.'

Researcher and Right2Know activist Dale McKinley says the corruption and mismanagement Fred endured 'sits like a leaden weight on people's lives, hopes and dreams. This is a history of the accumulated scourge of deep-seated political, institutional, governance and socio-economic problems and strife in Badplaas that continues to cast dark clouds across its beautiful landscape. It is a history that should have resonance across our country and the world because, at the centre of those clouds, is a hybrid political–business mafia who have shown time and again that they are really only interested in one thing: the accumulation of power and money at all costs.'

This book was supported by a Henry Nxumalo Grant, which is funded by the Millennium Trust and managed by the Wits Journalism Department. It is dedicated to all the journalists who tell stories that hold the political mafia to account.

REHANA ROSSOUW
MAY 2020

1
Standing his ground

The late winter sunshine evaporates in the chill, but red blooms flush up Fred Daniel's cheeks and settle on his forehead. It is August 2019, and in 11 months his massive damages claim against the South African government was due to be heard in the North Gauteng High Court. From his perch on the edge of his seat, Fred steals glances at the unlocked palisade gate at the end of the driveway from which his security gate motor was stolen overnight. He can't risk breaches in his home security. He is a whistleblower against corruption and a plaintiff in a damages claim amounting to just over R1 billion against politicians, government departments, agencies and their officials. He is exposing several rackets in Mpumalanga where many people who stood their ground against corruption were poisoned or gunned down. The Daniel family's location can't be disclosed.

Fred has witnessed how corruption cripples service delivery, increases unemployment, exacerbates poverty and widens the huge disparity between rich and poor. These social ills fuel crime – South Africa has one of the highest rates of violent crime in the world: around 58 people are murdered every day.

What scares him more than the dire crime rate is the target

on his back, drawn by politicians seeking to protect themselves and their business partners from the legal consequences of their misdeeds. Fred blew the whistle on land grabs that sucked the life out of taxpayer-funded programmes aimed at poor rural citizens. He sought protection from the police, the National Prosecuting Authority, the Special Investigating Unit and the Zondo Commission – to no avail. 'There is nothing scarier than a government coming after its citizens, using state resources and abusing their entrusted power,' he says.

The defendants in his damages claim include Deputy President David Dabede Mabuza, cited in his previous positions as Mpumalanga premier and member of executive council (MEC) for agriculture and land affairs. In his book, aptly titled *Eerie Assignment*, veteran *City Press* reporter Sizwe sama Yende writes that, as premier, Mabuza presided over 'a state infiltrated by quasi-politicians who subverted laws and policies with the sole intent of getting unbridled power to enrich themselves from the well of government resources'.

Fred's court action is based on his claim of corruption-related harassment – much of it already exposed in forensic reports, police investigations, the Carolina Magistrate's Court, the North Gauteng High Court and the Land Claims Court in Randburg, Gauteng and found to be credible. Corrupt politicians, government officials and their private sector enablers drove him off his 39,000-hectare conservation and tourism project between Badplaas and Barberton in southern Mpumalanga. It is a site of global historical and scientific importance, packed with ecological and cultural treasures and filled with natural wonders. He claims that the land has been substantially damaged as a result of the corruption.

The Daniel family has faced several violent attacks over the past decade and a half; their nerves are frayed. Shaken by an assassination attempt in November 2018, Fred, Linda and their 10-year-old son Jesse left their home six months later.

Although he lives by the axiom that failure is never an option, Fred had to throw in the towel. 'With the damages claim coming down on the fraudsters like a freight train, the harassment escalated, and I was advised by forensic and medical experts to get out of the firing line,' he says. 'I could no longer gamble with my family's lives and their future. I also realised that the massive effort I was putting into investing in Mpumalanga was a waste of time and getting me nowhere.'

Their new house is still a work in progress, but they have renovated it substantially. Fred and Linda are hard at work in the garden; it's their decompression and de-stressing zone. He is eagerly awaiting the spring rains that will nurture the grass seed he scattered in the brown patches of soil. She planted flowers and rose bushes and is planning a vegetable garden that she hopes will be as prolific as the one at their Mpumalanga home.

With the click of a remote button, lights illuminate their garden at night. 'It's so effective that you can read a newspaper outside,' Fred says. Motion sensors and hidden cameras in the garden record movement. The family tends to keep indoors after dark, locked behind formidable doors. A yappy small dog sleeps on Jesse's bed and a pack of large dogs roam the property.

Thick burglar bars stripe all the windows. The family sleep behind self-locking thick steel doors. In the main bedroom, a tall steel gun-safe is within reaching distance of the bed. Fred unlocks it and hauls out a semi-automatic shotgun (he has a valid licence) and a bullet harness filled with shells. He reaches into the safe again and brings out a box of 500 bullets. 'I have enough to start a war,' he says with a faint smile on his lips.

'There's a real risk that I will be permanently censored, either through protracted attempts by the government to delay justice, or by assassination. With either outcome, my story will be buried. I can't withhold this truth, it's too ghastly to allow that to happen. The truth, and my reputation, cannot be permanently smeared or covered up.'

Over the past 15 years, Fred has won 22 court cases against politicians, government officials, businessmen and journalists – all associated with his damages action. The North Gauteng High Court has granted him a trial; this is the first time the issues will be ventilated through testimony. The only result of his past legal victories was an escalation in the violence and harassment. 'It wasn't the corruption that drove me out of the province, although its effects were corrosive. It was the relentless retaliation that hurt my business and my family, and the absence of government protection. It was unleashed to protect vested interests and their ill-gotten gains so as to prevent a light from shining on them.'

His damages claim stems from events that followed his exposure of land scams concocted by politicians, government officials and businessmen. He is claiming compensation for the intimidation and violence that he faced, the damage to his assets and infrastructure, and the loss of his and his partners' investments and profits. He alleges in his court papers that the scam was orchestrated by Mabuza, working in cahoots with the provincial land claims commissioner and businessmen.

Deputy judge president of the Gauteng high court Aubrey Ledwaba set down a special trial from 27 July to 28 August 2020 to hear Fred and his business partners' R1 billion claim. Advocates representing the defendants insisted on a lengthy trial. Until recently, politicians defended themselves at corruption trials on a luxurious scale – D.D. Mabuza has been represented by the priciest senior advocates and state and private attorneys, all paid from the public purse. But it is no longer guaranteed that the state will pay the millions of rand that politicians squander as they attempt to side-step legal accountability for their actions. In December 2018 Judge Ledwaba ruled that former president Jacob Zuma could no longer receive state funding for the advocates and lawyers defending him at his corruption trial.

Advocate André Ferreira SC, who represents many of the defendants, also acts for Mabuza in his personal capacity. The deputy president has a busy schedule and his availability will have an impact on the trial date, Ferreira has warned. Is this an example of the common strategy among African National Congress (ANC) politicians facing corruption allegations to use every tactic possible to delay their day in court? State attorney Nelson Govender says Mabuza applied for state funding for his personal attorney, Ian Small-Smith, and to appoint Advocate Mike Hellens SC, who has often appeared for Zuma. Small-Smith says he is not the attorney on record for Fred's damages claim, and has not been paid by either Mabuza or the state.

From a distance, Fred appears to be an archetypal white farmer. At his home office, his daily uniform is shorts with a golf shirt tucked in at the hips. His thighs are as wide as a Springbok rugby player's. His takkies are dusty and nondescript. But he's no longer striding the plains and kloofs of his game reserve in Mpumalanga. Fred is stuck at a desk poring over thousands of pages of legal and business documents.

He is fluently bilingual; he can discuss science, conservation, religion, politics and much more in English and Afrikaans – with an endearing lisp. He is an avid reader of *City Press* and the *Mail & Guardian*, but he is no lefty. Fred was fiercely committed to South Africa after democracy arrived in 1994, until his efforts to build a spectacular teaching environment in a nature reserve were spurned.

The damages claim, brought by Fred in 2010, is ripe for hearing. The tide has turned in the struggle against corruption. The Zondo Commission of Inquiry into Allegations of State Capture has unmasked reckless mismanagement of the state, allowing for its capture and looting by rapacious businessmen. Marianne Merten reported in the *Daily Maverick* that the cost of state capture hovered around R1.5 trillion during the second term of the Zuma administration. 'That's just short of the R1.8 trillion budget for 2019,' she wrote. 'Put differently: state capture wiped out a third of South Africa's R4.9 trillion gross domestic product, or effectively annihilated four months of all labour and productivity of all South Africans, from hawkers selling sweets outside schools to boardroom jockeys.'

Listening to witnesses at his inquiry, Deputy Judge President Raymond Zondo shakes his head and says repeatedly, 'We can't go on like this. We have to ensure this never happens again.' He sighs heavily and often, especially when he adjourns for composure breaks when weeping former public servants relate how they attempted to put the brakes on corruption and were hounded out of government.

Fred was booked off from work for six months until the end of December 2019 by Nelspruit psychiatrist Dr L.T. Brauteseth, who wrote a report that will be submitted to the high court. It concluded that Fred was experiencing high levels of stress with 'recurrent, unwanted and distressing memories of the multiple traumatic events of the preceding ten years; recurrent flashbacks and reliving past traumas; upsetting dreams and nightmares; severe emotional distress; and situational panic attacks and physical reactions to intrusive recollections of traumatic events'. Dr Brauteseth diagnosed an anxiety disorder – post-traumatic stress disorder (PTSD). He prescribed anti-anxiety medicines and recommended that Fred leave Mpumalanga.

When the family moved, Fred packed every record of his business and legal battles into boxes. At their new home, he had the roof lifted by builders to create a 'war room' upstairs. A conference table that seats 10 people dominates the space. In the middle of the table is a wooden stand with a gold plaque, inscribed 'Nkomazi Wilderness'. A pair of rhino horns, studded with coarse brown and grey hair, is mounted on the stand. It was taken from the first rhino Fred introduced to his game reserve. The rhino fell down a ditch and twisted its colon. A vet performed emergency surgery, but the animal died a few days later.

The war room's walls are lined with bookshelves, and there are piles of heavy hardcover books scattered around. The shelves contain the best of the library he built on his reserve, crammed with titles by the world's top scientists and environmentalists. Stacks of cabinets in Fred's office, which leads off the war room, are filled with lever arch files, all neatly labelled, detailing the construction of his business and its spiteful destruction.

'Remaining silent about corruption or environmental degradation is not an option,' Fred says. 'The law requires all South African citizens to blow the whistle on corruption and to take care of the environment. It does, however, take courage to stand up against political corruption as there are serious risks to career, reputation and even personal safety for doing so. But if you love your country, this is not a good enough reason to avert your eyes, keep your mouth shut and suffer no consequences.'

'Despite the politicians, civil servants, conservation officials and big polluters knowing exactly the damage they were causing, they chose to chase profits. They have blood on their hands.'

2

The library of nature

Human behaviour, particularly the tendency to do business as usual, has led to the serious environmental problems facing the planet, Fred believes. He warns that politicians can't be trusted to protect the planet for the common good of all. 'Their greed trips up their responsibility,' he says. 'The earth's resources are needed to support life, but they are being raped, ravaged and consumed at a reckless rate to satisfy the greed of a few.'

Fred says his concern for the environment was sparked by a primary school teacher in 1974, who warned that, unless his generation took action to limit the human impact on the planet's resources, all life on earth would be in peril. A global oil crisis, which crippled supplies and sent prices soaring, had hit a few months earlier. 'I remembered my father driving slowly to cut down on his petrol use,' he says. 'So this warning from my teacher had a profound effect on my views about human behaviour in relation to the truth, business and the environment.'

He began reading about conservation and discovered Rachel Carson's ground-breaking book, *Silent Spring*, which led to the banning of the pesticide DDT in America. Fred was, and remains, struck by Carson's observation: 'Over increasingly large areas of the United States, spring now comes unheralded by the return of the birds, and the early mornings are strangely silent where once they were filled with the beauty of birdsong.'

He can recite by chapter and verse the history of the Anthropocene era, marked by the significant human impact on the earth's geology and ecosystems. Scientists had first warned in the early 19th century about the greenhouse effect, caused by rising carbon dioxide levels in the atmosphere. Decades later they realised that this pollution was leading to catastrophic global warming.

'We now face the greatest challenge in the history of the human race,' Fred says. 'There is a call to arms to halt, stem and reverse the ecological crisis as a matter of priority. But in this important endeavour, we are held back by corruption. Political hyenas have damaged the environment and stolen natural treasures from the generations to come. Corruption should be made a crime against the people.

'The rate at which the planet's natural resources are being stripped is leading to a rapid loss of biodiversity. Increasing levels of pollution have raised global temperatures and threaten the existence of all life on earth. The world is now confronted with an oh-shit moment, like the one I experienced in Mr Hand's classroom.'

To feed his growing interest in the environment, Fred's high school subjects included biology, geography and agricultural science. In 1982, he went to Rhodes University where he studied business administration, economics, accounting, geology and chemistry. He was forced to drop out halfway through his second year as his father could no longer fund his studies.

The South African Defence Force called Fred up after he quit university; studying had been a valid reason for deferring his compulsory national service. He was a court orderly throughout his national service, stationed first at the Johannesburg Magistrate's Court. In May 1987, Fred went into an office to give documents to a friend he had made at the court. Minutes after he left the room, a limpet bomb planted by the ANC's military wing Umkhonto weSizwe (MK) exploded. Half an hour later, a car bomb detonated outside the court. Three policemen died and 15 civilians were injured. Fred is still haunted by memories of that day.

After he completed his national service, Fred went to work with his father, Fred Daniel senior, who had been a game ranger until he discovered the strategic mineral fluorspar in the Richtersveld. He held vast mineral rights in the area and operated the Fluorspar Valley Mine. The Daniel family house stood on the bank of a riverbed near the mine. Fred senior was also involved in alluvial diamond mining on the Orange River in Namaqualand and later exported coal from South Africa, developed mining concessions in Kenya and Zambia and exported precious metals and minerals to Japan.

Fred settled in Johannesburg and, in 1992, built an advertising company, Adnamics, which provided above- and below-the-line advertising. His employees designed and manufactured billboards, provided copywriting services and placed advertisements in magazines and newspapers. He sold the company a year later.

In 1995, he established an IT company, which developed satellite tracking systems, wireless communications technologies, radio networks and radio transmitters. These four technologies were patented worldwide. He soon acquired big clients. Fred built a comfortable life in a neo-Georgian mansion in Bryanston. In 1998, he sold the technology and patents to a British consortium and founded the Fairview Investment Trust, which focuses on sustainable tourism and conservation projects. Fred says he had made enough money to choose what he wanted to do with the rest of his life and opted to embark on his 'true passion': the conservation of the natural world.

Fred believes that people have a warped understanding about technology and its uses. 'The continued belief in the wrong notions makes it even more dangerous,' he explains, 'especially where our sense of moral responsibility to our fellow travellers – human and non-human – is concerned. Scientific literacy and critical thinking are not just tools for professional scientists; they are basic life skills as vital to our personal and intellectual growth as reading, writing and arithmetic.'

'The fundamentals of scientific inquiry and critical thinking are concepts that lie well within the bounds of understanding by ordinary people. The fact that so many people don't understand science is the failure of the education system, not the students. Today's muddied thinking on issues of evolution and global warming is a result of the unreliability of information and the failure to teach everyone about nature.'

By 2009, many experts were warning that global warming had arrived at a faster and more dangerous pace than anticipated. By 2018, huge damage from droughts, floods, cyclones, wildfires and declines in wildlife had occurred sooner than scientists had predicted – and at much lower carbon dioxide levels than they expected.

The World Health Organization warns that carbon dioxide pollution increases the risk of stroke, heart disease, lung cancer and acute respiratory diseases. At the end of 2018, Mpumalanga had the highest levels of air pollution in the world, Greenpeace reported. It had the highest nitrogen dioxide levels measured across six continents. Coal mines, transport and Eskom's 12 coal-fired power stations were the biggest sources of the pollution in the province. In 2018, air pollution killed 550 people and hospitalised about 117,200 in Mpumalanga.

Fred opens the *Mail & Guardian* every Friday and turns to page two for the weekly report on the level of carbon dioxide pollution in the atmosphere. It is still climbing and is currently 370 ppm (parts per million). Scientists warn that life on earth will be threatened if it rises to 450 ppm. Fred recites their predictions that the increasing global temperatures will lead to 'massive crop failures, climate instability, mass extinctions and the mass migration of people as the polar ice caps melt and the seas rise to inundate coastal cities like Cape Town, Venice, New York and London.'

Fred believes that his generation fail their children when they cannot agree on what is true, what threatens life on earth and what should be done about it. 'What science has revealed about the nature of humankind – how great our similarities and how trivial the differences – is knowledge that completely destroys all claims to intellectual, racial or ethnic superiority. Anyone who truly understands the science of evolution would no more look upon their fellow human beings with disdain than they would kill an animal for sport.'

The library that Fred built on his Mpumalanga reserve to feed the minds of visiting school pupils and scientists contains several titles questioning whether science has replaced God. 'It is not true that the scientific outlook is emotionally impoverished and spiritually bankrupt,' he says. 'There is space for passion, poetry and love in the dispassionate mindset ruled by facts. There is much love around us: romantic love, love for our children, love for nature, love for our communities and love for our countries. But love also needs understanding. A library full of books allows ordinary people to stand on the shoulders of giants. We discover truth by building on previous discoveries.'

Fred was decades ahead of many of his peers in appreciating the threat humanity posed to the rest of earth's inhabitants. He built his dream project and healed 39,000 hectares of land in Mpumalanga before scientists reached consensus on human culpability for global warming. His project was derailed by corruption but his self-taught philosophy will not allow him to quit.

'The future of the human race is finely balanced right now,' Fred says. 'There is a race between the acquisition of knowledge and self-destruction. Like Adam and Eve, we acquired too much knowledge too fast and now we cannot cope with the power. Will this lead to our destruction or will we learn to live in harmony with other life forms on this planet?'

'Battling corruption for more than a decade meant that we had to divert our attention from caring for the environment. As a result, we are now well on our way to being too late to do anything about it. But when it comes to protecting life on earth and the environment for future generations, failure is not an option.'

Fred's decade-long battle against corruption has been joined by many others. The tide has turned against the ravenous political predators devouring his dream and the futures of many South Africans. He says he will not pause in his determination to present the best case he can.

'I set many precedents in the courts,' Fred says, 'but all I wanted was for civil servants to do their jobs. To do what it says in the Constitution. Why should I have to spend years in court and millions of rand to get them to do their jobs?'

Fred said that although he was promised investment of R2.6 billion in Nkomazi for high-end tourism, he had planned to preserve its teaching environment as a gift to the nation. 'I didn't need that money. I didn't want that money,' he says. 'It was an environmental project with the purpose of teaching people to be better custodians of the world. I wanted to teach people that they are part of nature, not apart from nature. It was my contribution to the world, to the cause of saving the planet.'

You can cut a slice off and chew on his frustration – it's thick and raw.

3

The race to the bottom

Fred came to Mpumalanga to invest in the rainbow nation. Using the money he had earned from the sale of his technology company, he spent millions of rand buying farms in Mpumalanga for conservation and a tourism business. In doing so, he trusted Nelson Mandela's African National Congress to keep their promises, and believed that civil servants served the best interests of the country and all citizens.

'It was a shock to discover that politicians had captured the state – its departments, processes and law enforcement – to repurpose the civil service,' he says. 'They did this to divert public funds to themselves at the expense of service delivery and to shield themselves from accountability.' Politicians were seldom prosecuted – many were instead promoted to the National Assembly or high office in the ANC headquarters after their scams were exposed – and the looting escalated from millions of rand to billions.

According to Auditor General Kimi Makwetu, Mpumalanga

lost R2.73 billion in irregular expenditure in the 2018/2019 financial year. Conducting audits in the province is a fraught business. Alice Muller, acting national audit leader at the auditor-general's office, might have been exaggerating when she told *Business Day* reporter Linda Ensor that the municipal manager at the Victor Khanye local municipality had warned the government's audit team that they could be kidnapped because of their probes into supply chain management tenders but many people believed this. Members of an audit team were asked by employees at the Msukaligwa local municipality what routes they took when they drove home.

At a media briefing in Johannesburg on the national and provincial government audit outcomes, Makwetu said only 18 per cent of Mpumalanga government departments and municipalities received clean audits in 2018/2019. Up to 76 per cent of their financial statements contained information that was untrue. In his annual report Makwetu warned about the emerging risk of increased litigation and claims. More than a third of departments had legal claims against them amounting to more than 10 per cent of their annual budgets.

The fuming auditor general said municipalities were being used 'as piggy banks to finance the operations of political parties and the lifestyles of politicians and their top management. The looting at state-owned entities, in government departments, intelligence, everywhere – from the president, from the ANC, from the top six officials and the national executive committee of the ANC – all of this is permitted and sometimes encouraged by them. People get phone calls and it is called a mandate that they must take an amount of money and give it to someone. Zondo is discussing that. What we now need is to recognise that we are busy finishing off this country.'

Mpumalanga was created in 1994, carved out of what was once the Eastern Transvaal and incorporating several apartheid-era homelands, formerly 'native reserves' used by successive white governments as labour reservoirs and dumping grounds for the unemployed, the elderly and the unwanted. The KaNgwane homeland was absorbed into Mpumalanga in 1994, as well as parts of Gazankulu and Lebowa. These so-called self-governing territories had never been transparent and financially accountable, and became bywords for corruption and inefficiency. In the homelands, bribery was prolific in government departments. Officials extorted payments from homeland 'citizens' for permits and government grants. Public housing officials evicted thousands of people to make way for residents who paid bribes to councillors to secure housing.

After the end of apartheid, about 400,000 former functionaries of the homelands were absorbed into the democratic government, most of them in provincial governments. While these provincial governments have no significant sources of independent finance and their budgets are allocated from central government, the disbursement of funds at the provincial level gives their politicians considerable real power.

As the political scientist Tom Lodge remarks in *South African Politics since 1994*, 'Political corruption in the strict sense of venality amongst elected politicians has been most evident in provincial administrations, notably in Mpumalanga. Some of the difficulties can be explained by the ANC's organisational character in the provinces, where it is often a disparate and awkward sum of its parts. The ANC between 1990 and 1994 expanded its organised following very rapidly and in doing so incorporated a multitude of different political cultures as well as contrasting styles of political leadership.

'This was an especially obvious feature of rural provinces, in which governments reflected uneasy coalitions of old-style homeland bosses, veterans of the militant and militaristic youth congresses which mushroomed in the 1980s, and technocrats returned from exile. Mpumalanga's MEC for safety and security (until his resignation in 1997 in a car licensing scandal) was the former police minister of KwaNdebele homeland, Steve Mabona. Such people, when moving into the ANC, often brought with them intact their patronage networks as well as grandiose expectations of privilege and deference.'

In Mpumalanga, the ANC elected Mathews Phosa as its chairman and first premier after the 1994 elections. Phosa, an attorney by profession, was among the first exiled members of the ANC to enter South Africa in 1990 to start discussions with the National Party. As the head of the ANC's legal department, he played an important role in the negotiations to dismantle apartheid.

Corruption scandals brewed in Mpumalanga soon after the first tranche of funding arrived from national government. Whistleblowers found themselves out in the cold as the ANC covered up the malfeasance of its members and deployees. Billy Cobbett, director general of the national department of housing, was fired in 1997 allegedly after asking the auditor general to investigate a suspicious housing project. The R185-million Mpumalanga Rural Housing Project – at the time the largest government housing scheme – was awarded to a company that wasn't registered, Motheo Construction. It is alleged that housing minister Sankie Mthembi-Mahanyele, complained to senior ANC officials that Cobbett was frustrating attempts to promote black economic empowerment (Mthembi-Mahanyele denies the allegations). Former MK commissar Thandi Ndlovu, who had worked in exile with the housing minister and Thabo Mbeki, owned Motheo Construction. Her company was eventually registered months after it received the contract – and after Cobbett was fired.

Mpumalanga's first education MEC, D.D. Mabuza – currently South Africa's deputy president – was mired in scandal during his first year in office. School principals were appropriating money budgeted for school meals, sharing it with members of their staff and depriving needy children of food. Mabuza said that he had 'tried to avoid taking drastic action while strengthening the system' but conceded that the corruption was embarrassing.

Mabuza, who had previously been a maths teacher and school principal in the KaNgwane homeland, announced in 1998 that Mpumalanga's matric pass rate had soared from 51 per cent to an astounding 71 per cent. An August 2018 *New York Times* article by Norimitsu Onishi and Selam Gebrekidan alleges that Phosa fired him in response to the bald-faced lie – cooked up in Mabuza's home with the help of department of education bureaucrats, some of whom were also dismissed and a statement which Mabuza has not seen fit to challenge so far.

Phosa's successor as premier, Ndaweni Mahlangu, brought Mabuza back from the cold into his cabinet after memorably asserting: 'It is acceptable for politicians to lie. It is nothing new. Many politicians publicly deny they did certain things but then later admit to them. It is accepted, and it is not unusual anywhere in the world. It wasn't the end of Bill Clinton's life and I personally don't find it to be a very bad thing.'

Despite the many scandals during his tenure as MEC for education in Mpumalanga, the only consequence Mabuza faced after Phosa dismissed him was rapid advancement up the ranks of the ANC. He became the MEC for housing in Mpumalanga in 1999 and was an MP (member of parliament) in the National Assembly two years later. He was elected chairman of the ANC in Mpumalanga in 2008, and became a member of the party's national executive committee. After serving almost two terms as Mpumalanga premier, Mabuza became deputy president of South Africa in February 2018.

Minister in the Presidency Jackson Mthembu also ascended the political ranks following misdemeanours in Mpumalanga. When he was MEC for transport in the province, Mthembu was criticised for allegedley spending R2.3 million on a fleet of BMWs for his colleagues. He said in response: 'I am a leader in my community and therefore have a certain status – you can't be saying I should drive a 1600cc vehicle.' He was dismissed in 1999 after allegedly driving a government-issue Mercedes-Benz without a driver's licence while on ANC business in Witbank. He crashed through two traffic signs and rolled into a tree. After he was fired from the Mpumalanga government, Mthembu became an ANC MP in the National Assembly and was later appointed chief whip.

Former National Assembly speaker Baleka Mbete nearly wrote off her political career when police officers fingered her in 1997 for being in possession of a fraudulent driver's licence. The scandal led to the establishment of the Moldenhauer Commission, which found that Mbete's licence had indeed been issued fraudulently and that Steve Mabona, the Mpumalanga MEC for safety and security, abused state resources to provide her with special treatment. Mbete said that she had been 'too busy to stand in queues' to apply for a licence and take the test. She rose up the ANC's ranks to become chairwoman of the party.

In a 1998 interview with the author and Professor Padraig O'Malley, who studies the problems in divided societies like South Afruca, Phosa, who was elected ANC treasurer general after he resigned as Mpumalanga premier, defended the corruption in Mpumalanga during his stint as premier by saying it had been inherited from the apartheid government. 'We found the culture of corruption in this system, we found it there. When you talk about transforming the civil service, it is introducing new ethics in the environment – but it is not only the government that has to be transformed, it's the whole society, the moral values of our society. Our society has been so brutalised and degraded, black and white … we are all traumatised in our own different ways.

'I am not making excuses for the new corruption by the new people. There is a culture of corruption in the system, in the society. It's there in the police force, in the civil service, in justice, it's there. It comes out from every pore of our society and we need to deal with that. The whole society must look at itself and say we need to take a new course.'

Yet Phosa's attempts to put the brakes on corruption, including the dismissal of Mabuza from his cabinet, came to naught. Mpumalanga, with a fairly small population and little economic clout, is one of the most corrupt provinces in South Africa. It is known as Mamparalanga – a 'mampara' is township slang for an idiot.

Although it reflects the losses he suffered, Fred worries about the size of his damages claim against the Mpumalanga government and its agencies. If the court awards him damages, it would be paid with funds diverted from service delivery. Judge Ledwaba has agreed to Fred's request to split the trial into two parts; he will only hear the claim and will not rule on the damages. 'All I want is peace and justice, to be treated equally and see my government using public resources wisely,' Fred says. 'If a court awards me only R1 in damages instead of R1 billion, that would be justice, it would be sufficient. The truth will be exposed and relationships will be restored. All I really want is for my story to be heard.

'After the root causes of the conflicts are identified and resolved in court, relationships will be restored, value can be created and the quantum becomes a minor issue. So I decided to split the merits and the quantum; only the merits will be dealt with now. The amount that has to be paid in damages can be dealt with later, by another court. This will make the trial more simple, and much shorter.

'After the court grants relief to the parties, it will immediately restore stability and certainty. After the conflict disappears, people will be able to see clearly how corruption-linked harassment destroys social wellbeing and economic opportunities. For more than a decade, I have attempted to mediate with the defendants. They have been unwilling to attend mediation because it benefits them to keep the conflict alive.'

Like so many Mpumalanga politicians, a succession of corruption allegations did not at all hamper Mabuza's career. He is cited in Fred's damages claim in his capacity as MEC for agriculture and land affairs in Mpumalanga. He served in that position for a year, from 2008 to 2009, when the biggest land scam in democratic South Africa was exposed.

4
The Dolphin deal

The template for some of the schemes hatched by Mpumalanga politicians and officials to destroy Fred's business was a scam dubbed by the world's press as 'the Dolphin deal'. In 1996 Nelspruit-based journalist Justin Arenstein uncovered the brazen R25-billion corruption scheme. Millions of rand were diverted from the Mpumalanga government's coffers to the ANC's elections war chest, leading to the near destruction of the province's conservation and tourism infrastructure.

After the establishment of Mpumalanga in 1994, the conservation assets of the Transvaal Game Parks were transferred to the new province's care. Four years later, its new steward, the Mpumalanga Parks Board, was dysfunctional and bankrupt. A string of front companies had been set up to milk its funds and feed the ANC's coffers for the national and provincial elections in 1999. The board, tasked with managing swathes of protected public land identified as important conservation and heritage sites, provided the ruling party with cash, T-shirts, marketing gifts, equipment, accommodation and conferencing facilities.

In 1997, a planned second round of theft of conservation resources was camouflaged as a much-needed commercialisation project. The board's budget was slashed from R57 million to

R11 million to force a privatisation project on the organisation. A new parks board was established, with a deliberate gap in its founding legislation to allow the then MEC for environmental affairs, David Mkhwanazi, to circumvent its board of directors and deal directly with its chief executive officer (CEO), Alan Gray. Makhwanazi had been minister of conservation in the KaNgwane homeland and Gray had been his consultant.

The Mpumalanga Parks Board signed a secret deal with the Kenya-based Dolphin Group to develop several of its game reserves. The parks board promised that the deal, involving 14 protected areas, would result in an investment of more than R6 billion – dwarfing Mpumalanga's annual budget at the time of R4.7 billion, excluding its social programmes.

The Dolphin Group had been selected because of its experience in running the Masai Mara game reserve in Kenya and its 'vast expertise' in the hospitality sector. The company was planning to invest R198 million in the flagship Songimvelo Game Reserve to transform it into a *White Mischief*-like period theme park. *White Mischief* is a film about a group of dissolute English aristocrats living in Kenya during the 1940s who drank heavily, used drugs and conducted fervent extramarital affairs that led to murder and suicide. The company planned to place an American paddle steamer on Loskop Dam and to build a cable car in the Blyde River Canyon – the third largest in the world – which has endemic and threatened plant and animal species.

Alan Gray, the Mpumalanga Parks Board CEO, had apparently brokered the deal during a 'secret visit' to London in August, the *Mail & Guardian* reported. From there he flew to the Masai Mara reserve, where he was impressed by the group's tourism infrastructure. John Hanks, one of the Mpumalanga Parks Board's most influential directors, resigned in protest against the way the deal had been 'steamrollered' without consulting the board or affected communities.

Arenstein established that Dolphin owned Delphis, a Kenyan bank under investigation for its participation in a gold and diamonds export scheme. Kenya had no diamonds and very little gold. The scam cost the country more than 10 per cent of its annual gross domestic product and as a result the shilling lost more than 50 per cent of its value. In the wake of the scandal, the group moved its head office from Nairobi to Dubai and its registration from Guernsey to Bermuda – an ownership structure that allowed Dolphin to disclose only scant information about its activities to British and Kenyan regulators.

Early in 1997, the South African ministry of public enterprises voiced concern about the Mpumalanga deal, as it was 'not in line with government principles on restructuring state assets'. The nature reserves were public property and the parks board was a parastatal company. Did the board have the right to give away jewels in the country's tourism crown? Mpumalanga was the 'wildlife heart' of South Africa, conservationists said. The endangered Taita falcon lives in the Blyde River Canyon. Would it survive daily helicopter trips and cable car rides?

Parks board chairman Patrick Maduna dismissed concerns about land claims lodged in the Blyde River Canyon and Loskop Dam reserves by communities dispossessed under apartheid. They were 'irrelevant issues and cannot be allowed to stand in the way of development,' he proclaimed in a press release. Land claims commissioner Durkje Gilfillan was aghast. The Mpumalanga Parks Board was a state body and its proposed development could not 'contradict central government policies such as the land reform programme', she said. The claims on the reserves were lodged in 1995 and could not be ignored. 'Anything, including the change of ownership, sale of commercial rights or physical development, which forestalls or otherwise compromises a land claim has to be frozen until the claim has been processed or the entire procedure would be defeated,' Gilfillan warned in a press release.

When the national minister of environmental affairs and tourism, Pallo Jordan, woke up and requested a copy of the Dolphin contract, Mkhwanazi responded by launching an inquiry into allegations that the Dolphin deal was 'unconstitutional'. He sent a delegation to Kenya and Dubai to carry out a due diligence. On their return, they gave Jordan a glowing briefing about the Dolphin Group.

On Valentine's Day in 1997, Mpumalanga legislators voted to approve the deal. But just two weeks later, Mkhwanazi announced that a review of the contract had identified serious flaws, and said he was leading a delegation to London to renegotiate the deal with the Dolphin Group. The flaws included granting the group the sole development rights to Mpumalanga's prime heritage sites for 50 years, keeping the terms of the contract a secret for 50 years and enabling the group to pull out of the deal without any liability. He was seeking to reverse the monopoly rights given to Dolphin on six state-owned sites and reserves, including Blyde River Canyon, Loskop Dam and Pilgrim's Rest.

After his team had flown to London to renegotiate the deal, Mkhwanazi announced that the terms of the contract had been shortened to 25 years and some resorts, including Pilgrim's Rest and the Manyeleti Game Reserve, had been excluded. Dolphin would have to secure private sector investment of R10 million over three years and at least 50 per cent of work would go to local companies. The development would be subject to environmental assessments and communities would be consulted. The contract was amended to allow two representatives of the Mpumalanga government seats on Dolphin's local board.

Allegations of fresh corruption in the Mpumalanga department of environmental affairs surfaced in March 1998 when the National Party, which was the opposition in the provincial legislature, gave the press a 'dossier of documents' proving that Mkhwanazi had appointed hundreds of employees in his department and at the parks board – in contravention of a moratorium on hiring. The board was paying almost R10 million in salaries to new employees in Mkhwanazi's home town of Badplaas, many of them related to him. The public protector, Selby Baqwa, investigated the complaint of nepotism, but cleared the MEC despite the employment of his wife Cecilia, daughter Thoko, brother Zenzo and sister-in-law Jane. Baqwa said they were all qualified for their positions.

In April, Mkhwanazi ended his budget speech in the Mpumalanga legislature with the abrupt announcement that he was resigning as MEC for environmental affairs.

In August, Arenstein reported that Mkhwanazi, Gray, finance MEC Jacques Modipane and parks board director James Nkambule had issued R1.3 billion in promissory notes to an investment company, using 31 of Mpumalanga's nature reserves as collateral for a R340-million loan. The notes were issued by Fenetic Investments, established in Sandton in 1995 by Israeli fraudster Moshe Regenstreich.

Finance minister Trevor Manuel sternly pointed out that using public assets as collateral for a loan was illegal. The Reserve Bank said it had not given permission for the scheme. The Special Investigating Unit obtained an interdict against the parks board preventing it from using public assets to secure loans. Members of the unit and forensic auditors raided the organisation's offices.

Regenstreich, whose mugshot appeared on Interpol's wanted list, was arrested in Sandton but charges were dropped after he cooperated with the state. It could not be proven that he knew the promissory notes had been fraudulently issued.

Finally, in September the Mpumalanga Parks Board's new chairman, Francis Legodi, recommended that Gray should be suspended. The new MEC for environmental affairs forced him to resign and dissolved the board of the Mpumalanga Parks Board, which he accused of covering up the promissory notes scandal.

Gray released a report on the Dolphin deal and the promissory notes to the media, claiming that the problems raised about the schemes were due to 'political interference, personal vendettas and disinformation'. He warned that he would expose a 'shadowy network of empowerment companies' set up to finance the ANC's elections campaign if politicians did not 'step in and mitigate' the charges of maladministration and fraud that he faced.

On the first day of October, Modipane resigned as finance MEC. He and Mkhwanazi were suspended from the ANC. In November, Nkambule resigned from the parks board, claiming that he had been embroiled in the scandal because he had 'no knowledge of financial dealings'.

Arenstein unearthed the business network Gray had said was meant for the 'benefit of the ANC's financial wellbeing'.

Three holding companies had been established in 1996 to secure government tenders. Gray, working with the Mpumalanga department of finance director general Sam Cronje, Mkhwanazi, Modipane and South Africa's ambassador to Mozambique Mangisi Zitha, had established Air Excellence. They signed a four-year contract with the Mpumalanga government guaranteeing charter flights of at least 20 hours a month. The most profitable company in the network was Phakamani Security Services, which won most of the Mpumalanga government's security contracts. Gray appointed another front company, Somalanga, to develop the province's flagship game reserve, Songimvelo.

Early in January 1999, Gray leaked new details about the corruption to the media, claiming he had Phosa's support when he set up the companies to siphon government funding to the ANC for its election campaign. Phosa threatened to sue Gray for defamation.

At the end of January, Phosa appointed Mkhwanazi, who had resigned as MEC for environmental affairs, as the new MEC for sports, arts, culture and recreation. Phosa also appointed Modipane as MEC for safety and security, who had resigned after his role in the promissory notes scandal emerged. The ANC said it had lifted the suspensions on the two men's membership, as there was insufficient evidence against them.

The parks board charged Gray with 54 counts of misconduct and abuse of power. The charges included issuing R1.3 billion in promissory notes and channelling parks board funds to the ANC. Records showed that the ANC Youth League received R105,000 while its leader, Nkambule, was paid hundreds of thousands of rand. Payments amounting to R1.4 million were channelled through a front company to the ANC and senior members of the party were accommodated in luxury hotels and treated to helicopter trips.

In February, the parks board was placed under curatorship after it overspent its budget by R48 million. The Mpumalanga finance department took over its day-to-day management.

In early May, an Idasa/Markinor poll unsurprisingly found that the ANC's support in Mpumalanga had dropped from 71 per cent to 58 per cent while the party's support had grown in the other eight provinces. The national and provincial elections were weeks away. Phosa was dropped from the ANC's list as its candidate for premier and Johannes Mahlangu, a former Lebowa homeland politician, became the party's preferred leader for Mpumalanga.

Phosa finally resigned as premier at the end of July, but not before threatening his successor, Mahlangu, with a R1-million defamation lawsuit for saying that he was implicated in the promissory notes scandal. Mahlangu reappointed Modipane as finance MEC, and Mabona and D.D. Mabuza were brought back from the cold into the provincial parliament. There were no political consequences for the lies about the Dolphin deal, the promissory notes and the front companies that funnelled money into the ANC's election campaign. The party won Mpumalanga with almost 85 per cent of the votes.

The fallout of the schemes cooked up by rotten politicians in 1995 dragged on as the new century dawned. In January 2001, the Mpumalanga Parks Board found Gray guilty of eight charges of gross misconduct relating to the abuse of its funds for personal and political gain. He was guilty of using parks boards funds to pay for three ANC Youth League conferences; paying vehicle, legal and medical expenses for Nkambule; and making two secret transfers of money to Phambili Construction, a front company established by the ANC. A day later, he was finally dismissed from the parks board. According to Arenstein, his two-year disciplinary hearing had cost taxpayers more than R1 million. Gray announced that he was appealing against his dismissal. He and Nkambule appeared in the Nelspruit Regional Court to face 77 theft and fraud charges amounting to R2.3 million.

In March, Phosa's former special advisor Pieter Rootman was arrested on charges of fraud relating to embezzling donor funds. Phosa issued a joint press statement with Rootman claiming that the arrest was part of a criminal conspiracy to discredit and silence them. They threatened to disclose 'explosive evidence' that implicated senior ANC leaders in corruption. Arenstein reported that they accused MEC for safety and security Steve

Mabona, MEC for economic affairs Jacob Mabena and South African Defence Force secretary January Masilela of fraud. Phosa said he had 'damning evidence' that would 'sink' them.

At the same time, the Scorpions, the elite police crime-busting agency, were investigating the former premier's business activities. Phosa had gone into joint ventures with Mkhwanazi after he resigned as environment affairs MEC, and with Jean Mopotu, who had been a director of Regenstreich's Fenetic Investments, Arenstein discovered. The dogged reporter had another fascinating angle on the story: South Africa's deputy president, Jacob Zuma, had finally voiced his opinion on the six-year saga. He said the matter should be dealt with 'internally' by the ANC and the Scorpions should drop their investigation.

A few days later, Nkambule went into hiding after writing a seven-page 'confession'. He claimed that Zuma had met Mpumalanga politicians to discover what evidence they had against Rootman. Zuma urged them to drop the prosecution and allow the ANC to deal with it internally. Rootman was accused of using donor funds to settle the bond on Zuma's house in March 1998, after he had been taken to court for failing to pay R120,000 in arrears.

Nkambule said he was receiving death threats from three different men. They accused him of betraying his comrades, warned that they knew everything about him and told him he would be lucky to see the sun rise again.

At the end of March, the ANC's top leadership summoned Nkambule to explain his threats to expose the party's systemic corruption. He claimed to have evidence implicating Zuma, Phosa, former defence minister Joe Modise and other senior party leaders in acts of fraud, theft, bribery, tender rigging, intimidation and tampering with official records. Nkambule told Arenstein that Phosa and Rootman had 'forced' him to sign an affidavit in which he retracted some of the testimony he had given an ANC inquiry into the political turmoil in Mpumalanga, which had been instrumental in forcing Phosa to resign as premier in 1998.

Arenstein described Nkambule as a 'teflon-coated man' who appeared to 'thrive on controversy'. The former ANC Youth

League leader and parks board director also claimed that Phosa, Cyril Ramaphosa and former Gauteng premier Tokyo Sexwale were involved in a 'plot' to overthrow Thabo Mbeki. The ANC's inquiry found Nkambule guilty of abusing his position in the party for personal gain and banned him from public office until their deployment committee determined that he had 'reformed'.

An investigation into Phosa by the National Prosecuting Authority was close to completion, Arenstein discovered. Conducted by private forensic auditors at Gobodo Inc, it was due to be handed over to national director of public prosecutions Bulelani Ngcuka. The auditors had 'stumbled' onto evidence of fraud while investigating financial irregularities at the Mpumalanga Parks Board. The new evidence included allegations that renovations to Phosa's official residence had been irregularly approved by the provincial treasury. A security wall and a gatehouse had cost taxpayers R835,000. The parks board paid R400,000 for an electric fence and R121,000 for landscaping.

November 2003 ended with a bang. A labour court judge reinstated Nkambule and three other officials who had been fired in May from the Mpumalanga government 'in an apparent retaliation for publicly challenging Premier Mahlangu's commitment to clean governance', said Judge Elna Revelas. 'The ongoing politicisation of government administrative structures in Mpumalanga is eroding normal managerial controls.'

Nkambule and Gray first appeared in court in January 2001 to face theft and fraud charges. By 2010 they had made 14 appearances in court, but hadn't yet been asked to plead. They changed lawyers several times, applied for legal aid and were refused. Their properties and other assets were seized by the Scorpions soon after their arrest, and they fought several legal battles against the seizure order.

In March 2010, Nkambule was arrested on further charges of defeating the ends of justice and conspiracy to commit fraud after releasing a sworn statement that he said was made to him by an alleged assassin called 'Josh'. In the statement, Josh confessed that he was the hit man behind several political murders and attempted murders in Mpumalanga. Speaking outside the

Nelspruit court after his appearance, Nkambule accused Mabuza of being behind the high-profile political murders. He told reporters that he had been used as a scapegoat to divert attention from 'the person who is behind the killings in the province'. He added that he would not shut up until the truth was known about an alleged hit list targeting whistleblowers in Mpumalanga. 'I am just a small lizard that is not capable of killing in this whole saga. The real crocodile that is capable of killing is hiding behind state resources in the premier's office: your premier, David Mabuza. That crocodile should be the one attending court, not me.' He also accused Mabuza of using state resources to intimidate him. 'I have been followed around by a policeman in the past few weeks and he only disappeared after I called the crocodile to ask him to remove his dog from my behind.'

Mabuza's spokesman Mabutho Sithole in a press release said Nkambule was 'crazy'. 'Nobody in his right mind can believe James, taking into account that in 2001 he accused Sexwale, Phosa and Ramaphosa of trying to oust Mbeki,' he said.

In July 2010, Nkambule appeared in court for the fifth time in relation to the charges that he had manufactured an assassin and defamed Mabuza. He had laid a counter-charge of intimidation against Mabuza, who he said sent him a threatening message on the night of 15 June. The SMS allegedly included the line: 'I will be around till mid-July, but you won't.' On the steps of the court, Nkambule accused Mabuza of being 'behind a hit list of people who were being murdered to prevent opposition or revelations about corruption emerging'.

In October, Nkambule died – the tenth Mpumalanga politician or official to die in suspicious circumstances in two years – after blowing the whistle on assassinations and corruption linked to the construction of the 2010 Soccer World Cup stadium in Nelspruit. An autopsy conducted by Mpumalanga's chief medical officer concluded that his death was unnatural. White, foamy material was found in his throat and windpipe and there was about 30 millilitres of brownish fluid, suggestive of poison ingestion, in his stomach. To this day, no one has been arrested for his murder.

Phosa weathered the storm that arose after Nkambule accused him of plotting to overthrow Mbeki. He was elected as a member of the national executive committee of the ANC in 1999, and in 2007 became the treasurer general of the party. He contended for the position of ANC deputy president in 2012 and was convincingly defeated by Ramaphosa. Five years later, he announced that he had accepted a nomination to be ANC president. Ramaphosa won that race again. Since 1999, Phosa has been a consultant for several local and international businesses and a board member for ten South African institutions and companies. He has not faced any charges relating to corruption in Mpumalanga.

David Mkhwanazi is a very wealthy businessman, known as the Mpumalanga godfather. He owns shopping centres in Elukwatini and has a passion for expensive cars. He has not faced any corruption charges.

Jacques Modipane was deployed by Mabuza as CEO of the Mpumalanga Tourism and Parks Agency, which replaced the bankrupt parks board. He faked his CV, claiming that he had tertiary education and was studying for his honours degree. Soon after he took up the post, rhino horn and elephant tusks valued at R116 million were stolen from the agency's offices, the biggest such robbery in the history of South Africa. He was paid an exit settlement of R5 million and left the agency.

It was into this cesspool of corruption that Fred ventured when he came to invest in conservation and tourism in Mpumalanga. Many of the politicians and officials fingered in the litany of wrongdoing were in positions of authority, which they could use to help build Fred's business – or seize control of it for their personal benefit.

5

In the lion's den

In 1998, when Mathews Phosa resigned as premier of Mpumalanga in the wake of the Dolphin deal, Fred Daniel arrived in Badplaas. His aim was to create an economically sustainable project to protect biodiversity by developing ecotourism, game farming, education and agriculture. 'It was planned to protect and preserve the natural world and all its variety of life, in a manner that sustains the ability of natural systems to provide healthy ecosystems and abundant natural resources to meet human needs,' he explains.

The project depended entirely on the acquisition of a large piece of land on which he planned first to develop a nature reserve. Before settling on Mpumalanga he had conducted a seven-year search across southern Africa for a suitable location. In the spring of 1998, a 916-hectare game farm, Boekenhoutrand, which lay between Badplaas and Barberton, went on sale. The Komati River flows through 20 kilometres of the property, which lies on both sides of its banks. Two other rivers also run through the farm. It had 2,000 hectares of available agricultural land with water rights from the rivers.

'This piece of land had mountains, kloofs, rivers and a variety of terrain ranging from lowveld to highveld, which is an extraordinary find on one property. I told Fred that he should sign on the bottom line as soon as possible,' says Professor Wouter van Hoven of the Centre for Wildlife Management at Pretoria University. Fred had phoned him out of the blue one day and asked for his advice in buying a wildlife farm.

Fred conducted a due diligence to decide whether it was feasible to invest in the area. It showed that Badplaas was suffering serious economic hardship. 'It had a high unemployment rate, mainly caused by the policies of the previous government, which had in the late 1970s settled tens of thousands of people onto this fragile area to form the KaNgwane homeland,' he says.

'Badplaas had brief renown as an agricultural area, but large-scale commercial farming collapsed dramatically during the 1980s, putting most farmers out of business and off their land. Some of the farms had been in the same family since 1865. But the harsh conditions – poor soils, hail and large inputs of fertiliser and water – rendered the land unsustainable. Many farmers were desperate to sell.'

With a former homeland on the outskirts of the land he was purchasing, Fred had to know whether black residents had been forcibly removed from the farm during apartheid and were entitled to justice. 'I was especially concerned about land claims,' he says. 'I did not wish to purchase land that might be or might become the subject of a claim. As part of my due diligence investigation prior to the purchase of my first property in Badplaas, I contacted the Mpumalanga department of land affairs.

'Their officials informed me that there were no land claims registered over properties in the Badplaas area. Because the cut-off date for claims was in a few months' time, in December 1998, they said it was highly unlikely that any would be registered. They informed me that a key factor in determining the validity of a land claim was that the claimants had to demonstrate that they were forcibly removed after 1913 due to racially discriminatory laws and practices.

'The officials confirmed that, according to their information, there were no records of any forced removals in the Badplaas area. I was informed that the previous government kept accurate records of all forced removals as part of their policy. I consulted the title deeds of Boekenhoutrand and some adjoining properties and I was satisfied that they were owned by white farmers since at least 1846.'

Fred dubbed the area flanking the Komati River the Great Nkomazi River Valley. He purchased the shares of Grand Valley Estates, which owned 12 farms including Boekenhoutrand. The farm is three hours' drive from Johannesburg, the perfect distance for short escapes into nature. There is no malaria. It is close to the picturesque town of Barberton, in a region known as the wild frontier of Mpumalanga. It is within comfortable distance of Swaziland, the Kruger National Park, Mozambique, South Africa's lake district, Sabie, Pilgrim's Rest, the Blyde River Canyon, God's Window and KwaZulu-Natal.

It lies on the edge of the escarpment, partly nestled in a section of the world-renowned Barberton Mountainlands – the oldest mountain range on earth – and partly on the Komati grasslands, the most threatened biome in the world. It is protected by the green foothills of the Makhonjwa Mountains on the escarpment and the Hlumuhlumu Mountains below.

There is an elevation of almost a thousand metres between the grasslands and the mountain plateau and the land has a range of soils, providing for a kaleidoscope of habitats. 'Its temperate climate, abundant fresh water, diverse habitats and high carrying capacity veld combine to make it a game breeder's paradise,' says Dick Wensing, who had been a consultant for the Mpumalanga Parks Board and understood the terrain.

Boekenhoutrand was fragmented, degraded and had suffered visible ecological damage. Fred commissioned Van Hoven to identify the correct use of the land, and to work with him to rehabilitate it into wilderness, a project he called the Healing of the Earth. With the conservationist's guidance he reunited the reserve's fragmented ecosystems, improving their ecological integrity and functioning.

He distilled his project into five main tasks. These were to create a new brand, the Cradle of Life, which would be internationally renowned; to rehabilitate his land back to its natural state, fence it, re-stock it with wildlife and name it Nkomazi Wilderness Reserve; to develop a visitor centre where people could celebrate and share the land's scientific significance; to create a development plan to ensure the sustainability of the project; and to build a new, exciting tourism destination.

Serendipity had brought Fred to an actual cradle of life to establish his dream. His farm was a living laboratory, recording the emergence of life on earth. 'The Barberton Mountainlands are arguably one of the most beautiful areas in South Africa, not simply because of their stunning aesthetic and natural appeal but, crucially, because they house some of the world's oldest volcanic and sedimentary rocks as well as sequences representing one of the world's greatest biodiversity hotspots and geological treasure troves,' writes researcher Dale McKinley, in a 2012 report on Fred's conflict with the government, titled, 'Beauty and the Beast: A Historical Timeline of Corruption, Greed and Conflict in Badplaas, Mpumalanga'.

In the mountains on the property, the rocks and fossils contain a record of the first atmosphere on earth, the first forms of biological life, the birth of the first ocean, and the evidence of the first tidal currents. The rocks and fossils date back 3.5 billion years. Geologists and other scientists have been teasing evidence out of these mountains since 1885 and regard it as a scientific mecca.

Fred was ecstatic when he discovered that he owned part of the oldest real estate on earth. 'It was here, in the ancient Barberton Mountainlands, where this incredible journey of all journeys really started,' he says. 'The rocks all around me spoke of the conditions and environments that prevailed at the most remote reaches of time … I learnt about the beginning of time … At Nkomazi I became the ultimate time traveller.'

He was eager to conserve a significant part of the Barberton Greenstone Belt – a site preserving the planet's first volcanic and sedimentary rocks – on his property and in the stretch of river dissecting it. The land was everything Fred had dreamed of since childhood, and much more. 'Here was a place where I could teach people to take back humanity's future,' he says.

The Barberton Mountainlands have a plant biodiversity second only to the world's richest floral kingdom, the Cape fynbos region. It is home to the much-admired Barberton daisy, the pride of de kaap shrub and an array of proteas. There are 2,500 plant species in the region, 410 bird species and about 80 animal species.

There were patches of fabulous plant and animal diversity on Boekenhoutrand when Fred purchased it. With Van Hoven's guidance, a team of employees and a squad of earthmoving vehicles, he began the painstaking work of clearing the land of rocks and debris to create a valley in which a South African Serengeti could take root, replete with grazing animals. To protect valuable soil from being washed away, they built rock packs, contour drains, dams and weirs. Alien plants that were poisonous to game and destructive of natural habitats were removed. 'Good veld management is the basis for good animal management,' Fred says.

He asked officials at the Mpumalanga Parks Board for the specifications of fences required to keep the Big Five animals on the reserve. He marked out his perimeter with the highest game fence specification in the industry and constructed a fire programme to protect the nutritional quality of the veld. The parks board certified his fences as adequate.

All that was left to do was wait and watch the heritage grass grow as the land returned to wilderness. The large mammals he planned to introduce would do the rest. All the ecosystems – the plants, animals and insects – would be restored to land from which they had been banished by hunters and pesticides. 'They will maintain it for their benefit and humanity's,' Fred says.

Van Hoven and his team of postgraduate students conducted a vegetation survey, nutritional assessment, soil survey, habitat analysis, grazing capacity and game survey to produce an ecological management plan for the land. They concluded that the highveld was suitable for springbok, eland, black wildebeest, blesbok and oribi while the lowveld was suitable for the Big

Five animals – lion, leopard, rhinoceros, elephant and Cape buffalo. 'After the Big Five are reintroduced to the scenic natural environment, the greater Barberton Mountainlands will become one of the most spectacular wilderness areas in southern Africa,' Van Hoven predicted.

Fred informed the Mpumalanga Parks Board of his intentions to develop the land. He planned a nature reserve with accommodation; a biopark; a natural history and geology museum with educational facilities; a safari park, animal sanctuary and an animal rehabilitation centre. Boekenhoutrand was proclaimed a private nature reserve and he renamed the property Nkomazi Wilderness Reserve.

Fred so loved his work and watching his vision coming to life that, a year later in 1999, he began buying surrounding farms as they came onto the market. Many had been abandoned and required painstaking work to rehabilitate them back into wilderness. The farmers left behind derelict infrastructure including tobacco sheds, drying ovens and disused power and telephone lines. They abandoned rusting farm machinery, cars and piles of scrap metal. Fred and his team dug deep trenches to bury old fences, broken irrigation pipes and other rubbish. Heaps of rocks piled on the edges of the degraded farmland had to be removed. Although there had been large-scale hunting and reckless animal slaughter on the farms, the wildlife had not been completely decimated.

The work required as much perspiration as inspiration, but Fred was exhilarated. He reclaimed 14,000 hectares of land from farming and brought it back to nature, to its original beauty. He set springbok, eland, zebra, waterbuck, nyala, oribi and blesbok free into the high-lying grassland area and purchased giraffe, rhino, buffalo and elephant, which he placed in the low-lying bushveld areas. Herds soon roamed the land, bringing insects and birds in their wake. It was restored to its former glory, harmony and balance.

'Fred is an inspiring illustration of how a visionary and determined individual can heal the earth,' Wensing wrote in a report on the project. 'Nkomazi was carefully restored and became a role model of an ecological, sustainable enterprise. Behind this transformation is one man's dedicated commitment and management.'

Fred expanded his vision. First and foremost, he wanted to help alleviate the poverty in the area by creating jobs on the reserve. He pledged to save and protect its ancient geology and rich biodiversity, and its cultural history and heritage. He wanted to create a wilderness area reminiscent of the era before humans interfered with nature.

He aimed to develop the most exclusive private nature reserve in the world. He intended to consult top experts to assist with attention to the smallest details in its development. He was going to create a wilderness masterpiece that combined virgin African bush with the latest building techniques, technology and architectural design for human relaxation. He wanted to establish an international research centre for the study of his property's geological and cultural treasures, which included some of the oldest human settlements and gold mines in the world. To ensure the venture's long-term survival, he needed to create and maintain an environment that ensured substantial capital appreciation of land value.

From April 1999 to November 2000, Fred bought another seven farms and increased the size of Nkomazi Wilderness Reserve to 14,572 hectares. He planned to expand it to about 30,000 hectares and to make it part of South Africa's seventh transfrontier park, consisting of up to 170,000 hectares of reserve land.

To ensure Nkomazi was viable and sustainable in the long term, he decided to develop the reserve into a private conservancy. He drafted a business plan that provided six mechanisms to raise the capital required to fund the reserve's activities. In 2002, Grand Valley Estates submitted an application to the Mpumalanga department of agriculture and land affairs for consent to establish a development area. The rezoning application requested the consolidation of the seven farms to form the Nkomazi Wilderness Reserve, the subdivision of some land to sell as lodges, and for the remainder to be used for game farming, especially for rare and endangered species.

The company also asked for consent to establish a private eco-tourism resort. It would include diving and accommodation facilities at the Victorian mining village at neighbouring Komati Springs; a 20-bed, upmarket, 7-star safari lodge; a 40-bed fly fishing lodge; game auction facilities; a tourism information centre and museum; an animal rehabilitation centre and an international research station. Consent was granted by the Mpumalanga government.

Fred joined local efforts to proclaim his unique landscape, and the surrounding area, a World Heritage Site. (It came about in June 2018). He worked on a strategy to join his reserve to others adjacent to it to form the Greater Barberton Mountainlands Conservancy. The Mpumalanga government and the Peace Parks Foundation prepared planning studies to link the land between Nkomazi and the Kruger National Park through a scheme of cooperative management agreements with nearby reserves, consisting of up to 170,000 hectares, to create the Barberton Makhonjwa Transfrontier Park. Nkomazi borders the Songimvelo Game Reserve, where the Mpumalanga Parks Board managed 49,000 hectares of unspoilt wilderness. The others to be linked were the Barberton Mountainlands Nature Reserve, Paranie Nature Reserve, Barberton Nature Reserve and the Mthethomusha Nature Reserve.

The 18,000-hectare Malolotja Nature Reserve in Swaziland borders Songimvelo. It showed a keen interest in joining the conservancy. 'This kind of sub-regional conservancy could provide exceptional eco-tourism possibilities,' Fred's business plan read. 'Nkomazi is in the centre of advanced initiatives that will form part of an exciting tourist destination. The region will offer an unrivalled choice of game viewing, birding, hunting, mountain and bush trails, angling … fossil hunting, canoeing, 4x4 trails and more. No other region anywhere has such exciting options.'

On land adjacent to the wilderness area, Fred built the Cradle of Life, Travelport and a biopark. It had a fuel station, museum, information centre, country shop, indigenous nursery, conference centre accommodating 120 people, an amphitheatre for live concerts and lectures, a restaurant, animal sanctuary, wildlife rehabilitation centre, wedding facilities and 15 cottages. Schools and scientific conference groups were regular visitors.

In his business plan, Fred identified only two threats: political instability and competition from other tourism destinations. The biggest threat, for which he had performed no due diligence, came from politicians, who feasted their hungry eyes on the fruits of his hard labour.

6

The One&Only deal

Fred's company Grand Valley Estates had bought 16 farms by the end of 2002. He found common ground with existing Badplaas farmers and negotiated reasonable prices for their properties. He had almost no competition for his land assemblage programme. With the spectre of Land Bank auctions hanging over failed farmers, it was a buyer's market.

His conservation project attracted the keen interest of property speculators. Rather than exposing his plans to them so they could push up prices, he bought the shares of three companies and used them to buy farms. He regularly informed the Mpumalanga Parks Board of his activities and checked with the regional Land Claims Commission to ensure there were no claims on all his prospective purchases.

In July 2001, Fred leased the Panorama Holiday Resort from the Mpumalanga Parks Board, with an option to buy it. It had 15 dilapidated chalets, an untended swimming pool and 12 hectares of land. The board had purchased it for the Dolphin Group in 1996 to develop as a casino. The property had been left to rot after the corrupt Dolphin deal collapsed. Instead of following their mandate to maintain the resort to attract tourists, conservation officials turned a blind eye while prostitutes used the Panorama's chalets to conduct their trade.

Fred's dream was becoming a reality and the prospects for its economic success appeared certain. His efforts drew interest and admiration from scientists, conservationists, non-governmental organisations and potential investors in South Africa and abroad. In June 2000, a valuator firm assessed the 2,000 hectares that he had assembled and pegged its value at R8.5 million.

He applied to the parks board for an adequate enclosure certificate that would qualify him for wildlife insurance. Fred also submitted an application for an animal rehabilitation permit and a transport permit that would allow Nkomazi to transport animals. 'I observed the law and its regulations at all times while developing Nkomazi,' he says. 'I informed the parks board about all my plans and applied to them for all necessary permits.' Fred submitted a comprehensive application to the Mpumalanga Parks Board for a permit to keep large predators, lions and elephants.

By the end of 2002, bolstered by the protection and support offered by the Mpumalanga government, he made contact with hotel magnate Sol Kerzner. It had been reported that his company, Kerzner International, was interested in investing in game reserves. It was seeking to secure commercial rights to build and operate at least three new resorts in southern Africa – at Zimbabwe's Victoria Falls, in Mpumalanga and Cape Town. They were to be 7-star resorts known as One&Only, aimed at the upper level of the leisure travel market.

'Kerzner International represented a potential investor that could bring large-scale capital investment for tourism infrastructure and initiatives into the depressed Badplaas–Barberton area – with Nkomazi as its centrepiece,' Fred says. His business plan had to be polished until it shone like a diamond bright enough to attract a man who had built the Southern Sun Hotel Group and Sun International in South Africa, and developed and owned luxury resorts around the world. Kerzner was a perfect match because Badplaas was a new area for luxury tourism and he was known for placing Mauritius and Bahamas on the tourism map. Kerzner International had also assisted with the creation of the Pilanesberg National Park when Sun City was built and so it also had experience in conservation.

Linda drove with Fred to Johannesburg and dropped him off in Randburg for his January 2003 meeting with the Kerzner Group. 'We were so filled with hope; we were so excited. It was possible that our dream was coming true,' she says. 'When I picked him up afterwards and heard that there might be a deal, I knew we were on our way. We had found a financial backer who believed in our dream.'

After commissioning a due diligence report on Fred and his project, the Kerzner Group decided to proceed. The company was also keen to get involved in Fred's planned development of the former asbestos mining village of Msauli, which lay at the heart of the Songimvelo Game Reserve. At the urging of parks board officials, Fred had put in an offer to buy the village from the Mpumalanga government in 2001, after being assured in writing that there were no claims on its land. The sale was crucial, as the property's running costs were more than R100,000 a month and the employees operating its golf course, bowling greens, guesthouse, water works and electrical systems were about to lose their jobs. The closure of the Msauli asbestos mine had cast thousands of men into unemployment, and the government was eager to find a buyer who would create jobs. Fred planned to establish a historical town similar to Pilgrim's Rest, with residential stands, a country hotel, conferencing facilities and a world-class golf course. It would be linked to Songimvelo and the Nkomazi Wilderness Reserve.

In February 2003, two executives of the Kerzner Group came to Nkomazi, one of them being Butch Kerzner, Sol's son, who managed the family's hotel empire. They also met Dr Delani Tiba, CEO of the Mpumalanga Parks Board, and Abe Sibiya, his deputy, who were keen to be involved in the project. Although Fred's relationship with the conservation officials had appeared rock solid, there were some signs that not all was well. He was not invited to subsequent meetings with the parks board about the proposed transfrontier park and biodiversity corridor, and in July Fred was notified that a land claim had been lodged on Msauli village.

'The only conclusion that could be drawn from the sudden appearance of this claim was that it had been manufactured to frustrate the transfer of the land to my company,' Fred says. 'Even when the claim proved to be for compensation only, the parks board and the regional Land Claims Commission ensured that the transfer was not finalised. The deal collapsed and the village has since gone to ruin.'

Despite this setback, the discussions with Kerzner International continued. 'On 3 August 2003, Kerzner gave the go-ahead for the Nkomazi Wilderness project and decided to have further discussions with the Mpumalanga Parks Board regarding the inclusion of Songimvelo into the development,' Bruce Hutchinson of the Kerzner Group later said. 'I arranged a follow-up meeting with Mr Abe Sibiya in order to get the commitment of the parks board for the greater project. Mr Sibiya specifically told me that he did not want Mr Daniel to be present at the meeting. Mr Sibiya brought with him Mr Nqana, the regional land claims commissioner. Why he did so remains a mystery because the land claims were not relevant to the business under discussion.

'During the meeting Mr Sibiya went out of his way to bad-mouth Mr Daniel and insisted that he should not be part of the discussions. I was shocked and annoyed since what he was telling me was totally irreconcilable with what I, and [Butch] Kerzner, had learnt from the due diligence. Mr Sibiya did not impress me at all. I was very upset at his attempt to discredit Mr Daniel, whom I have come to respect for what he achieved with Nkomazi Wilderness. I did not understand Mr Sibiya's conduct. I held the impression that the officials that attended the meeting with Kerzner expected some favour in return for their cooperation.

'I then proceeded with a very strong recommendation on Nkomazi Wilderness, without the Mpumalanga Parks Board and Songimvelo. I had concluded that Nkomazi Wilderness was viable on its own, and with the current attitude of Mr Sibiya and the parks board, it was better to continue without them.'

In October 2003, an agreement was signed between Grand Valley Estates and Kerzner International. The hotel company invested R10 million in Nkomazi to fast-track the project to heal the land. They pledged R283 million to acquire land on the reserve to construct a One&Only luxury safari lodge. This was a one-year option: Kerzner wanted to monitor Fred's progress in obtaining permits from the parks board for some of the Big Five animals – elephant, lion and leopard.

At a meeting in March, the parks board's manager of wildlife protection, Jan Muller, had given Fred the clear impression that his wildlife permits would be processed. Yet, it was apparent that the board's attitude to him and Nkomazi had, for some reason, altered drastically and without explanation. The regional land claims commissioner had previously attested in writing, when Fred first took up an option on Msauli, that there were no land claims on the village. Yet, claimants had since emerged, and their claims were seemingly being entertained. Something fishy was going on.

7

Hyenas gather

By 2000, Grand Valley Estates and Fred's other companies owned, or intended to buy, portions of a number of farms in the Badplaas area for the Nkomazi Wilderness Reserve. As part of the due diligence Fred conducted before committing himself to purchase, he checked whether any land claims had been lodged on any of the farms by people or communities who had been evicted under apartheid. In all instances, he had confirmation from the Land Claims Commission and the Mpumalanga department of agriculture and land affairs that there were no claims on the properties he intended buying.

But in 2000, to his shock and surprise, fresh land claims were lodged by the land claims commissioner – two years after the legislated cut-off date of 1998 for claims – on four of his farms: Boekenhoutrand, Theeboom, Stolzburg and Welgelegen. Fred asked his attorney, Richard Spoor, to write an opinion about the likely impact of the Restitution of Land Rights Act on Nkomazi and the farms he intended to purchase. Spoor had worked in the field of land reform and restitution since 1994 and gave advice to landowners, rural communities and non-governmental organisations. Members of his firm were seconded to the department of agriculture and land affairs and the Mpumalanga Land Facilitation Service to provide advice and training on the implementation of the law and its regulations.

The Act stated that a claimant had to be a person, a community or its descendants dispossessed of a land right after June 1913 because of racially discriminatory laws, without having been paid just compensation, who lodged a claim by December 1998. Labour tenants who had been evicted from farms were offered redress through land redistribution programmes that provided subsidies to previously disadvantaged people to buy land. There was no legislation on redistribution: it was a government programme.

'I have examined the title deeds of all the relevant properties and am satisfied that all were in private registered ownership of members of the so-called white group prior to 1913,' Spoor wrote in his opinion. 'All these farms were first registered in the 1870s. There can therefore be no question that any person has been deprived of a registered real right in the property since 1913.'

After a land claim is lodged, it has to be investigated by a regional land claims commission. If it is verified, a notice advertising the claim must be published in the *Government Gazette* to prevent a change in the ownership of the land until the claim is settled. Claims can be challenged, but before the matter is brought to court, there has to be mediation. Only if that fails, can the Land Claims Court be approached to hear the matter.

If the court rules in favour of a claim and orders the restitution of the land, the owner has to be compensated. There are alternatives to restoration – the claimants can be offered compensation or appropriate state-owned land or become beneficiaries of the state redistribution programme. It was unlikely that restitution would be given for large and valuable pieces of land, as the state was facing the settlement of tens of thousands of claims.

Spoor said that the regional land claims commissioner would have realised that the new batch of Badplaas claims 'did not meet the requirements of the law, had not been properly lodged and were frivolous or vexatious. I have examined the claims that have been filed in respect of the farms Theeboom, Boekenhoutrand, Stolzburg and Welgelegen. None of the claims have passed the first hurdle – certification that the claim has merit. None of the claims have been vetted.

'A perusal of the claim documents suggests that they all relate to farm workers, labour tenants or occupiers who were evicted from farms for private or commercial reasons by owners during the 1980s. Such claims are not validly within the scope of the Land Restitution Act. It is my considered opinion that there are no valid claims currently registered in respect of the properties and that it is extremely unlikely that any valid claim will be registered.'

After the Land Claims Commission had gazetted claims on various farms in the Badplaas area, both those belonging to Fred and those of other landowners, the department of agriculture and land affairs began buying up farms from those who were willing to sell. All of these were meant for restitution to evicted labour tenants. There were no new claims based on historical ownership by black individuals or communities. This was because, as Richard Spoor confirmed, white ownership in the area stretched back uninterruptedly to the late 19th century.

In a report on the land claims in Badplaas, University of the Witwatersrand professor emeritus of history Peter Delius and Dr Michelle Hay wrote that in the early 1800s the entire area under claim came within Swazi territory when Mswati, son of the Swazi King Somhlolo, established outposts there. 'Members of the royal family lived in a number of villages in the area ... although capitals and households were fairly mobile. Households lived in scattered homesteads and villages under a system of customary tenure in which their own rights to land would have been strong.

'However, when the borders of Swaziland and South Africa were drawn up in the nineteenth century, this land was included within the territory of the South African government. The land was subsequently surveyed into farms and they were granted to whites in the 1860s and 1870s. Evidence from the Natives Land Commission and Eastern Transvaal Natives Land Committee suggests that, by 1914, the system of labour tenancy was established in the area, but other sources suggest that the area was sparsely settled by white farmers and Africans lived "under tribal conditions" – suggesting a degree of independent or customary land use on the farms.

'Nevertheless, Africans derived their land rights from the white landowners and the system of labour tenancy became entrenched, which may have been before or after 1913. They lived under a set of rules and conditions relating to land, determined by the landowner. Households were vulnerable to eviction and this meant a breakdown of communities as people scattered around farms in the area.

'White authority also meant that African leadership was challenged, and the system of chieftainship and headmanship, while still important in dispute resolution, tribute and tax collection, was no longer concerned with the allocation of land rights and determination of land use. While African households in this area had generally been significant cattle and stock owners and had formerly had access to as much land for grazing and cultivation as they required, this was taken away.

'African tenants were prevented from accumulating, were forced to sell cattle cheaply when white landowners wanted to reduce stock on their land and many lost everything, or most of what they had, when they were evicted. The system of labour tenancy was extremely exploitative and caused many hardships. Most of the claimants in [Badplaas] share this history.'

The gazetting of claims on behalf of labour tenants added a new dynamic to the property market in the Badplaas area. It represented an opportunity for speculators to derive benefit, especially when the department of agriculture and land affairs began the search to acquire farms on which to settle the labour tenants. It also presented an opportunity for corrupt officials and politicians. Dale McKinley, in his report titled 'Beauty and the Beast', describes the people who became involved in the Badplaas land scam as 'a motley crew of opportunists, land speculators, greedy white farmers, politically-connected businessmen, an ANC councillor, provincial government officials and ANC politicians. They milked land reform funds with impunity, exploited beneficiaries and ruthlessly launched a sustained campaign against the person and properties of Fred Daniel [who] came into the firing line because he exposed the biggest land scam in South African history.'

The first culprits in the land scam that Fred uncovered were speculators, who gathered like hyenas to prey on distressed farmers and land claimants in the Badplaas area. In November 2000, Grand Valley Estates had purchased shares at a cost of R716,725 from L.M.P. Swanepoel in a company that owned Portion 1 of the farm Stolzburg. It provided a vital link from the main reserve into the Barberton Mountainlands and joined the Doyershoek valley and the mountain plateau into one block of land.

Before Grand Valley Estates could take transfer of the shares, Spoor informed Fred that Badplaas property developer Pieter Visagie, on whose farm Swanepoel was then staying, had phoned him to offer the same farm to Grand Valley Estates for R1.5 million. According to Visagie, Swanepoel had cancelled the sale with Grand Valley Estates and had sold the shares to him and his partner Tony Kennet.

'I was concerned that Mr Visagie's aim was to profiteer out of our efforts to create a viable and sustainable Nkomazi Wilderness,' Fred says in an affidavit. 'I felt that this was not the time to speculate against the efforts of one's neighbour, considering the economic state of Badplaas, and that our individual success would determine the overall success. I felt that it was more important to take a long-term view and work together as a community to reverse the economic woes of the area for once and for all and support each other in this aim.

'Since there were so many farms available for sale in the Badplaas area, I thought that this was unacceptable and Mr Visagie was exploiting our efforts. The department of agriculture and land affairs had been buying thousands of hectares of land next to Nkomazi Wilderness at about R300 per hectare without affecting land prices in the area. I met with Mr Tony Kennet at his business in White River to discuss the matter with him. When

I explained my thinking, he appeared understanding. He said he would use his influence to talk sense into Mr Visagie.'

When Fred spoke to the developer again, he agreed to lower his asking price. Visagie said he and Kennet had paid R900,000 for Swanepoel's farm, and would settle for R1 million. In April 2002, Grand Valley Estates purchased the shares and acquired Portion 1 of the farm Stolzburg. 'I was pressurised to supply the guarantee fast since I was informed that they needed the cash urgently to buy another farm,' he says.

'I later learnt that Mr Swanepoel had sold the property to Mr Visagie for the same price as he had wanted to sell it to Grand Valley Estates. Mr Visagie had misled me. Although the figure bandied about was not correct, I was naturally annoyed when it became publicly known in Badplaas that he had made a cool, quick R300,000 out of me.'

Fred also had an option to purchase Portion 11 of the farm Vygeboom for R1.2 million. And he was offered an option to purchase 809 hectares of Portion 1 of Vygeboom from the Potgieter family for R1.2 million. He issued a guarantee to the Potgieters, but then cancelled it to pay Visagie and Kennet when they pressured him to supply a guarantee for the Stolzburg farm. Then he discovered that Visagie's company had bought Portion 11 of Vygeboom, for R1.2 million, and that Kennet was renting Portion 1 of the farm.

Early in 2003, Visagie asked if he could rent portions of Sterkspruit farm. Because of their history, Fred was reluctant but the developer persisted and eventually he was convinced by the promise to work with Nkomazi Wilderness to facilitate the project. Visagie said he would give Grand Valley Estates an option to purchase Portion 11 of Vygeboom and he would persuade Kennet to cancel his rental of Portion 1 of the farm.

'In addition, Mr Visagie undertook to assist Grand Valley Estates with its public relations between the local farmers and Nkomazi Wilderness due to the many misunderstandings about our project,' Fred says. 'He believed he had the necessary influence and could get the farmers to understand the logic behind what we were doing.' He agreed to lease his land to

Visagie for R100,000 a year, believing that the benefits of long-term cooperation outweighed the short-term consideration of rental income.

Visagie was chairman of the Badplaas Development Forum. All the landowners in the Badplaas area were informed by the forum and the Badplaas Agricultural Union in 2003 about a deal made with the land claims commissioner, Nceba Nqana. All land claims in Badplaas would be settled on a voluntary basis – landowners who wanted to sell could do so and those who did not want to sell would not be forced to.

'In effect, the agreement meant that the land claims would be settled by the government buying the farms offered voluntarily and the claims over the farms of landowners who did not want to sell would be cancelled,' Fred says. 'Because there were so many farms that were voluntarily offered to the land claims commissioner and because Nkomazi Wilderness was a ten-year project, Grand Valley Estates opted not to sell. The company had already embarked, with the assistance of ABSA Corporate and Merchant Bank, on an empowerment deal.'

Fred says that Visagie tried several times to persuade him to sell his land to the commission, promising a huge return. 'Each time I explained to him what our project was, and also pointed out that there was already 40,000 hectares available to the land claims commissioner, which represented more than half of the farms in the Badplaas valley.

'It soon became apparent that Grand Valley Estates had made a grave mistake in working with Mr Visagie ... It came as a shock when he sold Portion 11 of the farm Vygeboom to the land claims commissioner, knowing full well the contractual obligations he had with Grand Valley Estates.

'Mr Visagie had access to our land at a discounted price and he was reneging on all aspects of the agreement as if he had never intended to honour them in the first place. Taking into account that he had other farms to offer the commissioner, and that the commissioner could pick and choose from 40,000 hectares in the Badplaas valley, his bona fides was seriously in question.

'I put pressure on him to come clean and threatened to cancel the lease agreement if he did not meet his commitments. During a meeting Mr Visagie said that if I wanted Portion 11 of the farm Vygeboom, I would have to offer him more than the land claims commissioner was prepared to pay him. He told me he wanted R4.8 million and produced a valuation.

'Knowing the true market value of this farm and understanding the land situation in Badplaas better than most, I was really shocked. I took the valuation and made a copy of it on the machine in my office. Mr Visagie tried to stop me and said the document was highly confidential. After the meeting, I studied the document and became aware of glaring irregularities and inconsistencies.'

The valuation had been done by Albert Roux of Lowveld Valuators. Fred made an appointment to see him and drove with his wife Linda to Nelspruit in February 2004. He explained his concerns about the inflated valuation and told Roux he believed Visagie was only interested in commercial gain.

'Mr Roux looked genuinely concerned,' Fred says in his affidavit. 'He informed me that he was angry with Visagie and that he was misled by him.' Roux admitted that he had inflated another valuation for Visagie, in exchange for R5,000 cash. The developer had waited in his office while he completed the task.

'Mr Roux told Linda and myself that he could fix the situation because he was the official valuator for the land claims commissioner. He agreed to come to Badplaas in order to look into the situation and see how it could be resolved.' Roux failed to show up at their next appointment and did not answer calls.

'At the time there was a legal dispute between Grand Valley Estates and the Swanepoel Boerdery Trust concerning Portion 8 of the farm Sterkspruit,' Fred says. 'My attorney Mr Spoor was contacted by Mr Swanepoel's attorney ... for an out-of-court settlement. I was once again confronted with an outrageous valuation of R4.8 million. The valuation had also been prepared and signed by Mr Roux and, more than any of his other valuations, had glaring contradictions.

'It was inaccurate in a number of material ways. Most noteworthy was that the turnover of the abandoned mine at

Komati Springs had been inflated from an average of about R2,500 per month to R30,000 per month. All the infrastructure on the farm had been stripped and sold by Mr Swanepoel and the land was valued by Mr Roux as if this infrastructure (such as irrigation pipes) was still in the ground.

'When Mr Swanepoel and his attorney were confronted with this, they blamed Mr Roux,' Fred's affidavit continues. 'They alleged that the land claims commissioner had approached them after their farm had been gazetted and told them that the government wanted a valuation done. Mr Roux was sent by the land claims commissioner.

'I have seen Badplaas suffer economically over the years and, at 68 per cent, the area has one of the highest unemployment rates in the country. I do not want to see Badplaas collapse again due to inflated and unsustainable land prices. I would also like to see that the restitution process is fair and previously disadvantaged people get fair value for their money. It is also important that limited taxpayers' money is used in the best possible way.

'I would like to see that the new owners [of the farms] contribute to the economic revival of the area. Badplaas is just starting to recover from the collapse of mining and large-scale farming and is entering into a new phase where tourism is starting to become an important land use. But much hard work is still required to achieve this, which will take large amounts of investment, time and commitment.'

8
Blow the house down

In March 2004, a fresh land claim was lodged and gazetted on a portion of Fred's land in the Badplaas area. Then in May, a second new claim against land he owned was published in the *Government Gazette*. As he was not informed about the claims, which is required by law, he kept on purchasing more farms. But there was one stumbling block to his land assemblage programme. Regional land claims commissioner Nceba Nqana began using his R50-million budget to buy land for claimants, sending prices rocketing into the stratosphere.

In May 2004 Fred instructed his attorney Richard Spoor to write to Nqana expressing his concerns about land inflation, after discovering that the department of agriculture and land affairs was buying the farm Vygeboom for far more than its real value. 'Our client has become aware of the pending transfer of the Vygeboom Portion 11 farm as well as other farms in the Badplaas area to the state on behalf of various land claimants,' Spoor wrote. 'We are aware that valuations commissioned for sellers are hugely inflated.

'Our client does not know the price offered by yourselves for Portion 11, but we are advised that you are paying more than

R3.5 million for the land. This is significantly above the market price. The property was purchased in 2002 for R1.2 million … No improvements have been made to the land since 2002. In fact, the farm has deteriorated significantly…

'Our client believes that the property forms part of a package of farms being purchased from V8 Cattle Ranch [Pieter Visagie's company] or associated companies. Our client has been advised that several of the properties are not owned by the sellers and that they have been secured only by an option. We are advised that the difference between the option price and the sale price to you is substantial. Our client is concerned that the sellers are selling to you at significantly inflated prices and are profiteering at the state's expense. As a taxpayer, this is of concern to our client, but as a landowner and active buyer, this is equally problematic.

'Our client's purchases for Nkomazi Wilderness pushed up local prices over the past few years; your purchases will, however, chase prices beyond all reasonable parameters and this is not a good situation for anyone other than profiteers. It makes the purchase of land for productive use impossible. It has the effect of driving commercial farmers off their land and is a hugely inefficient use of taxpayers' funds.

'The valuation our client has been provided with for Portion 11 is seriously flawed and is not a fair valuation at all. We would urge you to reconsider purchasing the property at such a price until such time as you have done a competent and independent valuation of Portion 11 Vygeboom and the other properties.

'Our client is interested in economic development, job creation and eco-tourism and has made a huge investment in the area towards those ends. You are interested in land redistribution. Both you and our client have an interest in paying a reasonable or fair price for land. Without some degree of cooperation and planning, our client and yourselves are likely to work at cross-purposes and frustrate each other's good intentions. Cooperation on the other hand may bring about a mutually beneficial situation where prices are contained and our client can assist your beneficiaries in a whole range of projects that empower them economically and with skills.

'Our client supports the restitution and redistribution processes and would welcome the new owners' participation in Nkomazi Wilderness. We have been asked to facilitate a meeting between you and Nkomazi Wilderness to discuss these matters. Please advise if you are amenable to this and when it may be convenient to meet.'

Nqana did not respond to the letter.

In June 2004 another obstacle emerged when the regional Land Claims Commission gazetted new claims on the farms Winkelhaak, Languedoc, Skimmelfontein, Sterkspruit, Vygeboom, Doyershoek, Groenvallei, Boekenhoutrand – and Nkomazi Wilderness Reserve.

'The land that was gazetted corresponded almost perfectly with the map attached to Spoor's letter in May 1999 to the Land Claims Commission, showing where I wished to establish Nkomazi,' Fred says. 'It appeared as though the claims were gazetted to frustrate us, rather than in accordance with the Restitution of Land Rights Act. They matched my land exactly. There were competing claims for the same piece of land.

'The commission at no time followed the procedures set out in the Act, which prescribes notice to the current owner of land over which the claim is gazetted. Its conduct was even more alarming because the commission had been in engagement with us when the land was gazetted.

'Spoor told me this was either monumental incompetence or fraud. The claims that had been submitted were frivolous and vexatious. I was advised not to admit any land claim on the strength of information available to Spoor. His advice gave me the confidence to continue with the creation of Nkomazi Wilderness by acquiring more properties and incorporating them into the reserve.'

There was other opposition to Fred's land assemblage programme. Dick Wensing, who had been a consultant for the Mpumalanga Parks Board, said in his report on Nkomazi that some Badplaas farmers and farm unions objected to Fred's message that their land was unsuitable for agriculture. 'They were suspicious of his motives for purchasing their land, as they could not (yet) comprehend the benefits of replacing cattle with wild animals,' he wrote. 'Tourism, especially eco-tourism, were swear words.'

In June 2004, Fred sent a letter to the regional Land Claims Commission asking for information about investigations they might have conducted into the claims on his land. He told Nqana that he wished to engage with him about the claims. There was no response. Spoor wrote another letter in September suggesting that an independent non-governmental organisation be asked to represent the claimants. He said Fred believed that the commission was unable or unwilling to deal with the land claims in the interests of the claimants or the community of Badplaas. Nqana did not respond.

Spoor and Fred blew the whistle on the Badplaas land scam. In September 2004, investigative journalist Justin Arenstein published a devastating exposé in *City Press* under the headline 'SA's own land grab'. 'Shrewd land speculators are milking the land reform programme by systematically selling farms to the Land Claims Commission at massively inflated prices,' he began.

'Mpumalanga land claims commissioner Nceba Nqana reluctantly confirmed that he had ignored pre-emptive warnings from concerned local farmers and professional land valuators and spent R25.7 million on six farms in the Badplaas district, which had originally been bought for a combined price of R4.3 million. This left speculators with a cool R21.3 million in profit. The prices on some of the sales, such as Onverwacht farm, represent a 300 per cent increase on their 2004 market value.'

Arenstein wrote that records at the deeds office showed that Onverwacht was bought from its owner for R1.2 million in May and sold to the Land Claims Commission for R3.3 million a month later. 'Nqana is unable to explain how the land could have tripled in value in so short a time. He also said he doubted if a transaction could take place in such a short period of time.'

Onverwacht was not the only farm sold to the government at grossly inflated prices. Engelschedraai had been bought for R650,000 in 2002 and sold to the commission for R4.1 million in June 2004 – speculators made a profit of 600 per cent. The

Vaalkop farm had been bought from Mondi Forests for R1.6 million in 2000 and sold to the commission in June that year for R4.1 million – a mark-up of 500 per cent.

The 306-hectare Vygeboom dairy farm was purchased for R1.6 million in 2002 and sold to the commission for R4.4 million. The neighbouring 516-hectare Doornhoek farm was purchased for R250,000 and sold to the commission for R5.7 million – 22 times the previous purchase price.

Arenstein quoted Spoor's letter of concern to Nqana, warning that profiteers were seriously undermining land restitution and wasting taxpayers' money. 'The letter focuses on the Vygeboom sale, warning that speculators paid the original owner R1.6m for the dairy and vegetable farm in 2002, with R1m of that price for the farm's 538 dairy cows. The farm's true land cost, Spoor argues, was therefore R600,000. The Land Claims Commission paid R4.4m for the land, without any cows or other moveable goods.'

Spoor told Arenstein that several farms offered to the commission were not owned by the sellers, but that speculators had merely secured options on the land. The difference between the option prices and sale prices was substantial.

Fred told *City Press* that he was spearheading calls for a re-evaluation of farm prices in Badplaas. 'I suppose I could keep quiet, negotiate a lucrative deal with the Land Claims Commission and walk away from this a very rich man. But the amounts of money we're talking about here are obscene; they are actually undermining the whole agricultural market. What happens when the bubble bursts?

'This matter is so clear-cut that I am deeply concerned that the local Land Claims Commission office is either incompetent or corrupt, because the prices paid bear no relationship to actual land values. They simply cannot be justified. My company, Grand Valley Estates, has purchased comparable properties in this area for just R350,000 over the past three years.'

Arenstein wrote that Fred was not the only farmer who was concerned about the massive inflation in land prices in Badplaas. Other farmers, fearing victimisation, had written anonymously to *Farmer's Weekly* magazine complaining that they were being pressured into selling their land to middlemen in return for 300 per cent mark-ups on actual market values.

Nqana responded: 'This kind of scam is common right across South Africa and we therefore do everything humanly possible to check land costs and ensure that the taxpayer gets good value for money. I'm also aware of Daniel's concerns and have asked for an investigation into the matter.' Arenstein noted that Nqana was unable to explain why he had authorised the purchases in Badplaas before the investigation was completed.

The corruption-busting reporter concluded: 'Ironically, the Department of Land Affairs warned this week that it needed to allocate a minimum of R12 billion a year to land claims settlements or the government would fail to meet President Thabo Mbeki's December 2005 deadline for settling all restitution cases.'

A week later, in the *Mail & Guardian*, Arenstein reported that the national government had ordered an urgent independent forensic investigation into 14 contentious land deals in Mpumalanga, which cost taxpayers R72.1 million. 'Chief land claims commissioner Tozi Gwanya has instructed senior independent property valuer Derrick Griffiths to verify whether sales prices for the 14 vegetable and dairy farms in Mpumalanga's Badplaas valley were inflated or otherwise manipulated by land speculators and government officials,' he wrote. 'Griffiths and other government investigators will also probe whether government-appointed valuers acted ethically during the deals and whether there was any conflict of interests for landowners to also serve as government advisors during negotiations.

'The ambitious Badplaas land restitution project is designed to compensate the fragmented Ndwandwa community of about 30,000 people for their deprivation under colonial and apartheid regimes. Mpumalanga land claims commissioner Nceba Nqana says white settlers used racist laws to systematically acquire ownership of the land, forcing the dispossessed tribes to provide child labour on farms before eventually evicting the Ndwandwa and related clans from the area.'

Nqana had written to agriculture and land affairs minister

Thoko Didiza, warning that the scattered communities were in danger of disintegration unless they urgently regained ownership of at least some of their original land. The minister approved a R71.6-million budget to purchase 35 commercial farms, totalling 15,247 hectares, for restitution to the Ndwandwa community.

Arenstein continued: 'All the properties would, Nqana said, be purchased as going concerns that would immediately provide the Ndwandwa community with livelihoods and security of tenure. Nqana appears, however, to have already overspent his approved budget on just 14 of the properties covering 6,500 hectares of the targeted land. The deals have primarily benefited land speculator and farmer Pieter Visagie, who is chairman of the local land reform and development forum that advises the government on land-claim priorities and economic development opportunities.

'He is also tipped to help the Ndwandwa community take over commercial farming enterprises on their new land as part of a R8.8 million additional support contract signed by Nqana and supported by community leaders. He concedes that the government paid a premium for the Ndwandwa land but insists nothing underhand occurred and the deals are good value for money.'

'Any investigation will prove this. We put a hell of a lot of work into this land reform thing,' Visagie told the *Mail & Guardian*. 'We hope to eventually see the government buy 40,000 hectares in the valley for the Ndwandwa community. These are really good farms, with excellent water, and we have worked hard to ensure that they are fully operational businesses for the new owners.'

Visagie's business partner Tony Kennet said criticism of the deals was 'absolute hogwash' to Arenstein and the *Mail & Guardian*. Kennet sold his farm, Engelschedraai Portion 6, to the Land Claims Commission for R2.2 million. 'What outsiders fail to understand is that there has been a dramatic change in local circumstances in Badplaas over the past three years,' he said. 'Farmers who traditionally concentrated on tobacco and sheep could not survive, and have made way for tourism, which has taken off in a big way. Property prices have therefore increased. I think we have, therefore, actually undersold ourselves to the commission. We should have held out for more money. But you can say we sold in the interests of land reform.'

Nqana came to Visagie's defence in a statement that dismissed criticism of the deals as 'sour grapes' by farmers opposed to land reform. He said substantive improvements had been made to each of the 14 farms purchased so far, which warranted the dramatic price increases. The improvements included new irrigation dams and pipelines, game fencing, livestock enclosures and gravel roads.

On the day the land scam story appeared on the front page of *City Press*, Abe Sibiya, recently appointed acting CEO of the Mpumalanga Parks Board, visited Spoor's law firm partner Obert Ntuli. He brought Nqana, whom he introduced as a friend, to plead for Ntuli's help in stopping Fred from speaking about the land purchases in Badplaas. Ntuli refused to help.

Land affairs minister Thoko Didiza appointed Ernst & Young to conduct a forensic investigation into the activities of the Mpumalanga Land Claims Commission and the Ndwandwa Community Trust land claim and restitution. As a 'precautionary measure necessary to ensure the complete transparency of the investigation', she suspended Nqana and the commission's regional project manager Linda Mbatha.

Briefing parliament's land affairs portfolio committee in March 2005 on the progress of the investigations, Didiza said that among the reports' findings was that market-valuation principles and standards had not been adhered to or were misconstrued by the valuers. 'The findings also indicate there was incorrect application of valuation methods, which resulted in flagrant overstatement of market value,' she said.

'It was very evident there had been misrepresentation of market conditions. It was also found that the Land Claims Commission project officers processed payment, despite having been cautioned by the deputy director general of finance of calculation errors in the claim.' Didiza described to MPs what she called an interesting scenario: 'One of the farms was leased back, at a price of R6,700 a month, to the original seller by the beneficiary. And the landowner, instead of using the land, actually sub-let the farm to a third party, at a price of R75,000 a month.'

She told parliament that the reports recommended that the national department of land affairs consider a criminal investigation into the Badplaas farm sales. Charge sheets had been finalised and an advocate had been appointed to consider 'civil action against valuers, land owners and, possibly, some of the commission's staff,' Didiza said. 'We are identifying areas that may require criminal action, and, as such, we have engaged the Commercial Crime Unit. We have also appointed high-level staff in the Mpumalanga regional Land Claims Commission to beef up our capacity to deal with some of the issues.' Didiza told the committee she could not yet release the reports, 'because of the charges and further investigation that has to be done by the Commercial Crime Unit'.

Arenstein uncovered the scant details available on the two reports into alleged profiteering in Mpumalanga land restitution deals. 'Ministerial spokesman Nana Zenani confirmed the receipt of an Ernst & Young forensic audit into a string of dodgy deals in Mpumalanga's Badplaas valley, as well as a separate investigation report from Institute of Valuers executive member Derrick Griffiths,' he wrote.

'Evidence uncovered indicates that land speculators, allegedly working with Land Claims Commission officials, fraudulently inflated prices on gazetted farms and then over-charged the taxpayer up to 2,000 per cent in one instance and 300 per cent on at least six other transactions. The revelations led to the suspension of Mpumalanga land claims commissioner Nceba Nqana and local project manager Linda Mbatha last year, as well as the restructuring of the commission's offices in Mpumalanga.'

'Local developers claim Mr Nqana irregularly helped land speculators set up the deals by allegedly issuing illegal financial guarantees to help them bankroll the alleged scam,' Arenstein reported. 'In one case, his office allegedly issued a guarantee in favour of local farmer Pieter Visagie, allowing him to purchase the Vygeboom farm for R1.6 million in 2002. Mr Nqana bought the farm from Mr Visagie just months later for R4.4 million, even though the Land Claims Commission's own experts warned that the property was worth a maximum of R2.9 million.

'Mr Nqana has since consistently refused to answer questions on the matter, but Mr Visagie has denied any wrongdoing and dismissed critics as opponents of land reform. The local farmers' union, Agri Badplaas, has come to Mr Visagie's defence and condemned the investigation as a smear campaign.'

The department of agriculture and land affairs asked Griffiths to prepare another report establishing how much money had been stolen. He concluded in March that 'the market values for the farms are considered by me to be overvalued by at least R40 million, or 50 per cent. The valuations of the properties bought by the regional Land Claims Commission were overvalued by more or less R14 million, or 72 per cent. The prices paid for these farms exceed market value by at least R20 million, or 107 per cent.'

In August 2005, *Sunday Times* reporter Prega Govender wrote an update on the fraud. According to him, Ernst & Young's report strongly recommended that the department of land affairs consider criminal and civil action against government-appointed valuer Dr Nkosana Makhaya for allegedly manipulating valuations in Mpumalanga. It recommended that disciplinary action be taken against Nqana and his project officer Linda Mbatha.

'Nqana defended the prices by pointing to recent improvements on the farms said to be worth more than R6 million,' Govender reported. 'He resigned last month after an internal disciplinary committee found him guilty of wasteful expenditure related to the sale of the farms. But he is not yet off the hook. Chief land claims commissioner Tozi Gwanya confirmed that he had asked the police to launch an investigation. Those found to have benefited unlawfully from the transactions, be they staff members, valuers or landowners, would face criminal charges, he said.'

The audit found that Makhaya did not have the expertise to conduct proper valuations and used the report of a valuer appointed by farmers selling their land to amend his valuations. The amendments increased the valuation of the farms by more than R6.3 million. Payments for Badplaas farms included moveable assets, despite a clear directive from Didiza that they be excluded. Nqana had instructed the department of agriculture and land affairs finance section to pay Visagie R898,593 for moveable assets on the basis that they were critical assets.

Half of the farms bought for the Ndwandwa claimants came from Visagie and his companies at a cost of R51 million, the audit also found. This payment was processed in one week and appeared irregular. Visagie was also paid more than 80 per cent of the province's restitution development grant, amounting to R8.8 million.

Despite Didiza's promise to parliament, to this day the prosecution of people involved in the Badplaas land scam has not been concluded and there has been no civil action to recoup squandered taxpayers' money. The corrupt officials, speculators and politicians pulled off a R70-million heist of government funds meant for poor, black victims of apartheid injustice.

A possible reason why they remain free as birds is provided in an affidavit by Mpumalanga Land Claims Commission manager Linda Mbatha: 'I am of the opinion that certain claims are treated with preference due to political pressures, resulting in the claims being processed quicker. The chief land claims commissioner and/or the minister exerts pressure over the process. There was pressure over the Badplaas claim. Politicians are interested in properties or have interests in other ventures. The properties owned by Mr Pieter Visagie are an example.'

In 2003, forensic investigator Paul O'Sullivan investigated the Badplaas land claims 'as a matter of public interest' and laid charges of fraud against Visagie and former Land Claims Commission employees for inflating farm prices. In his report, he said previously productive land around Badplaas had fallen fallow and agricultural infrastructure had been stripped and sold for scrap. Tourism infrastructure like guesthouses and a trout farm had been stripped and sold, with no accounting of the proceeds.

'Public funds, earmarked for genuine claims, were used to pay fake claims while genuine claims went unmet, resulting in a complete failure of restitution to deserving communities, simply because there was no upside for the corrupt politicians,' O'Sullivan reported. 'Thousands of people, previously employed in tourism or agriculture, have been put out of work ... To date, not a single suspect has been prosecuted for the loss of hundreds of millions of rand in public funds ... that has been diverted into the pockets of cadre appointees and their cronies, families and friends.'

9
Pariah town

Blowing the whistle on the Badplaas land scam had immediate and severe consequences for the Daniel family. Many people in the small town literally turned their backs on them and closed ranks to protect locals implicated in the corruption. Farmers already suspicious about the Cradle of Life and Nkomazi became openly hostile. Fred was vilified in the media.

The Badplaas scandal was cited by Thabo Mbeki in his state of the nation address in February 2006 as evidence of the flaws and constraints of the 'willing buyer, willing seller' principle in land reform. There would be a 'full-scale' review of the government's verification and evaluation procedures, Mbeki said. The government was considering the expropriation of farm land to speed up the reform process. Badplaas farmers hoping to score huge profit on the sale of their farms to the Land Claims Commission blamed Fred for Mbeki's threat.

Arenstein wrote in the *Mail & Guardian* in September 2004 that Agri Badplaas, which represented landowners in the region, tried to derail the investigation into the scam by attacking Derrick Griffiths, the land valuator appointed by the government to investigate the inflation of prices. Agri Badplaas chairman Jappie Middel wrote to chief land claims commissioner Tozi Gwanya claiming that Griffiths had previously worked for Fred. Gwanya said to Arenstein that he checked the allegations, and found them to be untrue.

Arenstein also discovered that Middel worked for Pieter Visagie and the Ndwandwa Community Trust. Visagie managed the trust's accounts and paid all its bills. Middel admitted this, but denied that there was a conflict of interest when he complained to the commission about Fred. 'My work is different from our complaints against Griffiths – because I represent all local farmers,' he told Arenstein. Middel added that the protest letter against Fred was authorised by Agri Badplaas's management committee after a request from 'affected farmers'.

In early 2005, Pieter Visagie brought a damages claim in the Carolina Magistrate's Court against Fred, for R100,000 in reputational damage based on the contents of Fred's sworn affidavit to Ernst & Young about the land scam. 'The affidavit was provided on a privileged occasion, as part of a government-instructed investigation into Visagie's actions,' Fred told the court. 'It is therefore part of a lawful objective, the facts contained in the affidavit are the truth, and publication thereof was in the interests of the public.' Subsequently, in January 2008, Visagie offered to withdraw the matter. Fred accepted this, on condition that Visagie paid his legal costs. The costs were calculated at R40,587.06. Visagie has not paid a cent.

By the last quarter of 2005, Visagie and the Mpumalanga Land Claims Commission had come under such intense scrutiny that they decided to divert attention from their corruption. They allegedly bribed the veteran journalist Chris Louw with cattle and free grazing to damage the reputations of Fred, Richard Spoor and Derrick Griffiths.

Fred was out of the country when he discovered that Louw, a freelance reporter for *Farmer's Weekly*, was interviewing his friends and employees. They believed the journalist was trying to dig up dirt on him. On 25 October, Louw met Spoor in Nelspruit and made several unfounded and prejudicial statements about Fred and the Nkomazi project. Spoor said the reporter was extremely hostile and believed a set of facts that were blatantly false.

Fred's bankers Imperial Bank drew his attention to a defamatory letter that Louw had written to them on 20 October, apparently on behalf of *Farmer's Weekly*. The journalist alleged that Fred was resisting land claims and facing criminal charges and asked the bank whether it 'condones such actions'.

At a meeting in November, Louw finally met Fred. The journalist said he had been invited to Badplaas by Visagie, had met Abe Sibiya at the parks board and Nceba Nqana, suspended regional land claims commissioner. He did not tell Fred that he was planning to publish an article, nor did he provide him with an opportunity to comment.

Louw was a respected journalist. He went into journalism in the late 1980s after his national service and worked at *Die Vaderland*, the *Mail & Guardian* and the South African Broadcasting Corporation. He became a freelance writer for *Farmer's Weekly* and *Beeld*. In 1987, he was part of a delegation of mostly white Afrikaners who held meetings with the then-banned ANC in Dakar, Senegal.

In late November 2005, Fred was outraged when he read an article in *Farmer's Weekly* headlined 'Criminal charges against Badplaas whistleblower'. Louw claimed that Fred and Spoor believed that no black people had any rights to land in the Badplaas area. He also alleged that Fred ill-treated his employees. Another article in the same edition falsely alleged that Griffiths faced charges of unprofessional conduct.

Spoor wrote a letter to the magazine's editor, Chris Burgess, saying that the allegations against himself and Fred were completely false and impugned his honour and track record as a defender of human rights and legitimate community land claims. He reiterated that Fred and his business entities were 'wholly supportive of land redistribution and the land reform process' and would admit all and any land claims filed against his properties, 'of which he is reasonably satisfied have merit'.

On 18 November, Fred called Burgess to bring to his attention the falsehoods in the article. 'In a stroke of luck, he was not in his office,' he says. 'His secretary mistook me for someone else and faxed me copies of a series of articles that was clearly designed to do massive damage and discredit me to take the heat off the probe into corruption and fraud in Badplaas.' The following article in the series, to be published in the next edition, had the headline 'The secret life of a whistleblower'.

'The articles consisted of shocking journalism, people were completely misquoted, and the facts were incorrect and blatantly false,' Fred says. His lawyers sent a letter of demand to Caxton, the publishers of *Farmer's Weekly*, to withdraw the articles and apologise for the first one already published. Their letter was ignored.

On 22 November, Fred and his company Grand Valley Estates brought an urgent application to restrain and interdict Caxton and Louw from 'publishing, disseminating, selling and distributing' an edition of *Farmer's Weekly* in which an article about Fred or his business appeared, or 'in any other publication; or in any form whatsoever'.

Within an hour of the papers being served on the company, Caxton's attorney agreed to provide a written undertaking not to publish the articles. 'The attorney told me Louw was not able to answer any of the facts set out in the article, which was why they came back so quickly to settle the matter,' Fred says. 'I wasn't objecting to freedom of the press, or even what Louw's opinion was about me. I was simply insisting that he and Caxton had no right to publish false and untrue facts and statements.'

Despite the undertaking, two articles about Fred were published in *Farmer's Weekly* in December under the headlines 'Emotions run high over Nkomazi Reserve' and 'New allegations against Badplaas whistleblower'. Fred brought an urgent application in the North Gauteng High Court for an interdict against Caxton on the grounds that the articles were defamatory and untrue. Paul Jenkins, an attorney representing Caxton, said Louw had been unable to reply to any aspects of Fred's founding affidavit. Caxton undertook to allow Fred, over a period of five years, to check any planned articles about him prior to publication, to ensure that they were factual and did not defame him. In February 2006, *Farmer's Weekly* published an apology under the headline 'Daniel wrongly slated in Badplaas saga'. Caxton agreed to abide by the court order that they desist from publishing defamatory articles about Fred and to pay R80,000 in costs.

After Kerzner International signed the agreement with Fred to build and operate a One&Only safari lodge at Nkomazi, the Development Bank of Southern Africa approved a R135-million investment in the reserve and paid the first R35 million. In November 2006 Louw sent the bank's CEO, Paul Baloyi, a letter similar to the one he had sent Imperial Bank, alleging that Fred was opposed to land claims and was facing criminal charges. Spoor sent another letter of demand to Caxton, and the company responded by firing Louw.

The journalist contacted Fred soon after his dismissal to complain. Louw said he had invested his pension in Visagie's butchery in Nelspruit and the cattle he received as payment for his defamatory *Farmer's Weekly* articles grazed on the Ndwandwa Trust's land. He said that he was broke because Visagie had slaughtered all his cattle and liquidated the butchery. He offered to meet with Spoor to give him an affidavit about his dealings with Visagie. On 30 November Louw committed suicide by shooting himself in the head with an AK-47.

10
The animals came in

Corruption and fraud pervaded the Mpumalanga Tourism and Parks Agency before, during and after D.D. Mabuza's short tenure of just over a year as MEC for agriculture and land affairs, when he had oversight of its work and budget. The agency was formed in 2006 after its forerunner, the Mpumalanga Parks Board, collapsed under the weight of political corruption.

As the owner of a private game reserve, Fred was required by law to cooperate with the agency. It had the authority to grant the crucial authorisations and permits for which he had applied to stock Nkomazi with animals. Without them, he could not grow and secure the value of his assets.

After he signed the deal with Kerzner International in 2003 to build a One&Only resort on his land – an investment that would secure Nkomazi Wilderness and the Cradle of Life for future generations – Fred redoubled his attempts to secure permits from the parks board for all the Big Five animals.

By 2005, Nkomazi had buffalo, leopard and rhinoceros, but Fred was still waiting for permits to keep lion and elephant to complete the Big Five animals. He also applied for permits for large predators like wild dogs and cheetah. As lion and elephants were available from Sabi Sabi, he asked the parks board to stamp his fence specification as compliant for the Big Five, 'to commit them and close the gap so they could not change the goalposts again. The fence specification was approved and stamped, but written in bold letters was a caveat that there was a ban on the introduction of lion.'

Ignoring the fact that their core mandate of biodiversity protection and tourism development extends to private reserves, officials of the parks agency sparked a conflict with private landowners that has not been resolved. Fred discovered in 2003 that officials, charged with the care of wildlife on state-owned and private reserves, were issuing permits to hunt valuable animals. A male and a female hippo came up the Komati River in 2000 and settled on Nkomazi, where they grazed on the lush new grasses, helping to preserve the riverbank ecology. Despite issuing an adequate enclosure certificate to protect Nkomazi's animals, the parks board issued a permit to Fred's neighbour to hunt one of the hippos. He sold the meat and kept the head for a trophy.

Attorney Richard Spoor wrote to the parks board to express Fred's anger. 'It is incomprehensible that you issued a permit to shoot the hippo. Please confirm that in the future no such permit will be issued until interested or affected neighbours are consulted and alternatives to killing the animals are considered.' There was no answer to his letter.

Fred sums up the death of his valuable animal in a clipped tone: 'Corruption leads to environmental degradation.'

THE CHRONICLE OF HARASSMENT waged by the parks agency against Fred is a long one. In August 2006, its officials threw a spanner into his plans when they refused to approve an application from Grand Valley Estates to be appointed as the management authority of the Nkomazi Wilderness in terms of the Protected Areas Act. Approval of the application would provide additional tools to protect the nature reserve.

In 2007 the agency launched another attack. It obtained a search warrant for the Cradle of Life animal rehabilitation centre, executed on 5 November. After attaching the animals, the agency laid 21 criminal charges against Fred for, among other things, keeping game without a licence, receiving animals unlawfully and unnecessarily disturbing animals.

Spoor sent a letter to Nelspruit Regional Court prosecutor Charles Lloyd, citing the 'unrelenting obstructionism' and complete lack of support for Nkomazi by the parks agency's manager of wildlife protection services, Jan Muller. The official had made it clear 'that there will be no accommodation on the release of Nkomazi's animals' and no permit for keeping large predators. Spoor asked for 'at least some assurance ... of good faith' in approving Nkomazi's management status; considering its permit applications on their merits and authorising the release of its animals. By doing so, it would 'go a long way to facilitating a plea, restoring good relations and allowing us to move forward together.' There was no response from Lloyd.

After they had attached the animals from the Cradle of Life, the parks agency could not find a suitable facility that was prepared or able to take them. Dr Ndayeni Ndamase, district deputy director of animal health, was asked by the agency to conduct an inspection of the animals. He said in his report that they were in good condition and recommended that they should not be removed as it would create unnecessary stress.

Lloyd wrote to Fred asking him to undertake to keep the animals pending the outcome of the criminal prosecution. He asked that none of the animals be removed from their enclosures, that they be fed and watered, that access to the rehabilitation facility be given to parks agency officials and nominated veterinarians, and that Nkomazi bear all associated costs. Spoor sent a letter committing Fred to all these requirements.

The prosecutor said he had instructions from the parks agency to settle the case. Fred should plead guilty, pay a R500,000 fine and undertake not to apply for wildlife permits for five years. If he did not plead guilty, further charges would be added to the charge sheet. The Mpumalanga Nature Conservation Act allows prosecutors to ask a court to declare a convicted person unfit to obtain permits to keep animals for up to five years. A criminal conviction could have had far-reaching consequences for Fred's management authority status. He refused to plead guilty to trumped-up charges.

In March 2008, Fred received an email from Dr Koos de Wet at the parks agency, who had planned to conduct veld assessments on Nkomazi for the introduction of elephant and lion. He wrote that his superior, Charles Ndabeni, on instructions from Jan Muller, the manager of wildlife protection services, had 'prohibited' any contact with Fred. De Wet therefore cancelled his site visit.

In an attempt to break the deadlock with the officials stonewalling his project, Fred commissioned an expert to confirm his belief that the conservation agency had been derailed by corruption. 'The Mpumalanga Tourism and Parks Agency has been known to be inefficient at the best of times,' Dick Wensing observed drily in his report. Wensing had been a consultant for the agency and understood the terrain.

He praised Fred for his nine years of careful restoration of Nkomazi, a 'role model of an ecological, sustainable enterprise. Behind this transformation is one man's dedicated commitment and management. For an operation with a current investment of almost R200 million and growing in excess of R1 billion within the next several years, it could be expected that the provincial government would acknowledge Nkomazi as a role player in the regional economy in terms of wealth generation, job creation, social upliftment, poverty alleviation, foreign exchange earnings and biodiversity conservation. However, little to no support was provided either financially, operationally or by streamlining bureaucratic procedures for the reserve's establishment and making these procedures less obstructive, hostile and untrustworthy.'

Merely with the flourish of a signature on a form, an official at the agency could help transform Nkomazi Wilderness into a 7-star reserve by allowing it to host elephant, lion and cheetah. Permits were granted for rhinoceros and buffalo, but the agency would not budge on providing paperwork for the rest of the Big Five animals – the major tourist drawcard. Fred had applied for permits to establish the game reserve; to keep the animals in holding facilities; to care for orphaned, injured and sick animals, and to erect multi-functional bomas.

Wensing posed the problem: 'Why is there an acrimonious relationship between the Mpumalanga Tourism and Parks Agency and Nkomazi Wilderness management and is this happening to other private organisations?' He investigated and reported: 'Nkomazi Wilderness has to deal with ... a civil servant organisation in total chaos, highly politicised and unionised, with no ambition to go full-out to support and promote private initiatives because there is no direct benefit for themselves.

'By making matters personal and with a racial undertone, it is easier to delay and frustrate processes on the basis of unwarranted technicalities, simply because they can.'

Wensing reported that other tourism organisations and businesses in Mpumalanga shared similar experiences. The agency's focus had shifted from issuing permits to settling land claims, while ignoring 'to a large extent their duty to verify claims', Wensing wrote. It had 32 reserves under its jurisdiction, with claims on most of them. 'Soon, thousands of hectares of land under their control will be handed to communities without any regard to nature conservation or biodiversity protection.'

Nkomazi should have been a flagship tourism project in Mpumalanga, Wensing believed. It could have 'set an example of what can be achieved by good cooperation between a private organisation with driven management and a statutory body that encourages and supports the project because they understand how it benefits the local community, the province and the country. Unfortunately, the opposite is true.'

IN MAY 2008, while Fred was contemplating solutions to the impasse between him and the parks agency, its officials obtained a search warrant, based on testimony by its employees that lions were being held in cages on Nkomazi Wilderness at a precise GPS location. The next morning police officers from the organised crime unit in Middelburg descended on the reserve.

When they arrived, a police officer grabbed a security guard through the reserve's gate, overpowering him and taking his cellphone. After going to the GPS location and finding no lions there, a helicopter flew low over Nkomazi for hours. Spoor sent a scathing letter to prosecutor Charles Lloyd, the organised crime unit and the magistrate at the Carolina court. The warrant was based on false and perjured information and the search was part of an 'unlawful vendetta' by the agency, he said. Nkomazi had no lions, the attorney pointed out again; for the agency had not responded to Fred's applications for a permit to keep them.

Spoor sent another letter in May to the state attorney in the Mpumalanga premier's office, Ansie Venter, advising her that the parks agency was deliberately spreading false information that Fred was breeding animals in cages and running a black market smuggling ring. He asked that the 'defective and unlawful' warrant be withdrawn immediately and requested a copy of the affidavit on which it had been based. He warned that if this information was not provided, Fred would bring an urgent interdict to set it aside. Venter responded that the warrant had 'expired'.

On 18 June, the parks agency and police officers descended on the Cradle of Life rehabilitation centre, with the defective and expired warrant, and confiscated several animals, including duck, wild dog and leopard. Fred says the raid appeared to have been carefully coordinated with his appearance on that day in the Carolina Magistrate's Court to answer the criminal charges brought against him by the agency. Fred then brought two interdicts against the agency, preventing them from removing any more birds or animals and ordering them to return those they had taken. The judge in one of Fred's cases called the actions of the agency's officials and police 'nothing more than common theft'.

In July some of the animals were returned, but many had died while they were being kept at the Rhino and Lion Park in Krugersdorp. Conservationist Kenneth Heuer, general manager of the section 21 company Great Cats in Crisis South Africa, trout breeder in Mpumalanga and Gauteng, and owner of a carnivore rescue centre in Krugersdorp, described how unnecessary and cruel the deaths were.

In January 2008, when he was applying for several permits for his farm in Mpumalanga, Heuer, who also owns Trans Africa

Aviation, had received a phone call from Jan Muller. 'He informed me that the parks agency had a donor with funds to purchase a helicopter … to patrol their reserves,' Heuer said in an affidavit. 'Muller is a helicopter pilot and he is currently funding his son's training to become a pilot as well, which is a very expensive exercise.'

They agreed that a jet ranger helicopter would be the most suitable for patrols and he told Muller that it would cost about R7 million. 'He proposed that once I had located such a machine … I could then sell it on to the agency, but with one condition … Muller wanted a commission out of the deal, since he controlled the deal.'

Muller called again to say the parks agency wanted to develop a trout farm on a property in Lydenburg that was owned by the Mpumalanga government. Heuer claimed in his affidavit that Muller 'and another person whose identity was not disclosed to me, wanted to have a slice in the company that did the development'. He did not enter into any of the deals with Muller, 'as I am not comfortable to do business by bribing officials since it has become a national disease. Because of blatant corruption, I do not believe that the Mpumalanga Tourism and Parks Agency acts in the interests of wild animals, conservation or tourism and they started making compromised decisions. That is why their reserves are collapsing and deteriorating and tourism in the province is rapidly declining.'

Heuer said Muller consulted him before they removed the animals from the Cradle of Life. 'I strongly advised him to leave the animals exactly where they were, especially in light of the fact that he himself had informed me that the Cradle of Life's facilities were world-class. There was no point in moving the animals, especially if they were well cared for. I was absolutely dumbfounded when I learnt that Muller had gone ahead and moved the animals. I was also saddened to learn that the large male leopard had been killed and I smelled a rat. The killing of such a magnificent animal is a barbaric, senseless and irresponsible action that one would never expect of those entrusted with the noble task of conservation.

'The motivation of selling the skin would have further clouded his judgement, as corruption does. This, the fact that Muller was not very complimentary of Fred Daniel, as well as what I learnt from Muller in further conversation, made me realise that he and the Mpumalanga Tourism and Parks Agency had a serious personal vendetta against Daniel.

'I find it truly amazing that Muller and the Mpumalanga Tourism and Parks Agency could openly defame and discredit Daniel in the manner they have done when his achievements and motives are clear for all to see, if they just took the trouble to look. I believe that the Badplaas area and Mpumalanga (which is steadily declining in tourism and conservation) are very lucky to have someone like Daniel investing there. Despite this, Muller informed me that Daniel was an arrogant asshole who thought he was above the law. Muller said that Daniel always sent his lawyers and experts to the agency to deal with him and the staff, and he was tired of this.'

Heuer helped Fred to bring his animals back to Badplaas after his urgent interdict against the agency was granted. He helped to find the big male leopard that Muller and his team had killed when they confiscated the animals. 'I was very keen to see the condition of the animal as what Muller had told me, and what I read in the press, was not consistent with the photographs I had seen or the people I had talked to concerning this animal,' Heuer said.

'It became clear to me that a great injustice had been done against Daniel, conservation and the wild animals. Nobody at the Rhino and Lion Park, the police or Mpumalanga Tourism and Parks Agency was cooperative in providing simple and clear answers to the question of where the leopard's remains were. I was very surprised when Daniel's partner John Allen informed me that he had traced the leopard to Life Form Taxidermy in White River where the animal's skin and skull were being prepared after the agency had asked the owner to do so and to tender for the skin. It was apparently worth between R15,000 to R25,000 to the agency.'

Fred issued a cutting rebuke to the agency: 'We are not keeping the animals in a zoo nor are we selling them; the animals are brought to us for medical care and treatment ... the agency's position is that the animals should rather bleed to death.'

The leopard was put down during the raid on the rehabilitation centre by a state veterinarian. It was then sold as a trophy and mounted on a wooden stand. While the agency issued a press statement claiming the animal had been in a poor condition, Fred insisted it was in a good condition. He has the stuffed leopard stored securely in his new home. In its mounted form, its dead eyes stare mutely above a gaping mouth ringed with sharp yellowing teeth, displaying a final snarl.

AFTER YEARS OF ignoring his correspondence, the parks agency finally responded to a letter of demand that Fred sent at the end of 2008. The agency's new CEO Charles Ndabeni instructed compliance officer Shukrat Makinde to thrash out a settlement agreement with Fred and Spoor. All civil and legal issues – Fred's damages claim against the agency and the criminal charges the agency laid against him – would be dropped. The agreement would constitute a 'full and final settlement' of any claims and disputes. This was signed on 15 May 2009, the day D.D. Mabuza was sworn in as premier of Mpumalanga. It was subject to the finalisation of a development and cooperation agreement to be drafted and signed within six months. Fred began work on developing an environmental and developmental framework for Badplaas and its surrounding areas.

On 26 May, the criminal charges brought against Fred for operating his animal rehabilitation centre were formally withdrawn in the Carolina Magistrate's Court by magistrate T.G. Netshiozwi. Three days later, the magistrate sent a letter to his superiors in Nelspruit saying that he feared for his life. He had received an anonymous phone call to tell him that there was a plan to vandalise property at Badplaas on 30 May by people from local rural townships. The caller said Netshiozwi's 'day-to-day life' could not be guaranteed. He requested 'urgent security' for himself, the court and the community.

It soon became clear that the gap between the Mpumalanga Tourism and Parks Agency's promises and their practice was as wide as ever. Spoor sent letters to the agency in June, and again in August 2009, citing concern about the lack of progress in finalising the development and cooperation agreement. In November, six months after the document was signed, he informed the agency that they were in breach of the settlement agreement.

Despite Fred's constant legal action against them – and his clean sheet of court victories – the parks agency did not relent in their harassment and attempts to shut down his projects. In February 2012 he was informed that they had decided to close down the Cradle of Life biopark and revoke his zoo licence after an inspection due at the end of the month.

His lawyers fired off a letter to the agency informing them that they were breaching their undertakings to the North Gauteng High Court to assist him, conduct regular inspections of his facilities and keep dialogue open. The next morning an undertaking was received from the office of the state attorney in Pretoria to abide by the judgment. The inspection went ahead and the agency found no fault with the biopark.

In 2009 the investigator Paul O'Sullivan was hired as a forensic consultant by parks agency CEO Charles Ndabeni 'to assist him in bringing the organisation under control after years of nepotism and corruption, and to put controls in place that would help him fulfil his mandate of increasing tourism, improving conservation and creating sustainable jobs'.

During his investigations, O'Sullivan discovered that the agency's game rangers were involved in poaching. 'The situation was so bad that the more rangers a reserve had, the higher the levels of poaching,' he reported. 'In some cases, the rangers were so involved in poaching that a whole industry of bush-meat butcher shops had sprung up around the reserves that fed the demand for cheap meat in the local communities.'

The Problem Animal Fund had been set up by the parks agency's employees to receive funds from the sale of hunting rights over escaped dangerous animals. According to O'Sullivan, the agency's interest in protecting animals 'was outweighed by the income derived by the fund and the decision makers were the same people.' Officials at the agency charged hunters tens of thousands of rand for a permit to kill hippo, buffalo, leopard and other animals. In 2009, the fund had R1 million in its account. 'This led to the wholesale hunting for profit of so-called problem animals and the cash being taken off-balance-sheet for use in private hunting activities,' O'Sullivan reported. 'Most of the wildlife protection officers were registered as professional hunters, in direct conflict with their duty to protect the wildlife. Rehabilitative farms were prevented from operating as they conflicted with the unlawful need to raise cash by hunting these so-called problem animals.'

The agency was also entrusted with storing and legally disposing of rhino horns and elephant tusks. Its officials were required to tag them and keep a register. O'Sullivan took photographs of shelves of tusks and horns in the agency's offices and warned that there was inadequate security. In 2014, over the Easter weekend, the stockpile was stolen; clearly the result of an inside job. It was valued at R116 million – the biggest stockpile theft in South Africa. To this day, despite an investigation by the police special crimes unit, no one has been arrested or prosecuted.

Not even the fauna they were tasked with protecting was safe from the agency's looting employees: 'Bio-conservation officers were stealing and selling protected plants such as cycads,' O'Sullivan reported. He concluded that the agency was 'rotten to the core and the blame can only be laid at the feet of the corrupt politicians who have been the overseers of 20 years of pillaging'.

It was only after Fred read O'Sullivan's report on the Problem Animal Fund that he understood why the Mpumalanga Tourism and Parks Agency's officials, particularly Jan Muller, manager of wildlife protection services, kept such a pythonesque grip on his permit applications. He was not the only private reserve owner who experienced the agency's refusal to issue permits to transport animals, erect fences to keep them enclosed, and rehabilitate them when they were injured. It was not in the officials' interest to grant permits to protect animals. They were issuing permits to hunt them instead and pocketing the proceeds as the bank records detailed in O'Sullivan's report seemed to show very clearly.

Despite O'Sullivan providing the agency with several reports and substantial evidence of corruption, to this day no one has been arrested or prosecuted. After Ndabeni submitted the forensic report to the agency's board, its members asked for his resignation. No internal or criminal action was taken against the agency's employees involved in fraud or other crimes and none of O'Sullivan's recommendations for tighter financial control were implemented.

Subsequently, the agency invited O'Sullivan to tender for the work of vetting candidates for a replacement CEO. 'As I had still not been paid in full [for the investigation into corruption], I thought it wise to curry favour and decided to carry out the vetting free of charge,' he said. 'Naturally, I won the tender. I then vetted the three short-listed applicants and, to my amazement, the candidate I had clearly stated to be a problem was appointed, despite the fact that he had embellished his CV, claiming an honours degree that he did not have, which amounts to a misrepresentation. I'm talking about Jacques Modipane.'

Modipane was the finance MEC who had allegedly issued R1.3 billion in promissory notes to an Israeli fraudster's investment company, using 31 of Mpumalanga's nature reserves as collateral for a R340-million loan. He resigned from his position in the provincial government. In 1999, Mpumalanga premier Ndaweni Mahlangu reappointed Modipane (and D.D. Mabuza) to the government. Deploying Modipane to the position of CEO of the parks agency was one of Mabuza's first actions as premier of Mpumalanga. Mabuza was still premier when Modipane was paid R5 million to leave the agency in 2015 following the theft of its ivory and rhino horn stocks.

In 2017, O'Sullivan received a series of phone calls from Jan Muller, which he transcribed. Over the phone, Muller confessed that he had been threatened with losing his job, his career, his pension and his life. He had been instructed to block Fred's permit applications and forced to invent reasons for doing so.

'My work is on the line, my career is on the line, my whole pension is on the line and everything is on the line,' he said in a call to O'Sullivan. 'You know, all the politicians involved in this stuff, I am not going to name them, but it is a war; that I know. I think that Fred is the biggest war. I am quite worried, you know. They have tried to take me out a couple of times. I withdraw all my statements. I am *klaar*, they will hang me. They will shoot me on the corner or let somebody drive with a truck over me.

'You know this, you know how politicians work and how guys just disappear. I can assure you, I will be on their hit list. Ja, I don't want to be on their hit list. I still want to live. I have seen what happens to people that turned against the government, especially in this province. They make people disappear, these guys.'

Muller did not defend himself against Fred's application for protection from harassment. Shortly afterwards, he was boarded because of work-related stress and retired from the parks agency in August 2017.

11

A heist and a hijack

In October 2005, the man fingered by both the Ernst & Young and Griffiths reports as being at the centre of the Badplaas land scam, Pieter Visagie, organised a meeting of the Ndwandwa Community Trust, the biggest group of claimants in Badplaas, at an office he made available for them on his farm. The trust's land claim had been settled in February 2004 and they were awarded the farms Grootkop, Engelschedraai, Onverwacht and Doornhoek in Badplaas as restitution. The founder and chairman of the trust, Robert Nkosi, walked out shortly after the meeting began when he realised that its sole purpose was to get him to agree to a fraudulent amendment of the trust's deed and to force his resignation. Visagie then appointed his farm manager, Steve Skhosana, as CEO of the trust but expected him to do his bidding and kept all the trust's land for his own use.

The office on Visagie's farm was used by three trustees who joined his 'Ndwandwa team'. One of them, Mangisi Nkosi (not related to Robert), was installed as the new chairman of the trust. A letter was sent to Robert Nkosi in November, on a Ndwandwa Community Trust letterhead, raising concern about his 'irregular activities'. One of the charges was that he was 'guilty' of being in possession of a copy of the original trust deed.

On 1 December, a well-planned demonstration, for which no police or municipal permission had been granted, took place at the entrance gate of Nkomazi. A large tent was erected and people arrived in buses, taxis and cars. The gathering, ostensibly called to voice dissatisfaction with the slow progress of claims lodged on Nkomazi and alleged human rights abuses on the reserve, was addressed by chief land claims commissioner Tozi Gwanya and his colleagues. Several verbal threats were made against Fred and pliers were brandished in the air as an indication that his wildlife fences might be cut, but the gathering ended peacefully.

In a letter to acting Mpumalanga land claims commissioner Harry Mboa on 5 December, Richard Spoor wrote that Fred had no knowledge about human rights abuses on Nkomazi Wilderness and had received no complaints or communication about any. The allegations that people were denied access to their family graves and that the graves were being demolished were false. He said he had been at pains to communicate to the Land Claims Commission and the department of agriculture and land affairs that anybody seeking access to Fred's land was welcome to contact him and consent would not be unreasonably refused.

Spoor told Mboa that information gathered on who organised the meeting outside Nkomazi pointed to the ANC Youth League. The Mpumalanga department of agriculture and land affairs had hired the buses and tent. One of the convenors of the meeting was Steve Skhosana, formerly employed by Visagie as a foreman, now a 'prominent figure in the land claims structure of Ndwandwa'. Badplaas businessmen who illegally grazed cattle on Nkomazi were also spotted in the crowd.

'This illegal gathering took place just after I alerted the authorities about the unlawful inflation of land prices in Badplaas,' Fred says. 'I believe that the protest was arranged as part of the retribution strategy by the parties involved in the land scam because of the pressure arising from the media scrutiny. It was aimed at prejudicing me and my project. When I exposed the unlawful actions behind the false land claims, I experienced increased pressure to force me to either admit to the claims, despite their lack of merit, or to leave the area.'

On the day that Spoor sent his letter to the commission, Visagie's attorneys wrote to Robert Nkosi's attorney claiming that he was not a chief as prescribed by the Traditional Leadership Act and, unless he provided a 'full explanation of the allegations' made against him by the new chairman of the trust by the end of the month, the Ndwandwa Community's trustees would approach the high court for an order to amend the trust deed and to 'formally terminate' Nkosi's role as founder and trustee.

The lawyers wrote that the matter was urgent, 'in lieu of the fact that the trust has financial obligations to meet ... and at present cannot effect any of the above without the signature of your client at the bank'. They said Mangisi Nkosi had been elected as the new chairman of the Ndwandwa Community Trust. The letter was accompanied by a resolution apparently taken at an annual general meeting of the trust on 12 November to institute criminal charges against Robert Nkosi for 'fraud, dishonesty and theft'.

In January 2006, Robert Nkosi's attorneys responded that Visagie was influencing the Ndwandwa trustees to further his own financial interests and that he, Visagie, had told Nkosi that he would see to it that he was removed as a trustee because he did not want to work with him. They noted that Visagie had arranged for all the trust's bank statements to be sent to his own address and had made offices available to fake trustees and encouraged them not to attend meetings. They said Visagie had taken over the herd of cattle belonging to the trust that had been bought with government restitution funds and had failed to render accounts regarding the animals. A copy of the original trust deed was available, but Robert Nkosi refused to part with it because Mangisi Nkosi and the other trustees wanted to make irregular amendments to the document.

In November, the regional Land Claims Commission sent a notification to the master of the high court about the 'registration of the Ndwandwa Community Trust', accompanied by a new, fake trust deed. Ernst & Young had reported to the department of land affairs that the original trust deed had been removed from the master's file, but no action had been taken to correct the problem. The inertia allowed corrupt officials, colluding with Visagie, to insert a new deed in the file with the same registration number as the original.

Visagie's attorneys sent a letter to the master in the first week of December, requesting a copy of the trust's letters of authority, which was provided to them. 'The cabal – that's what I call them – needed a vehicle to transfer ownership of farms valued at R300 million,' Fred explains. 'They achieved this by hijacking the Ndwandwa Community Trust by literally stealing the original trust deed from the master's office. They replaced the original with a fake trust deed and fake trustees. The master had no idea that this had been done and issued new letters of authority.'

The trust's founder, Robert Nkosi, laid criminal charges at the Badplaas police station against the group that had hijacked his organisation and was siphoning off its money. He had been threatened and intimidated. There had been an attempt to burn down his house but the arsonists did not succeed. He read in a newspaper about his neighbour Fred's stand against the corruption and came to Nkomazi. Fred immediately agreed to help.

A month later, Nkosi filed an application at the North Gauteng High Court for the removal of the new trustees of the Ndwandwa Community Trust and for the fake trust deed to be declared invalid. In his application he explained some of the background to what had happened. 'I objected when I learnt that a speculator was offered a lease of the trust's land in circumstances where he was to make substantial profits by subleasing the land to a food producer. Pieter Visagie entered into an agreement with McCain Foods without proper authorisation from the trust. He was making R75,000 a month and paying the trust R6,500 a month. I also objected when I learnt that the regional Land Claims Commission was influenced to purchase land that the Ndwandwa claimants did not claim as restitution. This caused conflict between me, the speculator, the regional land claims commissioner and certain of his officials.

'In order for the land transactions and lease agreements to

be finalised with the trust, the speculator and the regional Land Claims Commission required trust resolutions. I was opposed to the transactions and was not prepared to pass the resolutions. In order for the perpetrators of the land scam to continue with their plans, it was therefore imperative to get rid of me as a trustee. I believe that this is the reason for the registration of the false 2006 trust deed.'

On 4 November 2011, Judge Eberhard Bertelsmann granted an order against the new trustees. He ordered that the trustees operating from Visagie's farm resign immediately from the Ndwandwa Community Trust, restored Robert Nkosi's letters of authority and ordered that the beneficiaries of the the trust elect new leadership.

The forensic investigator Paul O'Sullivan established that the fake Ndwandwa Community Trust had been used as a vehicle to lodge fraudulent land restitution claims to farms. Lists of members of community trusts which submitted land claims in Badplaas in 2007 included 'fake names and identity numbers, as well as many duplicated identity numbers. This was based on a selective sample; a full audit would be required to determine the precise number of fictitious claimants.'

O'Sullivan went to the farms bought by the Land Claims Commission for the Ndwandwa Trust. They were occupied by small numbers of people, 'not part of any previously dispossessed community, who have, for the most part, allowed the farms to fall fallow and have sold anything of value. The farmhouses have been stripped of geysers, copper pipes, electrical wiring and fitted furniture. Farm equipment, including pumps, pipes, boilers, sprinklers and machinery are all gone.

'It is clear that [Pieter] Visagie colluded with corrupt officials from the regional Land Claims Commission and the government. He received financial assistance from the commission for his purchase of Portion 11 of the farm Vygeboom. Contractual conditions were set for the back-to-back sales of the farm to Visagie and the commission. He did not meet these conditions and, when the owners threatened to cancel the deal and take back their farm, Mpumalanga land claims commissioner Nceba

Nqana stepped in to assist him. An amount of R1,380,152.18 was unlawfully paid by the Department of Agriculture and Land Affairs to assist Visagie to buy the farm, which he immediately sold to the Land Claims Commission at an inflated price.'

O'Sullivan established a link between Visagie and D.D. Mabuza while the latter was MEC for agriculture and land affairs. Visagie sent an enquiry, via Mabuza's business partner Sonnyboy Maphanga, about payments for the balance due from the sale of land restored to claimant communities. Mabuza commissioned a joint task team to investigate and determine whether payments were owed to Visagie.

'The joint task team claimed to have carried out a comprehensive and in-depth investigation into this historic case,' O'Sullivan reported. 'It then unlawfully came to the conclusion that Visagie's company was underpaid due to the discrepancy between moveable and immoveable assets. It was agreed by Mabuza that Visagie should be paid R3,347,629. It was patent that the ... investigation was nothing more than a fraud, as it failed to discover that the land was settled by white Afrikaans farmers in the early 1870s and could not therefore have been subject to restitution claims.'

FRED'S DIFFICULTIES WITH the Mpumalanga Land Claims Commission continued. In early January 2006, he again instructed Spoor to write to the commission requesting mediation on the land claims against his properties. They did not reply. Three days later, the commission issued a notice for an inspection of Nkomazi. Spoor asked for copies of the land claims relating to the inspection but, again, there was no reply.

The commission gazetted another land claim in February in the name of Josia Ncongwane, acting on behalf of the Dhlomo Dhlomo Community. The claim covered more than a hundred properties in the Badplaas area and its owners included black and white farmers, family trusts, private companies and community property associations. Included were three properties totalling 120 hectares that Fred owned, all of them portions of a farm he had purchased in 1999 – Kees Zyn Doorns 708 JT.

Mpumalanga's new land claims commissioner Peter Mhangwani issued a press release on 31 May warning that where there were difficulties in processing land claims, 'we may employ provisions of the law which may require criminal proceedings or expropriation of land'. He said the 'Wilderness Game Farm' was one of the properties that his office was having difficulties with in settling the claims on it. He averred that a delegation from the commission had been barred from inspecting Nkomazi. In a speech later to the provincial legislature, Mhangwani said the 'impasse between us and the owners of Nkomazi Wilderness represented by Fred Daniel' provided an illustration of 'landowners who are not cooperative'.

The next onslaught came a few weeks later when the regional Land Claims Commission approached the Land Claims Court for access to Nkomazi. The application was dismissed by Judge J.P. Bam, who instructed the parties to enter an agreement on times and conditions of access to Nkomazi. 'It was an ill-conceived application,' says Fred, 'bound to fail because it was an irregular step in the land reform process and demonstrated the extent to which these people wanted to get rid of me.' Over the next few months, Spoor wrote three more letters to the commission requesting mediation on the claims on Nkomazi. As ever, there was no response.

But the biggest, and most tragic, setback for Nkomazi came in October 2006 when Butch Kerzner, who had been passionate about building a luxury resort on Nkomazi, died in a helicopter crash. His death put his company's plans on hold until 2007, when a new deal was negotiated to build One&Only resorts on the reserve.

In 2006, one of Fred's companies purchased eight further portions of the farm Kees Zyn Doorns from the Roesch family. Fred signed an agreement to purchase early in December and Roesch appointed a conveyancer to arrange for a transfer of the deeds. As Roesch detailed in an affidavit submitted to the court, Land Claims Commission official Harry Maboa phoned Roesch on 30 December, threatening him with arrest if he did not cancel his agreement with Fred and sell his land to the commission.

The conveyancer prepared documents for the transfer and lodged them at the deeds office in July 2007. A few weeks later, he contacted Roesch and said the deeds office was refusing to transfer the farm as caveats had been issued. Land affairs minister Thoko Didiza had issued two notices of possible expropriation against Roesch in May, stating: 'The property has been sold contrary to the provisions of the Restitution of Land Rights Act. The Commissioner was never been [*sic*] consulted on the purchase of the property. The office of the State Attorney must first be consulted before dealing with this property.'

The Restitution of Land Rights Act does not confer powers or authority on the commissioner to prevent the sale and transfer of any farm in this manner. Spoor consulted the state attorney's office and established that there was no basis in law for such caveats. He prepared an application to the high court against the Land Claims Commission and Didiza. But before he could file it, the deeds office contacted Roesch's attorney and advised that the caveats had been removed. The property was then transferred to Fred.

Fred and Spoor doubled their attempts to discover who the Nkomazi claimants were by using the Promotion of Access to Information (PAIA) Act. In February 2007, Spoor filed a request in terms of the Act, directed to the Mpumalanga Land Claims Commission. He asked for all relevant land claims and investigation reports, any other records related to claims lodged against Fred's properties, and the details of all properties acquired by the commission on behalf of claimants.

Instead of a response to the PAIA request, the land claims commissioner served a notice of referral to the Land Claims Court of new claims involving 23 farms, some of them owned by Fred. They covered almost 70,000 hectares and included two rural townships with a combined population of tens of thousands of people.

Only two of the new claims lodged in 2007 had been included in previous notices issued by the commission, and there was no information about them in the referral. Nor was there any information about the identities of the claimants. The commission also denied Fred's PAIA request on the basis that the claims had already been referred to the department of land affairs for restitution.

After several amendments, which focused primarily on Nkomazi and included nine claims by different communities and trusts, the notice of referral was lodged in the Land Claims Court by Mpumalanga land claims commissioner Peter Mhangwani. He stated in the motivation that the owners of the land had denied the legitimacy of the claims, and had refused to negotiate or mediate with the claimants and the commission, which he said had 'tried in vain to enter into negotiations/mediation with owners'. The commission concluded that it was not possible to resolve the disputes and was referring them to the court for adjudication. Most of the claims presented by Mhangwani were lodged by the Ndwandwa Community Trust, despite Robert Nkosi telling the high court that their claims had been settled in 2004.

Fred lodged an appeal in May against the commission's refusal to divulge the information he requested. PAIA requires the government and its agencies to respond within 90 days of a request, but there was none. Instead, the commission published a notice of amendment in the *Government Gazette* that added even more properties and claimants to the enormous and bogus Ndwandwa land claim. They explained that the farms had been 'erroneously excluded' from the gazetting of the community's original claim in 2004. Again, the owners of the land were not informed of the intention to gazette the claim.

THE FRESH BATCH OF land claims accepted and gazetted in 2007 by the Mpumalanga Land Claims Commission were made on behalf of poor, black labour tenants. During the course of the 19th and 20th centuries, they had been granted small plots of land on white-owned farms in exchange for six months of their labour every year. They were evicted at whim and often lost their livestock when they were forced off farms. Many of the claims were lodged by leaders or chiefs who said they were acting on behalf of communities which had owned or lived on farms that, coincidentally, perfectly matched the boundaries of Nkomazi.

In a research report on the Badplaas land claims, Wits

University historians Dr Michelle Hay and Peter Delius described how they examined official reports on the claims, interviewed many of the claimants and conducted literature and archival research before they concluded that some of the claims had no merit. The Mpumalanga Land Claims Commission was charged with investigating the validity of all claims before recommending to the department of land affairs that they be gazetted. Hay and Delius found that some of the reports compiled by the commission's researchers were based on poor investigations or none at all, and many contained similar details.

The commission's research reports on claims to the farms Vergelegen, Theeboom, Doyershoek and Boekenhoutrand – all owned by Fred – had neglected important sources and details, and 'critical information, such as the dates when the farms first came under private ownership, and exactly who those owners were, is missing,' the historians wrote. 'The report is based entirely on oral evidence, and contains no deeds research, archival research or secondary literature relevant to the particular area under claim ... It is impossible to know exactly where the information comes from as no footnotes or sources are provided.'

Delius and Hay reported that the commission's researchers made no attempt to assess the merit of each claim against others, even though some conflicted with others. No explanation was given for overlapping claims. 'For example, the Mdumane Community's claim to Vergelegen is accepted as valid, even though in the report it is stated that only one family (the Masina family) now represented by the claimant community actually lived there and that family had actually got permission to stay there from the Nhlabathi family, who were there already. Both claims are simply accepted as valid.

'Similarly, the Maseko Community and BakaNkosi-Ginindza Community claims to Theeboom are both accepted as valid, even though both groups provide different narratives of the history of that land. The report does not discuss the nature of land rights in any depth, and does not raise any questions about the actual extent of the land lost by each group, for example, how much land each family is likely to have actually used.'

The historians reported that the commission's researchers ignored the significance of the 1913 cut-off date for claims laid down in the Restitution of Land Rights Act. No attempt was made to assess whether the claims were based on a loss of customary rights before 1913 to force black farmers from their land or the substantive nature of the land rights that the Badplaas claimants lost after 1913. 'Despite [these] issues, and the lack of information on all of the farms and claimants, all of the claims are accepted as valid and recommended to be taken to the next phase of restitution.'

The 2007 referral report on which the Mpumalanga Land Claims Commission based its legal action against Fred was 'very limited and suffers from many of the same problems' as the reports on the claims to his farms, Delius and Hay discovered. It relied predominantly on information provided in the claimants' application forms and from interviews with claimants. It used no archival material or information from the deeds office.

The commission's report on Theeboom stated that when the Thwala family arrived there around 1913, 'the farm at that time was not owned by any white person', which was not true. The farm had been divided in 1911 into three portions inherited by Ockert Tobias van Niekerk, Anna Sophia van Niekerk and Hester Maria van Niekerk. Their deed number was 2905.

The only information in the commission's report on the Mabuza family's claim to the farm Sterkspruit was the land claim form. It recorded the dispossession date as 1914, and that the family had unregistered ownership rights on the farm. 'Notwithstanding the lack of research in this regard, the land claim was published in the *Government Gazette*, accepted and referred to the Land Claims Court,' Delius and Hay reported. 'The referral of this land claim is in our view improper as the investigation into the land claim is not complete. From the documents before us the Mabuza family's entitlement to restitution is at this stage tentative.'

The historians found abundant evidence that members of the Kwaliweni claimant community or their forebears lived for years on Sterkspruit. Some of them were evicted and also lived on

Boekenhoutrand, Doyershoek, Goedehoop, Rous and Vriesland. 'However, there is no evidence that people who are currently part of the claimant community lived on Stolzburg specifically,' they reported. 'There is no evidence that the Kwaliweni claimant community represents all of the families who were evicted from this land over time – in fact on some farms (like Sterkspruit) it is clear that they do not as there are overlapping claims.'

The Ginindza claim was based on a 're-interpretation of the history of the area to favour the Ginindza family', Delius and Hay wrote. 'There is no historical evidence to suggest that they exercised the control and authority they did over the land they are claiming or, even, aside from Theeboom, that they were definitely living there.'

The Mdumane claim did not have merit, based on the evidence the historians collected. There was no evidence linking the group historically to the area under claim. 'Sadly, we were not able to get any evidence from the Mdumane community when we met with them,' they reported. 'The community urgently need to present evidence (including oral history of individual families) of where exactly families involved in the claim were living, in order that they may be converted to labour tenancy claims.'

Delius and Hay reported that the Badplaas claims were based on two phases of dispossession. The first was the imposition of a private property system on land on which they lived and the failure to recognise the land rights of their households. Black people then became labour tenants for white farmers. The second phase of dispossession involved the eviction of families unwilling to provide labour. In the 1970s, families who had lived on Badplaas farms for generations were removed to the KaNgwane homeland.

Despite unearthing several fatal problems with many of the Badplaas land claims, Delius and Hay believed that some of the 'community claims' deserved compensation – but not the restitution of the farms they were claiming. There were questions about the extent to which these groups had land in common in the 19th century. Headmen and chiefs had no land rights then, and property ownership belonged to households. 'These households were dispersed over large areas of land and seem to have lived quite independently of each other.'

Most of the farms under claim were granted to white owners in the 1870s. A system of labour tenancy was imposed. 'Thus, whatever the nature of customary land rights had been, by 1913, they were no longer recognised. Families lived scattered and did not come together frequently. They legally and practically had to ask white landowners for permission to settle on land, to use it for cultivation. Evictions also meant that families moved away from ancestral homes and away from their communities. This happened over a 100-year period and the effects were profound.

'This may help to explain why there are so many separate claims to the same farms. Most of the claimants to Sterkspruit, for example, clearly have connections with each other and share a similar history. They were all labour tenants on the same farm, and many of them have roots in the area stretching to the 19th century before whites arrived. Given the history of the area, and based on the evidence, there are likely to be many more families who are eligible for compensation for lost informal rights on all of the farms under claim.

'Rights to the land were rooted exactly where families lived. They were not defined by farm boundaries. Redress is therefore most likely to be credibly achieved through purchasing the relevant farm portions (not whole farms) where appropriate, or through financial compensation.'

'Fair compensation would also need to take into account the fact that these families have very deep historical connections to the land, and were treated inhumanely throughout the twentieth century,' the historians concluded.

12

The gatekeeper

D.D. Mabuza arrived in Fred's orbit as the land claims battle in Badplaas began heating up. Appointed MEC of agriculture and land affairs in 2008, he had oversight of the government's land reform programme. His election that same year as chairman of the ANC in Mpumalanga brought him into contact with shady businessmen seeking to milk government funds. One of their corrupt schemes was the Badplaas land scam.

After he was fired from the Mpumalanga government in 1998 for cooking up false matric results, Mabuza was 'rehabilitated' by the ANC. For the next two years he served as a member of the provincial legislature and worked tirelessly for the party, building its membership. Many of his former allies and other senior members of the ANC claim in court papers and reports to the party that he paid the annual fees of 'ghost members' and used duplicate identity numbers to swell the ranks of branches in the southern regions of Mpumalanga that he controlled. These were the same tactics used to create fake land claims in the Badplaas area while Mabuza was MEC for agriculture.

The ANC deployed Mabuza to the National Assembly in 2001

where he served as a backbench MP for two years. He returned to Mpumalanga in 2004 and began a second term as a member of its legislature. A year later, he was elected deputy chairman of the ANC in the province. In 2007, he was appointed MEC for road and transport and, in the following year, MEC for agriculture and land affairs. He supported Jacob Zuma's successful campaign to become president of the ANC and was elected onto the party's national executive committee at its Polokwane conference. He donated R400,000 towards the costs of Zuma's 2008 wedding and, a few months later, in 2009, he was appointed premier of Mpumalanga.

His early political career was magnificently sketched in a *New York Times* article published in August 2018 as he embarked on a new career as deputy president of the country. The headline above the article by Norimitsu Onishi and Selam Gebrekidan posed the question 'South Africa vows to end corruption: Are its new leaders part of the problem?' It opened with a hideous description of the consequences of government neglect and corruption.

'The little girl hated going to the bathroom at school. The pit toilets were so dark, dirty and crumbling. Many children were so afraid of them that they relieved themselves in the schoolyard to avoid the ordeal,' the article began. 'But as she played with her best friend during recess the girl, Ziyanda Nkosi, a six-year-old first grader, really had to go. She stepped warily inside the closet-like latrine.

'Even with the gentle pressure of her tiny frame, the floor caved in. Ziyanda flailed wildly, clinging to the edges of the hole, frantically trying to keep herself from falling in and drowning in the fetid pool below. Mommy! Mommy! She screamed, managing to hold on long enough for an older boy to run in and save her.' This happened at a school in Middelplaas, Mpumalanga, while Mabuza was premier. The article described him as 'a former maths teacher who had become one of the most powerful figures in the ANC'.

When he became MEC of education in Mpumalanga in 1994, he promised to liberate black people by providing them with quality education. 'But under the ANC, the education system has been in shambles, so gutted by corruption that even party officials are dismayed at how little students are learning, in schools so decrepit that children have plunged to their deaths in pit toilets,' the leading US newspaper lamented. 'The rage in Ziyanda's town grew so intense that protestors hurled stones at a local ANC leader, who narrowly escaped by whipping out his handgun and shooting randomly into the crowd, wounding two children and roiling the community all the more.

'Mr Mabuza never came to the school or met with the parents – and for good reason, local officials contend. The dangerous conditions were a clear reflection of his control over the province, where millions of dollars for education have disappeared into a vortex of suspicious spending, shoddy public construction and brazen corruption to fuel his political ambitions, according to government records and officials in his party.'

Onishi and Gebrekidan wrote that Mabuza seemed a strange choice for deputy president of the ANC and the country as the ruling party rid itself of President Jacob Zuma and attempted to end its reputation for corruption: 'after all … rural Mpumalanga is fairly small, has little economic clout and is widely regarded as one of the country's most corrupt [provinces].' They explained Mabuza's spectacular climb up the political ladder through interviews with former and current ANC members. They claimed that he siphoned off money from schools and other public services to buy loyalty and amass enormous power, 'putting him in a position to shape South Africa for years to come'.

'He didn't become what he is now because of his political capability,' Mpumalanga ANC leader and National Assembly MP Fish Mahlalela told the *New York Times*. 'No, no, it was out of money and the manipulation. Nothing else.'

In a speech given weeks after he was sworn in as deputy president, Mabuza lamented the poor state of schools and the 'tragedies that take away the innocence of our children'. He spoke about a toddler who drowned in a broken pit latrine. And of a five-year-old boy whose body was discovered by his mother at the bottom of a pit, his hand sticking out of a pool of faeces.

Such deplorable conditions were common, Mabuza said. It symbolised the failure to provide black South Africans with a decent chance in life. 'Where is our care? What has gone wrong with our nation?' he asked.

The *New York Times* listed several of Mabuza's major governance failures: millions of rand allocated to schools were misspent year after year. Mpumalanga routinely spent less on poor students than required by national government. School construction projects were riddled with inflated costs. Nearly a quarter of primary schools in Mpumalanga had pit toilets, despite ample government funds made available to replace them with safe and modern plumbing. Mabuza had fabricated the province's matric pass rate.

He pushed to build big boarding schools and the budgeted costs tripled to R450 million each. According to ANC officials and anti-corruption groups, this provided an easy way to funnel large amounts of money through front companies into politics. Mpumalanga politicians were using the scams they developed in 1999 to skim ever larger amounts of money from the public purse and divert them to their party's accounts. They were still getting away with it.

'Some construction was so shoddy that roofs sprouted leaks, toilets barely worked, students lacked water, retaining walls collapsed and dormitories were missing doors, according to a provincial report,' Onishi and Gebrekidan wrote. 'Over the years, Mabuza's province became known as one of South Africa's most dangerous. Nearly 20 politicians, most from inside the ANC, were assassinated in the past two decades, some after exposing graft in public works projects.'

The *New York Times* reported that Mabuza attracted legions of new ANC members with government contracts, cash handouts and KFC meals. Mpumalanga had the second-highest number of delegates at the ANC's 2017 conference, where he was elected deputy president of the party. His delegates switched sides on the eve of the leadership elections, abandoning Nkosazana Dlamini-Zuma to whom they had pledged their support and voting for Cyril Ramaphosa instead.

The *New York Times* said the 'unpleasant truth' was that Ramaphosa owed his victory at the ANC conference, in part, to corruption. Political analyst Ralph Mathekga told them that Ramaphosa's presidency relied on Mabuza. 'We are being reluctant as a nation to face the reality of Mabuza. If Ramaphosa gets hit by a bus, Mabuza is going to be the president.'

Mabuza had the perfect résumé to become education MEC in 1994. The son of farmers, he grew up in the village of Phola Trust in Mpumalanga, walking long kilometres each day to primary school in a nearby town. 'Though he often had no shoes, he always tucked in his shirt and buttoned it up to the neck,' his childhood peer Reginah Mhaule recalled.

A bright student, he obtained a national teacher's certificate from Mgwenya College of Education in 1985, followed by a BA in psychology from the University of South Africa in 1989. His profile on the presidency's website reads: 'A trained mathematics teacher by profession, [he] became a school principal before moving to politics. His passion remains education and he established the D.D. Mabuza Foundation in 2014, focusing on education and the social upliftment of the vulnerable groups such as children, child-headed households, the aged and persons with disability.'

Mabuza was fired as education MEC in 1998 after he falsified the province's matric pass rate. Although Premier Mathews Phosa thereafter dropped him from the provincial government, Mabuza has never admitted to wrongdoing in the matric results scandal. After Phosa was ousted by the ANC in 1999, the new premier, Ndaweni Mahlangu, appointed Mabuza MEC for housing. He failed to meet the government's targets for building houses for the poor.

In 2003, while Mabuza was an ANC MP in the National Assembly, Scorpions investigators arrested Mpumalanga's chief director for textbook procurement after he allegedly accepted a R500,000 bribe. Jan Kriel appeared briefly in the Nelspruit Magistrate's Court on multiple corruption charges, Justin Arenstein and Jabu Mhlabane reported in the *Mail & Guardian*. 'Kriel has been under investigation for months following courtroom revelations that he allegedly set up a network of front companies to milk multi-million rand textbook and stationery tenders. The scam contributed to massive stationery shortages and poor exam pass marks in Mpumalanga schools between 1997 and 2001 and could implicate former education MEC David Mabuza.

'Scorpions investigators questioned Mabuza, after Bronkhorstspruit businessman Egbert van der Westhuizen testified in May that he had paid a R1-million bribe to Kriel and Mabuza. He allegedly received a R24-million stationery contract in return. Van der Westhuizen and his attorney Hennie Grobler were arrested for the alleged scam and face seven fraud charges, four theft charges and one of money laundering.'

'Mabuza has consistently refused to comment on the issue. His political career ended in disgrace in 1998, when he and crooked officials illegally inflated the province's dismal matric pass rate. Forensic investigations proved the massive jump was fraudulent, and appeared to be designed to win political glory. Mabuza escaped criminal and disciplinary charges, but department head Faith Sithole was dismissed. She later sued for unfair dismissal and won a secret R2.6-million damages settlement.'

Almost every ANC election in Mpumalanga – at branch, regional and provincial level has been marred with allegations of fraud and infractions of the party's procedures, policies and its constitution. ANC leaders in Mpumalanga have been accused of buying bulk branch membership to boost their support. Political violence is a common outrage at its meetings. The province with a tiny population takes more delegates to ANC conferences than Gauteng does. The party's national leadership admits that delegates' votes are sold to high bidders at its conferences, and has resolved to end the practice.

The *Mail & Guardian*'s Paddy Harper reported in June 2018 that disaffected Mpumalanga ANC members wanted the party's national leadership to dissolve its provincial executive committee and call a general council to elect new leaders. The group, led by Ronnie Malomane, a former campaign manager for Mathews Phosa's fruitless ANC presidential bid in 2017, said they would go to court if the ANC's national dispute resolution committee, to which they had presented a dossier on ghost ANC branches and corruption, failed to act.

The disgruntled ANC members said their dossier contained evidence of corruption in the Nkomazi local municipality and other areas, and information about the cloning of 34 branches in the Ehlanzeni district municipality. 'For every branch that is registered there is a cloned branch,' Malomane told the *Mail & Guardian*. 'We will wait for the national dispute resolution committee. If nothing comes in our favour, with the evidence we have, we have a winnable case and we are going to court with it.'

He said the ANC had more than 3,500 bogus members in Mpumalanga, and this influenced the outcome of conferences. The murder of a former MK member at the Gert Sibande ANC Youth League regional conference in June was linked to contestation for political positions. 'What is happening in the mother body is happening in the youth league. Over the weekend [in June 2018] three regions did not sit and one person was killed. People are no longer interested in supporting this. People can see what is happening here is wrong and unprincipled.'

The matter was withdrawn from the South Gauteng High Court after the ANC agreed to investigate the group's concerns. 'The ANC will form a task team in Mpumalanga in order to track each and every … branch and check all of their complaints,' Malomane said, adding that he could not divulge further details because of an agreement with the party's leadership.

The party's task team disbanded the eHlanzeni and Bohlabela regional committees after establishing that there were ghost members and cloned branches. A new, electronic membership system was implemented, to prevent fraud ahead of the party's conferences in 2020, which have been postponed because of the Covid-19 pandemic.

IN AN ARTICLE headlined 'David Mabuza: A portrait of power', Sama Yende wrote in *City Press* that, in Mpumalanga, the former premier was 'the gatekeeper of power'. 'He is notorious as a ruthless politician who has destroyed opponents and dumped the closest of his allies after using them.' Mabuza's close ally Peter

Nyoni said: 'He's a calculating character ... good at planning behind closed doors. He knows where he is going and had the ambition to be where he is now many years ago. He understands chess. He knows you can sacrifice certain pieces for the king.'

Mabuza was known for playing chess alone at his Barberton farmhouse, and translating his moves into political action. He repeatedly read *The Art of War* by Sun Tzu. Nyoni fell out with him and then lost his position in the ANC provincial executive committee. But he said Mabuza was a kind-hearted person: 'The problem is his character in politics ... He can give you a job, a tender to keep you busy, for you to lose focus while he makes his next big political move. He's not the kind of man to empower you ... Everything is about himself.'

Sama Yende asked Mabuza point-blank: 'How have you managed not to lose a single conference despite having so many political activists as your opponents, and despite so many scandals?' Mabuza attributed his political success to 'loving people. I have a big heart and I'm forgiving and honest.'

The reporter said there may be some truth in the reply. 'Despite what his rivals and former allies say, Mabuza is loved by ordinary people. He forgoes sleep to receive people from all over Mpumalanga at his home who come to raise ANC branch issues or ask for assistance like bursaries for their children. Two years ago, he started the David Mabuza Foundation to offer educational funding and build houses for the poor.'

Mabuza denied dispensing patronage, keeping stacks of cash at his house or playing chess games with allies whom he uses and dumps in the political wilderness. 'I never dump people, that's not correct,' he said.

The rumours about large amounts of cash held at Mabuza's farm began in 2010 when a case was laid at the Barberton police station claiming that R4 million was stolen. 'But the provincial organised crime unit insisted that the case involved the theft of only R1,200,' the *Mail & Guardian* reported. 'Constable Mxolisi Nyundu of the Barberton Police Station confirmed that a complainant, identified as Captain P.M. Khoza, opened a case, number 237/12/2009.'

Organised crime unit spokesman Captain Leonard Hlathi said R1,200 was reportedly stolen from the premier's farm. He denied knowledge of a Captain Khoza laying a charge. 'I wonder if this guy is a police captain or a miner somewhere,' he said. Khoza was in fact head of security in the premier's office and was replaced by Welcome Nkuna. The *Mail & Guardian* could not reach him for comment.

Collen Sedibe, who grew up on the same street as Mabuza and worked with him at the housing department, told the *New York Times* how Mabuza allegedly looted government funds. Government officials were stripped of their decision-making powers, and a Rapid Implementation Unit in the premier's office adjudicated all tenders. 'That's how he managed to loot,' Sedibe said.

'Treasury officials in Mpumalanga say that irregular expenditure more than doubled in the previous two budget years, particularly in education, housing and health,' the *New York Times* continued in its 2018 article. 'Wages account for most of the education and health budgets. Money is usually siphoned off by politicians and business allies through contracts for services or construction, ANC officials say. When costs are suspiciously high, schools are poorly built or facilities are badly maintained, they say, it is a warning that money is being skimmed, at the students' expense.'

On Mabuza's farm in Barberton, near Badplaas, his power was on full display, current and former ANC officials told the paper. 'He received contractors there and took his cut before projects were awarded, they said. Those who refused to participate often faced exile.' Sedibe said young ANC workers went to the farm to collect wads of cash from Mabuza to help wage his recruitment drive for the party. 'He always had money in his house,' he said.

A week after the article appeared, the *New York Times* published a letter from Mabuza, denying its 'laughable' allegations. 'Your article unfortunately furthers a divisive narrative. It spins a tale of baseless exaggerations and claims that have been peddled by those who have sought to tarnish my name, as well as that of the ANC, my birth province Mpumalanga, and our country. A

2016 Mpumalanga Community Survey indicated that within our province 77.3 per cent of households reported that they had access to safe drinking water, 79.8 per cent had access to electricity and 84.7 per cent reside in formal dwellings. Over the past four years in Mpumalanga, we built many thousands of homes.

'Before I was a politician, I was a math teacher and a political activist, a thorn to the apartheid government that jailed me without trial. I believe that education, based on a responsible curriculum, is a fundamental human right. The backlog in our schools' infrastructure reflects the sad history of apartheid and of misdirected policy priority. Curbing this remains at the top of our agenda.

'We have been implementing rural development programmes focusing on meeting basic needs, such as building new schools and connecting those schools to communities. We introduced free education. We are placing emphasis on maths and science education in the spirit of inward investment, quelling the brain drain of our brightest and best. President Cyril Ramaphosa recently launched a high-level intervention to combat a persistent lack of proper sanitation in schools across our country.

'I am no kingmaker. I serve in government at the behest of President Ramaphosa, a man I admired well before he stood shoulder to shoulder with Mr Mandela and the forefathers of our revolution. I abhor corruption. Any fiction to the contrary or fake news is laughable.'

Sama Yende, in a December 2010 *City Press* article, fingered Mabuza in another dodgy deal concocted in 2008, when he was MEC for agriculture and land affairs. It was one 'among many mega-bucks tenders ... awarded irregularly under a cloud of cynicism, cronyism and nepotism. The aim of the tender was noble – to provide poor rural families with farming machinery and implements in order to assist them with food security.'

Mabuza's friend and former business partner Patrick Chirwa received the R230-million tender to supply tractors and other equipment to farmers, Sama Yende reported in *City Press* in 2010. A forensic audit found that the project, for which nearly 100 tractors were bought, was not part of the department's plans and had not been allocated a budget.

'Mabuza and Chirwa were business partners in a close corporation, Above Average Trading Corporation 45 CC, that has since been deregistered,' Sama Yende wrote. 'The two men are still very close. Mabuza's department gave Chirwa's company, Sizwangendaba Investment, a three-year contract to supply tractors, and manage, operate and maintain the fleet for the province's food security initiative, Masibuyele Emasimini (Let's go back to the fields).'

A probe into the deal found that Sizwangendaba Investment was not a tractor dealer. After they won the tender, the department contracted Laeveld Trekkers as an intermediary, thereby increasing the costs. The other eight companies that bid for the contract were told the budget was R150 million but the highest bidder, at R230 million, was selected. Because of this tender, the department overspent its budget by R65.7 million during the 2008/2009 fiscal year and the following two years until the contract expired.

In November 2011, the *Sowetan* reported that the integrity management unit, located in the premier's office which investigates corruption, found that the award of the tender to Sizwangendaba was irregular. No disciplinary action was taken, however. 'The company has been awarded the contract again this year, even though opposition parties and business people complain that the government should have reversed the original tender,' the article read. 'The provincial government does not want to reveal how much the new contract is worth. Head of the agriculture department Nelisiwe Sithole could only say that the project was based on a rate per hectare.' Sithole insisted that Sizwangendaba deserved the contract. It had, after all, been appointed after a 'rigorous evaluation'. They were paid on a 'rate per hectare basis for different activities. There is no fixed contract amount.'

Mabuza did not deny that he was friends with Chirwa, the *Sowetan* reported. He denied he had anything to do with the award of the tender while he was MEC for agriculture, as it was 'not the duty of MECs to decide which company got tenders'.

In his capacity as MEC for agriculture and land affairs,

as chairman of the ANC in Mpumalanga and, especially, as chairman of the Greater Badplaas Land Claims Committee, Mabuza was very much involved in the conflict with Fred Daniel and the attempt to drive him off Nkomazi.

13

Fences and defences

Soon after D.D. Mabuza was appointed MEC for agriculture and land affairs in 2008, he helped establish the Greater Badplaas Land Claims Committee together with ANC councillor Pro Khoza and others. He was elected as its chairman. Ostensibly a lobby group for people seeking resolution of their land claims, it terrorised Fred with a spate of organised violence, aimed at forcing him out of Badplaas.

According to Mpumalanga website 013News, Khoza was born in Badplaas and still lives there. He was elected as an ANC ward councillor for the town in 2006. He was known for 'leading very violent protests where protestors would duck rubber bullets from cops and end up in jail for public violence, and him for inciting it,' the website reported. 'Most of his protests centred around land issues…'

In March 2008, Mpumalanga Tourism and Parks Agency official Johan Coetzer announced that Nkomazi's exemption certificate, which was valid until 2009, was to be withdrawn with immediate effect. Such a certificate grants game reserves 'ownership' of the animals contained on their fenced land.

The animals can't be hunted, captured or traded without the landowner's permission.

In a two-step with the parks agency, the so-called land claimants represented by the Greater Badplaas Land Claims Committee drafted a memorandum of grievances against Nkomazi Wilderness. The chairman of the fake Ndwandwa Community Trust, M.J. Nkosi, invited Fred to receive their memorandum at the Badplaas police station. Fred's partner John Allen went to accept it, but left the gathering when people in the crowd tried to assault him.

Then, on 22 May 2008, more than 200 members of the Badplaas branch of the Young Communist League marched on the agency's head office in Nelspruit to stage a peaceful protest against its 'failure to sustain and promote the tourism industry in Badplaas'. The protest's convenor, league leader Livion Khumalo, said the agency had for years frustrated the community's efforts to promote tourism and prevented the creation of jobs for young people. He had interacted with conservation projects like Nkomazi, but the agency hampered these efforts with 'inexplicable bureaucratic nonsense'. Before dispersing, the protestors called for the powers and influence of the agency to be restricted and for the immediate resignation of its CEO Abe Sibiya.

The Lowvelder newspaper reported that many employees at the Mpumalanga Tourism and Parks Agency complained about the organisation's 'pandemonium ... mismanagement and non-performance'. People were employed without job descriptions, 'most managers don't have any background in the areas in which they operate, and all they do is attend workshops, short courses and purposeless meetings'. The agency told the paper that 'turn-around processes' were ongoing.

After the protest, CEO Sibiya met Douglas Nkosi, chairman of the Songimvelo Community Property Association, to ask him to mobilise support for his leadership of the agency. He told Nkosi that Fred had instigated the Nelspruit protest. If he was forced to resign from the agency, he would no longer be in a position to help the association claim land on the Songimvelo Game Reserve.

Nkosi warned Khumalo that he would die young if he continued his protests 'in support of Fred'. A few days later, petrol bombs were hurled through the windows of his house. Fortunately, Khumalo wasn't home. Unfortunately, his house was badly damaged and most of its contents destroyed.

On the night of 29 July 2008, about 6 kilometres of game fencing on Nkomazi, valued at R500,000, was torn down. A few days later Fred received information that a march had been planned to Travelport, his retail centre, petrol station and gateway to the Cradle of Life. He asked John Allen to report this to the Badplaas police station. Allen went there at 8 am on 2 August and found only one policeman on duty, who said they had been told not to interfere in the demonstration as it was a political matter. All the other police officers had left town, leaving him alone in the charge office.

During the demonstration, a crowd barricaded the intersection of the main roads to Barberton and Badplaas by setting tyres alight. Traffic was forced to a standstill. By 9.30 am another group of protestors gathered at the Machadodorp–Badplaas junction, about 100 metres from Travelport. They burned tyres and toyi-toyied around the flames. Allen called the Badplaas police station. There was no answer.

At 10.30, the crowd began pulling down Nkomazi's game fences. Allen took many photos that clearly identify the vandals, but to date no one has been arrested. He took many photos of Pro Khoza among the protestors. He was assaulted by men in the crowd and his camera was grabbed, but he managed to hold onto it. Allen called Badplaas police station again and again, but no one answered.

Fred then called a local security company and asked them to send armed guards to protect the petrol station after the protestors began marching on it and threatened to petrol bomb it. The police arrived at 11.30 am, two hours after the protest started.

The tensions were finally defused when D.D. Mabuza arrived and addressed the crowd. He praised them and promised they would get their land. He told them to go home. They left on the buses that had brought them to Nkomazi. The police officers cleared the barricades and traffic flowed again. Mabuza's spokesman issued a press release confirming his presence at the protest.

'The protestors were not locals, land claimants or occupiers,' Fred says. 'They were bused in from a tavern and were given brandy and dagga. When journalists interviewed them, they did not know why they were at the protest. It was orchestrated by criminals perpetrating fraudulent land claims. They pulled down about a kilometre of my fencing. They marched towards my petrol station threatening to burn it down. They wanted to carry out a citizen's arrest – of me!'

An editorial about the protest in the *Elukwatini Guardian* asked: 'Why have the claimants not directed their aggression, frustrations and anger to the Land Claims Commissioner … why attack the subjects of the claims? No one subjected to a land claim in the entire Badplaas area has resisted when the process has been done properly.'

Allen went to the police station and laid charges of vandalism. 'Later we discovered that, a few days after the case was opened, it was closed by the police,' Fred says. 'Police officers told me that they had been ordered by politicians to keep out of the way during the demonstrations.' When Fred called D.D. Mabuza to complain, he recalls that he was told by the MEC for agriculture and land affairs to 'take care of your life as land is a sensitive issue'. He advised Fred to admit to the claims on his land.

Detective Inspector Johannes Vermeulen, stationed at the Badplaas police station for eight years, later described in an affidavit the havoc that the Greater Badplaas Land Claims Committee had unleashed on the 'peaceful rural town'. He and a colleague saw a group of people climbing through the game fence at the Cradle of Life. This had been 'deliberately cut with a pliers in a neat square to allow access. Mr Pro Khoza, the leader of the Greater Badplaas Land Claims Committee, arrived on the scene and prevented us from doing our police work. He gathered together a group of people and followed us to the police station where I was held hostage by them. This incident was the most traumatic of my life because it happened inside the police station and all law and order broke down to such a level that ordinary citizens had zero respect for the police and the law.' Police officers from Machadodorp raced to Badplaas to rescue their colleagues. Khoza was arrested for holding policemen hostage and assaulting one of them.

Later that month, about 6 kilometres of fencing at Nkomazi and the Cradle of Life was destroyed, Vermeulen said. 'Since then, a number of criminal attacks have happened against various businesses in Badplaas resulting in damages amounting to millions of rand. This lawlessness and criminal actions are matters of grave concern to the police and have a negative impact on tourism in our area, which is the lifeblood of our economy.'

In September, a group of vandals attacked the property of Chief Mnisi of the Majolo Trust. The damage to his house and cars amounted to tens of thousands of rand. Vermeulen collected evidence that showed a group of businessmen, known as 'the cabal', who had extensive interests in cattle and land in and around Badplaas, were behind the violence. They used criminal methods to attack legitimate businesses.

'The attack on the fences and other property of legitimate businesses and individuals in the Badplaas valley is not as a result of relationship issues between Fred Daniel and land claimants. I say this because the police have been confronted by a wave of lawlessness that resulted in violence, damage to property, racism and other crimes perpetrated not only against Mr Daniel, but also against other companies, individuals and community leaders that have business interests in Badplaas. This includes appalling crimes against members of the community who have stood up against this lawlessness and who have made it public that they want development and progress for the area. In response to this, the cabal have burned down their houses and threatened their lives as well as those of their families.

'It is clear from intelligence and evidence that has come to my attention that the riots in Badplaas are ... a well organised, funded and instigated initiative whereby the cabal try to muscle into business interests. The cabal is abusing and milking the land reform process and manipulating and extorting benefits from the legitimate beneficiaries. Despite the fact that thousands upon thousands of hectares of land have been restored to these communities, they have seen very little benefits due to corruption, infighting and mismanagement.'

Fred went to court to interdict the Greater Badplaas Land Claims Committee from damaging his property and intimidating or harming him or his employees. This was granted by Judge Ebersohn on 6 August. But despite the court order, there was no pause in the vandalism on Nkomazi. 'The police showed absolutely no interest in investigating and arresting the perpetrators,' Fred says. 'Many of them are influential figures in Mpumalanga politics and business.'

In the early hours of the morning on 23 August, a 3-kilometre stretch of fence along Lochiel Road was attacked and damaged. Fred reported it to the Badplaas police station, but later discovered that this investigation had also been shelved. Fred then appointed a security a company that specialises in nature conservation to track and trace the people destroying his fences.

On 25 August, a security guard spotted five people destroying fences. Douglas Nkosi, the chairman of the Songimvelo Community Property Association, had transported the vandals and joined in the wire cutting. Two days later Radio Alpha conducted interviews with Khoza and Bongani Mwali, representing the Greater Badplaas Land Claims Committee. The programme was broadcast in Siswati, and Fred arranged for it to be transcribed and translated into English.

Khoza called in: 'We are going to go and bring down that fence, whether it's broad daylight or it's night-time, and any other time. He can use his money against us, he can shoot us, but in the end we'll have our land back as black people.' Khoza and Mwali threatened war, and said 'people will die'.

On 5 September, Fred received a call from Mabuza, who confirmed that he was the chairman of the Greater Badplaas Land Claims Committee, and asked for a meeting with the organisation and the land claimants. 'I was reluctant to meet the people who had damaged my property and assaulted my staff,'

Fred says. 'Mr Mabuza responded by threatening that he could not guarantee my safety if I did not accede to the land claims.

'I agreed to send my attorney Richard Spoor and business partner John Allen to the meeting arranged by Mr Mabuza. At the meeting chaired by him in his dual capacity as MEC for agriculture and land affairs and chairman of the Greater Badplaas Land Claims Committee (which is unlawful), Mr Mabuza watched as the so-called claimants intimidated Allen, who had to leave the meeting in fear for his life.'

Spoor waited outside until the meeting ended, and had a brief chat with Mabuza. The MEC said he would set up another meeting to discuss the claims. This never happened.

Khoza led another protest outside the Badplaas police station in October. He accused the police officers of being racists who did not investigate any charges laid against white farmers for abusing black workers. He warned the officers that the Greater Badplaas Land Claims Committee would 'shoot to kill' them. 'We are also marching to remind the premier to follow the law, to tell the legislature to follow the law of land restitution together with the MEC for agriculture [Mabuza],' Khoza told a reporter for *The Lowvelder*.

Land Claims Commission spokesman Lucas Mufamadi said in response to the protests that 'the main concerns of the community members are the delay in the settlement of their claim. In order to deal with their challenges, we decided to involve the MEC for agriculture and land affairs, and local politicians to assist communities in understanding the challenges that we are faced with.'

In a formal complaint sent to the Human Rights Commission and Mpumalanga's South African Police Services commissioner, coupled with a request for protection following the committee's death threats, 19 Badplaas policemen stated that Khoza had only 'a handful of followers ... and incites attacks on other members of the community'.

Fred dubbed the Greater Badplaas Land Claims Committee the 'political extension of the fake Ndwandwa Trust'. Pieter Visagie's former foreman and the fraudulent chairman of the

Ndwandwa Community Trust, M.J. Nkosi was, along with Mabuza and Khoza, a founder of the committee.

The year ended with Fred serving a 'shot across the bow' letter of demand on the Mpumalanga Tourism and Parks Agency, the regional Land Claims Commission, Mabuza, the national commissioner of police, and five provincial and national government officials and departments. He set out an exhaustive decade-long history of how he and his businesses had been 'prejudiced, harassed, intimidated, attacked and legally undermined' by officials and government bodies. As a result, he had suffered huge financial losses, calculated at R667 million. The respondents were informed that if the amount was not paid within 30 days, court action would follow. This is the case that was scheduled to be heard in August 2020 in the North Gauteng High Court. Fred claims that his damages have ballooned to more than R1 billion since then.

But, despite all his attempts to secure peace, the harassment and vandalism did not stop until Fred left Mpumalanga in 2019.

14

Worlds apart

With his dream of 7-star resorts on his land stalled by a number of factors including the death of Butch Kerzner and the onslaught from government officials, Fred decided to sell 50 per cent of his shares in Nkomazi in 2008. His sale negotiations were conducted and concluded during a barrage of spurious legal action brought by the Mpumalanga Tourism and Parks Agency and the Mpumalanga Land Claims Commission.

In the late 2000s, Kerzner International's One&Only 7-star resort was under construction on the V&A Waterfront in Cape Town, timed for completion before the 2010 Soccer World Cup. Dubai World owned both the Waterfront and 30 per cent of Kerzner International, and that is how they heard about Nkomazi and considered it a prospect for their expanding portfolio of African hotel and resorts.

In a December 2007 cover story, the *Financial Mail* reported on the company's plans: 'Dubai, the small emirate, one of seven that make up the United Arab Emirates, has enjoyed double-digit growth in recent years and created a regional trade and finance hub that has attracted most of the world's top corporate names. In recent years, the inward focus of the emirate shifted and Dubai is starting to make its presence felt on the global stage. The mechanism: an array of state-owned companies that are building impressive investment, financial and property portfolios around the globe.' One of these was Dubai World.

Dubai's ruler Sultan Ahmed bin Sulayem planned to invest about $1.5 billion in Africa over the next five years. Dubai World was seeking a return of 'at least 20 per cent a year and believed Africa's strong economic growth enabled such returns. Since the company acquired Cape Town's V&A Waterfront from Transnet for more than R7 billion last year, Dubai World's expansion into Africa has been meteoric,' the magazine gushed. 'It created a new company Dubai World Africa, with headquarters in Cape Town, to consolidate its portfolio on the continent.'

Fred was introduced by a former chief executive of Kerzner International to James Wilson, chief executive of Dubai World Africa's subsidiary Istithmar in early 2007. After a visit to the reserve, Wilson commissioned a thorough due diligence on the project. In the report that issued from this, Nkomazi was compared to other high-end private game reserves and lodges in South Africa. It scored equal to the luxury Sabi Sands Game Reserve bordering the Kruger National Park and the equally prestigious Singita Lebombo concession inside Kruger. Sabi Sands and Singita had the Big Five animals. Nkomazi could trump them after its 7-star lodges were constructed and its wildlife permits were approved.

Cliffe Dekker Hofmeyr Attorneys investigated the land claims lodged on the reserve and found they had no merit. Fred's black empowerment partner, Simon Huba of the Inkaleni Land Owners Association in Badplaas, green-lighted the sale. His organisation would join part of their 30,000 hectares to Nkomazi and their beneficiaries would be employed at the luxury resorts during and after its construction.

Istithmar agreed to invest in Nkomazi as a 50 per cent joint venture partner. The sale was concluded in May 2008 and the company committed itself to providing capital and expertise for the reserve's expansion. Kerzner retained the right to design, build and operate two 7-star safari lodges on Nkomazi. A new joint venture company was established, Business Venture Investments 1145.

'The only conditions I cast in stone in the contract were that I retain full management of the reserve and wildlife for life; that I retain Paperbark as a free-hold title owned by my family trust and full traversing rights over the reserve would be registered against the title deed,' Fred says. He lived with Linda and Jesse at Paperbark, in a restored farmhouse on the banks of the Komati River.

Wilson told the *Financial Mail*: 'Dubai World Africa Conservation has been established as a holding company for what is expected to be a number of prime game reserves in Africa. In South Africa, the group bought pockets of land to create a 30,000-hectare game reserve – Nkomazi, near Badplaas in Mpumalanga – for $25 million and is planning to spend a further $75 million to restock the property with game and develop a number of 5-star private lodges. Its partner in the venture is local property developer Fred Daniel. The One&Only group is also considering building a commercial lodge there.'

Wilson said talks were being held with the Mpumalanga government and community trusts to align Nkomazi with the 50,000-hectare Songimvelo provincial game reserve. 'If successful, it would make it the largest private reserve in South Africa,' he said. 'The province and the local community land trust could become shareholders in the venture.'

Fred sold half of Nkomazi to Dubai World for R75 million. 'The project was valued at R250 million,' he says. 'My new partners drew up a R2.5-billion investment plan that included a hotel and golf course. The Development Bank of Southern Africa pledged that it would match the first R100 million that Dubai World invested. It committed a further R75 million to facilitate the Inkaleni community's inclusion in the deal.'

The day after the deal was sealed, 18 March 2008, the Mpumalanga Land Claims Commission filed an interdict in the Land Claims Court in an apparent attempt to derail the joint venture between Fred and Dubai World. It sought to prevent the erection of fences on several properties on which land claims had been lodged; to have the fencing declared a contravention of the Restitution of Land Rights Act; to interdict Grand Valley Estates from acquiring any properties under claim; and to have its acquisition of properties under claim declared a contravention of the Act.

Fred filed opposing papers, along with Dubai World. He pointed out that the commission had been informed of the sale of Nkomazi to Dubai World and did not respond. 'The land purchases were bona fide and it was absurd to make the contention that I bought farms solely to frustrate the land claims process,' he said in his affidavit.

'The commission seems to be labouring under the impression that, because a land claim has been gazetted, it is a valid claim and the claimants are entitled to restitution. It also seems to be labouring under the impression that, because a land claim was gazetted, this precludes the development of the land, even to the extent of replacing or erecting boundary fences without its permission.'

The commission's application was dismissed for urgency and postponed to April. No further affidavits were filed and the Land Claims Commission took no further steps to have the matter heard.

The partnership deal that Fred struck with Dubai World, intended to secure the future of Nkomazi Wilderness and the Cradle of Life, collapsed soon after he signed the contract with the investment company in May 2007. Instrumental in destroying their relationship was the Mpumalanga Tourism and Parks Agency.

The first order of business, Dubai World Africa CEO James Wilson announced, was to prepare for a visit from the emirate's ruler, Sultan Ahmed bin Sulayem, who was planning to come to Mpumalanga to seal the deal. Wilson proposed that a luxury tented lodge be built on Nkomazi for the sultan and his entourage. Fred was flabbergasted when construction started. The lodge was being built alongside the river, below its flood line. 'I had done everything on Nkomazi strictly according to the book, and more,' he says. 'I commissioned environmental impact studies and applied for permission for every weir, road, dam and every other structure that I built. The lodge would never have passed muster; it was within the 1:10-year flood line of the river. I could not believe that a plan had been lodged for it with the authorities and permission was granted.'

He withdrew his objections when Wilson said that the lodge was only a temporary structure. After the sultan's departure, it would be dismantled and moved to a more suitable site. The ruler did not come, but the chairman of Dubai World brought three friends to Nkomazi for three days in October 2007. Other guests included cabinet minister Jeff Radebe and his wife, and parks agency CEO Solly Mosidi. At the end of the visit, Wilson proposed that the lodge be opened to visitors. Fred was livid when his new partners commercialised their shortcut, shoddy tented camp, and got away with it. In terms of their joint venture contract, Fred was the manager of Nkomazi, but Wilson seemed to be calling the shots, and doing so badly.

Government officials and parks agency employees turned a blind eye to Dubai World's many contraventions of law on the reserve. They allowed the construction of a tented camp lodge that broke eight environment laws. They ignored tourist bookings into tents erected below the flood line. When some of the tents, half of the staff facilities and the swimming pool were washed away in floods, the lodge was allowed to continue operating. No action was taken when raw sewage ran into the Komati River. The parks agency and other government officials ignored the construction of illegal airstrips, roads and river crossings on Nkomazi, and damage to its wetland areas. Fred's heated opinions about the crass development of Nkomazi were ignored.

In an opinion on Fred's R1-billion damages claim that was to be heard in August 2020, Advocate Willem Heath said Fred's agreements with Dubai World were void 'precisely due to a fraudulent scheme that came into being as a consequence of the corrupt activities, conduct and relationships between Dubai

World staff and government officials. His dispute is therefore as a direct consequence of this corruption, the string of unlawful acts that followed and the constitutional breaches that were perpetrated by officials who set about covering up the corruption with deliberate, unlawful acts aimed to criminally silence, discredit and victimise [Fred].'

Despite the sale agreement giving him traversing rights over the reserve, Fred's new partners instructed their guards to stop him from entering Nkomazi and the cottage site that he owned. Dubai World instructed their staff not to meet or speak to Fred. The company's employees urged Fred's neighbours and other people to break off business ties with him.

Fred was unaware when he sold his share of Nkomazi to Dubai World that they were colluding with the parks agency. Heath says, 'Daniel was unaware that secret meetings and correspondence were already taking place between James Wilson [the Dubai World Africa CEO] and Solly Mosidi, the new CEO of the agency. The discussions covered Dubai World's investment in Nkomazi Wilderness. One email from Mosidi promised them development rights over game reserves the agency controlled, and all the permits Dubai World required. Its staff testified in sworn affidavits ... that they were told to get rid of Daniel, as he is a problem, in order to qualify for the permits. A corrupt and collusive agreement developed between Dubai World staff and the agency's officials, with the object of removing Daniel from Nkomazi and chasing him out of Badplaas.'

This collusion is very similar to the Dolphin deal. Mpumalanga's conservation agency was plotting to give a Dubai-based company the development rights on state-owned reserves, without permission from the provincial legislature.

Battered by his conflict with Dubai World and the parks agency, in March 2008, less than a year after their joint venture was sealed, Fred sold his share of Nkomazi Wilderness Reserve to Dubai World. The purchase price was R245.5 million, 'a much lower price than it would have been had it been a Big Five reserve with all the required permits', according to Heath. The 'unlawful actions of the parks agency and its employees were crucial and instrumental' in assisting Dubai World to purchase the reserve at a much lower price, he added. The company renamed the property Nkomazi Game Reserve. Fred retained ownership of the 1,000-hectare Cradle of Life on the edge of the property and moved with his family to its lodge.

On 13 June 2008, the day the land was transferred and possession had been handed over to Dubai World, the parks agency granted permits to Dubai World to keep predators, including lion, on Nkomazi Wilderness on the strength of the very same applications that Fred's company Grand Valley Estates had submitted. Grand Valley's name was simply replaced with the trade name of Dubai World by the parks agency.

A sworn affidavit by Nico van Schalkwyk, employed by Dubai World as a manager at the Nkomazi Game Reserve, explained how he was instrumental in ensuring that they received their animal permits. He lived in Nelspruit, where the agency's manager of wildlife protection services, Jan Muller, was his neighbour. He arranged for Bruce Maine, employed at the Shamwari Game Reserve in the Eastern Cape and recently appointed as Nkomazi's acting general manager, to meet Muller at his home in 2008.

'Maine advised Muller that Nkomazi Game Reserve had instructed him to prepare permit applications for the introduction of lion, elephant and cheetah,' Van Schalkwyk said. 'Muller advised Maine exactly what steps he had to follow to ensure that the permits could be issued. In other words, he would facilitate the process for Maine and the Nkomazi Game Reserve.'

Van Schalkwyk also said that he was instructed not to cooperate with Fred. 'I hasten to add that I had no idea why, but I assumed at the time that there was some animosity.'

The former Nkomazi manager said there had been a 'mad rush' by Dubai World to release lions onto the reserve. The animals were brought to Mpumalanga from Shamwari and were held in a boma. The outer fences of the reserve enclosed 13,840 hectares – the area stipulated in the permit applications for the release of lion, cheetah and elephant that had been granted to Dubai World on the day it took ownership of Nkomazi.

The farms Sterkspruit, Doyershoek and Stolzburg,

incorporated into Nkomazi, were occupied by invading herds of cattle owned by Badplaas businessmen. A new fence had to be erected between them and the rest of the reserve before the lion could be introduced. Van Schalkwyk was placed in charge of the project. 'I [had] clear instructions to erect the fence as fast as humanly possible along the easiest and quickest route. I was specifically instructed by Nkomazi management to leave a concealed gap of about a kilometre in the fence so that when the Mpumalanga Tourism and Parks Agency came to inspect it, an illusion would be created ... that the lion would be released into the entire reserve, which was 13,800 hectares.

'Immediately after the inspection, I was instructed (I cannot now recall by who of Dubai World) to fence the gap to create a camp into which the lion, elephants and cheetah would be released. The camped area was approximately 5,500 hectares instead of the whole of Nkomazi Reserve. I thought this was just an interim measure that would last a month or so, but it was to last to at least the end of 2013.'

Van Schalkwyk had been present at several meetings where Dubai World senior managers disparaged and threatened Fred. 'It became a running joke by Bruce Maine that, after the handover of the business, Frans Loubser of the Nkomazi Game Reserve was going to put up signs showing where our fences were and where Daniel's fences were. This would ensure that the community did not make the mistake of cutting the wrong fences, if they were so minded to cut fences.' He heard Wilson say that 'the community was breaking the fences because of Daniel and that steps needed to be taken to get rid of Daniel from the Nkomazi Reserve'.

Despite its boasts of luxury for discerning nature lovers, Dubai World local director Willem Dreyer approached Fred in December 2010 to ask if he, Fred would buy Nkomazi. The company was beating a full retreat from South Africa. After the global financial crisis of 2008, Dubai World had debts of $59 billion and ran out of cash to invest in the properties it had acquired in Africa. It was keen to dispose of the reserve, a loss-making, non-core asset into which it had sunk R340 million.

When Dreyer made the offer, he was at the same time practically begging the regional Land Claims Commission to buy Nkomazi. 'The ultimate irony was', Fred points out, 'that after all those years of playing dirty politics to get the property, the provincial government had no money to buy it. With all the land reform projects in Badplaas going sour and large tracts of land lying fallow, pressure had mounted for politicians to rescue those failed land reform projects and to recapitalise them.'

Clearly sensing the gap created by the mismanagement, abuse of power and corruption in the Badplaas land reform project, notorious conman Gustav de Waal allegedly devised a scheme to make money from the sale of Nkomazi. He had been a foreman on a farm that Fred bought and incorporated into Nkomazi.

De Waal had been involved in the earlier Badplaas land scams with Pieter Visagie and the fake Ndwandwa Trust after they tossed out the trust's founding chairman Robert Nkosi and obtained options on land in the area for land claimants. In an affidavit, Astrid Christianson, in support of two fraud cases laid by Nkosi, said that she acted on behalf of De Waal to acquire options on as many farms in Badplaas as possible, in conjunction with Visagie, in the early 2000s. She set up a shelf company that had no funds to buy land and no mandate to become involved in such transactions.

Mpumalanga journalist Bheki Mashile took up the story in a March 2010 article headlined '"Con man" De Waal eyes Nkomazi', published in the *Guardian yase Mpumalanga*. 'In what can only be described as highly mysterious and inexplicable, Dreyer is said to be in negotiations for the sale of the reserve to one Gustav de Waal, a reportedly shady, self-proclaimed agricultural development businessman. De Waal, who operates a company called Investment for Agricultural Sustainability in Africa (Ifasa), is alleged to specialise in exploiting rural communities by making grandiose promises of funding major agricultural projects with the sole aim of accessing government grants. He has operated several companies, both domestic and international, over the years.

'He has been involved in a number of failed projects such as the Namibian Jatropha biodiesel project, in which Okavango

Bio Energy, based in England, and Prime Investment Holdings – the project's executing company – would invest N$3 billion in the project. De Waal was the controlling shareholder in both companies.'

The Namibian newspaper reported in June 2010 that De Waal fell out with his partners 'who accused him of double dealing and, despite a finalised integrated environmental assessment, his Prime Investment Holdings failed to realise the Jatropha scheme as a result'. A former employee of De Waal described him to the paper as 'the sweetest con man you will ever meet'.

'Ifasa has now partnered with the Ndwandwa Community Trust, which is facing serious legal challenges to its legitimacy,' Mashile wrote. Ifasa claimed to have R2.5 billion, which would be invested in the Badplaas area – including for the purchase of Nkomazi Game Reserve.

'De Waal and M.J. Nkosi's illegitimate Ndwandwa Trust claimed that they were seeking to purchase the reserve on behalf of seven communities supposedly represented by MJ's trust. De Waal not only went into a partnership with an illegal entity, he seemingly ignored the fact that most of the land comprising Nkomazi Game Reserve is subject to a land claim, and could not be legally put on the market by Dubai World.'

Nkomazi general manager Willem Dreyer told Mashile's inquiries: 'The reason we embarked on this route (with Ifasa) is that relying on the court process proved to be tedious with a long and protracted timeframe. Legal counsel opinion supports our view that these claims are spurious in nature; however, they remain a land claim until proven to be spurious in the Land Claims Court or de-gazetted.'

The Ifasa boss was 'constantly hosted' at the Nkomazi Game Reserve, Mashile noted. 'Recently De Waal hid from police officers when they paid a visit to the reserve. When the *Guardian* asked him whether he was still involved in any sort of negotiations relating to the Nkomazi Game Reserve, he said no.'

In November 2010, with Dreyer's backing, De Waal sent a written proposal on his company Ifasa's letterhead to Lucas Mufamadi, operations director at the Land Claims Commission, and to the Mpumalanga department of agriculture and land affairs. He proposed to buy Nkomazi from Dubai World, and other properties in the Badplaas area, and then offer them to the commission for land restitution.

Fred's cottage site on Nkomazi, Paperbark, which he wanted to retain after the original sale to Dubai World, had not yet been subdivided as agreed. His traversing rights over the reserve had also not yet been registered. It would be a disaster if a fake land claim was used to sell the property to the Land Claims Commission. He consulted an advocate and discovered that his 2008 amended sale agreement with Dubai World was void as it failed to comply with two pieces of land administration legislation and one piece of company legislation. By not transferring ownership of Paperbark to him, the agreement also became void.

Fred sent a letter to Dubai World in February 2011, informing them that he had been advised that the agreements were void. He asked that the matter be sent to arbitration, as stipulated in their agreement. He warned that Ifasa was a front for a fake land claim lodged in a fraudulent scheme to grab the land. An official working in the regional land claims commissioner's office had given him a memory stick with all Ifasa's presentations, correspondence, business plans and minutes of meetings; Fred knew they were up to no good.

Dubai World refused to go to arbitration, and Fred brought an urgent application in the North Gauteng High Court to interdict the sale and refer the dispute to arbitration. The company responded by refusing outright to sell Nkomazi back to him. In a meeting with the deputy judge president in November 2011, Dubai World's advocate gave an oral undertaking that his client would not sell the reserve until the urgent application had been heard.

The company's local directors realised that they could circumvent the legal problems by selling the reserve to the Land Claims Commission, for a much higher price than Fred was prepared to pay. In this scheme, De Waal, the parks agency, the regional Land Claims Commission and the Ndwandwa Trust would play key roles.

In April 2011, Ifasa called a meeting with the fake trustees of the Ndwandwa Community Trust at the Forever Resort in Badplaas. The agenda included 'establishing the real needs and development goals' of the trust and allowing Ifasa to assist it as an 'investor and developmental agency'. De Waal claimed that he had an undertaking from the government to purchase and develop Nkomazi on behalf of Badplaas claimants as a ten-year project. He said he had R2.5 billion to invest and decided to purchase Nkomazi on their behalf 'to ensure that the property does not fall into the wrong hands'. He promised to deal with conflicts about the land claims and told the fake trustees that they faced no financial risks or debts.

Former Mpumalanga regional land claims commissioner Tumi Seboka was introduced at the meeting as a facilitator for Ifasa and the Greater Badplaas Land Claims Committee. She said D.D. Mabuza had sent her to raise money to buy Nkomazi. She offered to work for the communities for free; all she needed from them was a resolution of support. A few days later M.J. Nkosi, chairman of the hijacked trust, sent a letter to Seboka confirming her appointment 'to act as consultant on behalf of the trust to restore claimed land and to negotiate for investment'.

Many leaders of the Ndwandwa Community Trust, including its founder Robert Nkosi, found it hard to persuade their beneficiaries that Ifasa was making wildly exaggerated promises. They asked Fred and his partner John Allen to conduct a due diligence on Ifasa. The organisation had said at its meeting that anyone was welcome to check it out.

Despite heavy stonewalling and obfuscation by Ifasa, including an urgent application in the high court by Dubai World to interdict him from finding out more about the organisation, Fred together with John Allen blew the scheme right out of the water by exposing Ifasa as a group of shelf companies. They provided the master of the court with evidence that the fraudsters were using fake letters of authority for the trust. Fred contacted Ifasa's attorney J.G. Venter, who confirmed that there had never been R2.5 billion available to invest in Badplaas and said that De Waal owed him money.

Ifasa was promised access to government funds, through the politically connected Seboka, and with the help of the fake Ndwandwa trust. As the leaked details on the memory stick show they were paving the way for a R350-million government-backed bank guarantee for the company, at 8 per cent interest a year, payable after ten years. Ifasa intended to cash the bank guarantee overseas, pay Dubai World R300 million for Nkomazi and pocket R50 million, which would be shared with the Greater Badplaas Land Claims Committee, the fake Ndwandwa trustees, Seboka and Dreyer.

As had been the case with Visagie's deals with the Mpumalanga government, the beneficial use of the restituted land would not remain with the claimants but with Ifasa. The company would pay the beneficiaries a modest rental for Nkomazi for a decade while it used government grants to train them and transfer skills. 'It was akin to one of those ubiquitous 419 schemes, but covered in a veneer of professional and political respectability,' Fred says.

Robert Nkosi laid two criminal cases of fraud at the Badplaas police station. The first was against, among others, the 12 fake trustees of the Ndwandwa Community Trust and their accomplice Visagie. The second was against Ifasa and their three directors. This was followed up by letters sent to the regional Land Claims Commission, Ifasa, the putative Ndwandwa trustees and Dubai World Africa. They were informed about the fake Ndwandwa trust deed, the unlawful trustees and the dodgy nature of their new land deals.

In October 2011, Robert Nkosi's complaint bore fruit. A letter was sent from the master of the high court to the 'trustees of the Ndwandwa Community Trust' – addressed to M.J. Nkosi – confirming that the trust's 2006 letters of authority were issued in error. The deed's original letters of authority were valid, although the copy had been removed from the master's file when a new one was issued. The master informed the fake trustees that their letters of authority were revoked with immediate effect, and M.J. Nkosi was instructed to immediately return them.

True to their past form, the fake trustees refused to hand over the Ndwandwa files, records and documents to the lawful trustees. Seeing that they faced fraud charges and possible jail time, there was a threat that they would destroy records and evidence. Police officers, acting on the charges Robert Nkosi had laid against Visagie and the fake trustees, removed three bakkie loads of computers, documents and records from the office on Visagie's farm. In appreciation for his assistance, the reinstated chairman of the trust gave Fred access to all the files. He made copies of emails between M.J. Nkosi, Seboka and Ifasa, and reconstructed their fraudulent scheme.

The fake trustees launched an urgent application in the North Gauteng High Court in November to review the master's decision and have their records returned. The court upheld the decision of the master and appointed interim trustees pending the election of new trustees at an annual general meeting, to be held after the verification of the trust's beneficiaries. The master issued new letters of authority to Robert Nkosi, and the police handed all the records to the interim trustees.

In November, an attorney acting on behalf of the Ndwandwa Community Trust and its interim trustees sent a letter to Ifasa and the fake trustees setting out their new framework. It stated that formal verification of beneficiaries would be conducted by the trustees, with assistance from government structures, and those with no title to any benefit would be excluded.

Robert Nkosi's victory was a major blow to the Ifasa scam, but it did only half the work of clearing the land claims on Nkomazi. The 2008 court case brought by the Mpumalanga Land Claims Commission against Fred and Dubai World to set aside the reserve's sale hung over his head like the sword of Damocles. Seboka meanwhile approached the presiding judge J.P. Bam, saying that she had permission from the parties, to ask him not to hand down judgment because the matter had been settled. Judge Bam closed the file, fell ill soon afterwards with cancer and passed away. The matter is still pending 12 years later and a new judge has not been appointed.

In August 2015, *Sunday Tribune* journalist Phalane Motale reported that charges had been withdrawn against five people facing charges of fraud and theft in connection with the land restitution deal in Badplaas. 'The investigation has since been widened and top politicians have been implicated,' Motale wrote. 'The accused, who last appeared in the Nelspruit Regional Court in 2013, were three officials of Investment for Agricultural Sustainability in Africa (Ifasa), Gustav de Waal, Gert Pienaar and Ferdinand Odendaal; Ndwandwa Community Trust chairman Mangisi Nkosi; and land speculator and farmer Pieter Visagie. The Hawks accused them of being involved in fraudulent land claims and of theft of the Ndwandwa Community Trust deed.'

Hawks spokesman Brigadier Hangwani Mulaudzi said the state had withdrawn the case due to lack of evidence, reported Motale. The prosecutor had, however, recently told the investigating officer that an advocate needed the cases for review. 'It is unknown what happened thereafter but, according to our system, the cases were filed at the Badplaas Police Station,' Mulaudzi said.

An investigation by Paul O'Sullivan established that the charges were withdrawn before forensic evidence was examined that showed that the network of alleged fraudsters was wider than the state anticipated. 'This evidence implicated Mpumalanga Premier David Mabuza, who was then the MEC for agriculture and land management,' O'Sullivan told the reporter. 'It's either the state hit a wall or there has been political interference not to continue with the prosecution. But I am not going to rest until someone goes to jail because that money could have been used to uplift the lives of poor people. We have ample evidence for a successful prosecution.'

AFTER FRED WON THE high court case that interdicted Dubai World from selling Nkomazi, and another legal victory that compelled them to arbitrate, the company signed an arbitration agreement in December 2012. Fred filed his statement of claim and other documents in preparation. A year passed while Dubai World's attorneys tried to separate the issue of the alleged breaches of its agreement from the allegedly fraudulent manner in which its permits and permissions were obtained. The mediation was finally set down for 29 July to 15 August 2014.

Fred's statement of claim had to be amended three times when forensic investigators found proof that fraud and corruption had been committed during Dubai World's development of Nkomazi and attempted sale to Ifasa. 'But because arbitration has no jurisdiction to hear matters of fraud and corruption, it was no longer viable to keep amending the statement of claim,' he says. 'The only viable option was to suspend arbitration with them and issue a summons for damages in the high court.'

UNTIL THEY LEFT Mpumalanga in 2019, Fred and Linda watched as the land he had restored and carefully stocked with wildlife became degraded under the stewardship of Dubai World. In September 2007, the Mpumalanga Tourism and Parks Agency approved Dubai World's application to keep elephants at Nkomazi. The permit was issued subject to the condition that the area in which they were kept would not be smaller than 12,700 hectares. In July 2008, Dubai World wrote to the agency that the reserve would be 14,740 hectares and 'the elephants will have access to the whole reserve'. The agency granted a permit for ten elephants. A month later, its officials inspected Nkomazi's fences and issued an adequate enclosure certificate.

In May 2016, Professor Wouter van Hoven of Ecolife inspected Nkomazi and was appalled by what he found. 'From the records provided to us, it is clear that a 10-kilometre fence had been erected which had the effect of illegally shrinking the entire Nkomazi Reserve from 14,700 hectares into five smaller camps. The area into which the elephants and lion were being released, the so-called main reserve, had shrunk to 5,654 hectares.

'The motivation for doing this is not based on ecological principles but based on satisfying tourist sightings. Prime elephant habitat area was fenced out, setting the Nkomazi Reserve on a collision course with its biodiversity, and reversing years of ecological rehabilitation.' By releasing ten elephant into a small camp, Dubai World violated their permit conditions, overstretched Nkomazi's carrying capacity, and caused biodiversity loss and environmental degradation.

When Van Hoven returned to the reserve in April 2017, the herd had increased to 18 elephants. He watched them for months and recorded the damage to the environment. 'On Nkomazi big trees are very few and far between. These are the first casualties of over-stocking elephant. Trees like kiepersols are targeted and quickly disappear. In areas of significant damage the trees are replaced by invader species like lantana. Large trees, such as marula, that take many years to grow magnificently tall have been pushed over and may not grow back again.

'The decline in the health of the reserve's vegetation … deleteriously affects the entire ecosystem as many birds, insects and mammals rely on trees for sustenance and shelter. On Nkomazi, all of the biodiversity must be considered in order to effectively manage the environment.

'The reckless management of Nkomazi's biodiversity is having a devastating effect … and is reversing all the positive steps taken over the last decade to rehabilitate, restore and heal its ecosystems and habitats back to health,' Van Hoven reported to Fred. 'In addition to the damage caused, the elephants have become frustrated with being confined in such a relatively small, sub-optimal habitat. This could have contributed to the female elephant named Knysna overturning a game vehicle carrying tourists.

'Despite the fact that the Mpumalanga Tourism and Parks Agency knew about these breaches of the permit conditions, and the negative impact by the elephants that were exceeding the carrying capacity of the Nkomazi Reserve and damaging its biodiversity, a blind eye was cast and the damage has been allowed to compound from year to year. Much of the damage can never be fixed in our lifetime.'

15

World-class corruption

Corruption in land restitution programmes was central to one of the biggest scandals that rocked Mpumalanga during D.D. Mabuza's short tenure as MEC for agriculture and land affairs and his two terms as premier. The construction of the stadium in the Mbombela Municipality for the 2010 Soccer World Cup provided corrupt politicians with an opportunity to ramp up their crooked schemes. The stadium built in Mbombela (formerly Nelspruit) led to massive theft from the poor and a tragic loss of lives.

After Mbombela was confirmed a host city, the first task was identifying and securing a site for the stadium through a transparent public process. But that is not what happened. According to Dale McKinley in his report entitled 'Mbombela: A tale of corruption, murder and resistance': 'Instead, opportunistic local politicians quickly moved to get their hands on what they knew would be a lucrative source of political prestige, economic patronage and personal accumulation.'

In 2003, thousands of beneficiaries, mainly workers on Mataffin farm on the outskirts of Mbombela, members of the Matsafeni community, successfully claimed 6,000 hectares of land. By early 2006 – without informing most councillors and the community involved – Mbombela mayor Justice Nsibande identified a section of the Matsafeni land for the stadium. He announced that a deal had been struck with the trust's beneficiaries and the municipality moved in to clear the site, evicting students from their primary and high schools and providing them with prefabricated classrooms. Nsibande appointed project managers and a professional team, and put out a tender for the main construction work.

'By this stage, things were already bad enough for Mpumalanga MEC for local government and housing K.C. Mashego-Dlamini to appoint a team to investigate allegations of fraud, corruption and maladministration with a specific focus on allegations of procurement irregularities and the failure to keep proper financial records in relation to the 2010 World Cup stadium,' McKinley wrote.

'It did not take long for the Matsafeni community to figure out that something was seriously rotten and questions began to be raised. In response Nsibande, Mbombela municipal manager Jacob Dladla, councillor Differ Mogale (unilaterally appointed by Dladla as Mbombela's 2010 co-ordinator) and other officials who were part of what had clearly become a cabal, threatened to forcefully remove the community to a new settlement 21 kilometres away in virgin bush, while secretly negotiating an illegal sales agreement for just R1 with the chairman of the Matsafeni Trust.'

Mbombela council speaker Jimmy Mohlala told reporter Justin Arenstein that he was opposed to his colleagues' threats of forced removal; it was illegal. He questioned payments of millions of rand to the stadium project's professional team, Lefika Emerging Equity. The municipality denied any wrongdoing and placed a gag on all officials about the stadium project.

The land sale agreement signed in June 2007 was 'a classic example of a shakedown', McKinley said. In return for R1 as the price for 118 hectares of land, the Matsafeni community was promised 'no less than one third of the job scope and value in respect of work to be performed and services rendered of the whole development and construction of the soccer stadium' and 'preference ... for sub-contracting work'. The document stipulated that 'no party may make the agreement public or issue any statement about it without the written consent of the other party' and that each party 'shall keep confidential any information in relation to the agreement'.

A stadium sod-turning ceremony was held in December 2006. Bobby Motaung's Lefika Emerging Equity splashed out R1.45 million on a party to celebrate. (Durban spent R300,000 and Cape Town R35,000 on their sod-turning parties.) The bash in Mpumalanga was attended by the political elite and guests from other parts of the country, who were wined and dined in air-conditioned tents. For the few members of the Matsafeni community in attendance, all that was on offer was a plate of pap and meat to be eaten outside.

In its report to the Mbombela municipal council in early 2007, the investigating team appointed by the provincial government said there were serious problems with the management of municipal funds for service delivery and the municipality's over-extension of its stadium construction budget; and major irregularities in awarding tenders for the stadium. They found that required supply chain procedures, particularly in relation to the evaluation and adjudication of tenders, were not followed in the appointment of Platinum Sport as the stadium project managers and Lefika Emerging Equity as the professional team.

Lefika had irregularly adjudicated the tender for the construction of the stadium, and fraudulently invoiced the municipality R2.9 million for work on the stadium business plan. The main partner in the consortium for the construction, Basil Read, irregularly chose subcontractors. The investigating team recommended to the municipal council that a forensic team probe all Mpumalanga's World Cup projects and expenditure.

The council fired its World Cup co-ordinator, Differ Mogale. They claimed he had been irregularly appointed at a salary of R480,000 a year by municipal manager Dladla. When the investigation team pointed out that the council would be liable for up to R4 million if they prematurely terminated his employment, Mogale was reinstated.

The council ordered a full forensic investigation into suspected unauthorised payments of up to R50 million by Mogale to Lefika and Platinum Sport. They sent Dladla on compulsory leave and passed a vote of no confidence in Nsibande. Dladla's appeal to the Labour Court was dismissed with costs.

'These actions of Mr Dladla only serve to remind one of the power-drunk actions of a crazed Gestapo,' the provincial report read. A resident on Matsafeni land, Sarah Shabangu, told the investigators: 'We really don't care anymore about the World Cup or the stadium. We have been promised that we will benefit … but it looks like we are getting poorer and the only people who are benefiting are greedy and corrupt politicians.'

A new front opened in the campaign to loot millions of taxpayer rand. ANC regional secretary Sabelo Shabangu angrily accused his party's councillors in Mbombela of acting 'without our support' and warned that 'internal procedures' would be taken against them. The ANC's chief whip in the council, Mfana Nkosi, refused to back down. He told reporter Justin Arenstein: 'The 2010 project is a cornerstone of growth for our city's future and the mayor began endangering it by breaking legislation and regulations governing municipalities. He stopped consulting his executive committee or the ANC caucus, and started taking decisions on his own.'

The majority of the Matsafeni Trust's 750 beneficiaries met with attorney Richard Spoor and announced that they would be asking the North Gauteng High Court to dissolve the board of trustees and overturn the R1 land deal they claimed they didn't approve. Any land deal needed a 60 per cent majority vote from the Matsafeni beneficiaries 'as required by law', Spoor told the media. 'There was no alternative plan for the students whose two schools were going to be demolished or for residents who would be forcibly removed from their homes.'

The Mbombela council passed a resolution stating that the

land sale 'agreement' secretly concluded with the Matsafeni Trust was null and void. Council spokesman Vusi Sibiya said 'no such contract exists. Mogale was not authorised in terms of the regulations, or by anyone, to buy or sell land.' Chief land claims commissioner Tozi Gwanya declared the deal illegal.

Construction work on the stadium began and quickly ran into trouble. The municipality said there was a sizeable shortfall in its budget for the infrastructure and less than a year after the first sod was turned, more than a thousand workers downed tools in protest about pay and working conditions. Their strike continued for days until they won annual bonuses.

The MEC for local government and housing K.C. Mashego-Dlamini, citing the findings of the investigation into the municipality that found its executives had failed to fulfil their constitutional obligations, sent a letter to Nsibande informing him of the province's intention to invoke section 39 of the Constitution and directly intervene in the running of the municipality.

The investigation unit made their report public in January 2008. It told a story of managerial malfeasance, outrageous conflicts of interest and unmitigated greed. Noting that Dladla considered himself and his associates to be 'untouchable' and that he was largely responsible for the 'systemic failure' of the Mbombela Municipality, the report found that he had failed to declare any of his extensive business interests as required by law, failed to sign a performance agreement with the municipality, and employed 'a cloak of secrecy and collusion' over the stadium project.

They described his actions as 'stemming from greed in order to ensure that his and certain other people's pockets were lined from the coffers of the Mbombela Municipality'. He had also used his position to ensure that the illegal Matsafeni community land deal benefited a private company, Blue Nightingale. Nsibande, Mogale and Matsafeni Trust chairman Terry Nduli were its directors.

Dladla had approved a R1-billion contract to build the stadium despite the Mbombela Municipality being allocated

R975 million by National Treasury. He had oversight of the award of the tender to Lefika to act as an intermediary between the project managers and contractors – the only contract of its kind in the country as it prepared for the World Cup. There was a clear conflict of interest in Lefika's participation in the tender evaluation and adjudication committees – which met after hours – while it was in a commercial relationship with Basil Read and Bouygues Travaux Publics, which made up the consortium that was awarded the tender.

Lefika's failure to disclose his commercial relationship with Basil Read and Bouygues Travaux Publics constituted fraud and 'collusive practices', the investigators concluded. A payment of R43 million to Lefika, processed hours after the submission of an invoice, was unauthorised and irregular. Several contractors, subcontractors and municipal employees received threatening phone calls and death threats. The investigation unit recommended that criminal charges be laid against Mogale and Nsibande, and that Dladla be dismissed.

The provincial government stripped the Mbombela Municipality's executive committee of all their powers and placed the council under curatorship. Local government MEC Mashego-Dlamini issued a statement: 'The municipality failed the population of Mbombela, and the province, so we are taking over control.' One of the key tasks of a curator mayor was to 'revisit the independent forensic report into suspected tender irregularities in the construction of our 2010 stadium'.

Speaker of the Mbombela municipal council Jimmy Mohlala, the main whistleblower on corruption and managerial incompetence in the stadium project, was instructed by Mashego-Dlamini to resign. He refused and issued a public statement: 'I look forward to rebuilding Mbombela after so many hardships ... now it's about taking the municipality forward, it's not about rumours of vengeance and ulterior motives against certain individuals ... we only carry out the mandate of the Constitution.'

McKinley wrote that Mohlala's principled bravery raised the hopes of many Mbombela residents, especially the Matsafeni community, that a corner was being turned. 'Once again, they were to be disappointed. No sooner had Mohlala stood his ground than the top leadership of the ANC in the province, in an obvious fit of political pique and opportunistic self-preservation, recommended that he – along with Nsibande – be fired and that Dladla be allowed to continue in his position. Again, to his public credit but personal vulnerability, Mohlala refused to budge and received support from many other councillors and Mbombela residents.'

Motaung's lawyers dismissed as 'groundless' all the findings of the investigation in relation to Lefika's role in stadium tender irregularities. They blamed the media for 'consistently trying to undermine Lefika's reputation'.

Most of the Matsafeni Trust's beneficiaries signed a memorandum of understanding with their leadership, the municipality and the provincial government, agreeing that a separate process would address the issue of the dodgy sale of their land. New primary and secondary schools would be built, and the stadium would be completed on time. They demanded the resignation of their trustees; the finalisation of a list of all beneficiaries by an independent task team; a forensic audit of the trust's financial affairs; the right to cancel contracts prejudicial to their rights and the election of new trustees at a properly constituted annual general meeting after the forensic investigation had been completed.

The department of agriculture and land affairs under the leadership of D.D. Mabuza convened a meeting with the 'illegitimate trustees' of the Matsafeni Trust who had sold the land for R1. When Spoor and Phineas Mdluli, representing the majority of beneficiaries, tried to attend, they were 'physically threatened' and forced to leave.

A letter was sent to the Matsafeni community from lawyers acting for the Mbombela Municipality. The national department of land affairs would review and possibly reverse the 2003 land sale, only if the stadium site was 'surrendered' to the municipality, it read. Any attempt to resist would prompt intervention from the national government and the community would suffer. Their demands, it was claimed, were 'fuelled and financed by an outside party'.

As with the fake Ndwandwa Trust in Badplaas, Mabuza was at the centre of a land deal concocted with trustees to wrest control from the true beneficiaries of restitution – the rural poor – and to steer the proceeds of its sale to politicians and officials.

The trust's beneficiaries applied for an urgent interdict in the North Gauteng High Court to stop the municipality from transferring ownership of the land. 'In one last pathetic attempt to delegitimise the community's actions, Mbombela's caretaker manager Khayalihle Mpungose tried to defend the municipality's actions by insisting that they had done nothing wrong and that the Matsafeni community were undermining the province's 2010 preparations and thus subverting the national interest,' McKinley wrote.

In June, the interdict was granted by Judge Moses Mavundla, who accused the municipality and provincial cabinet of acting like colonialist-era land-grabbing politicians. He stated angrily: 'I will not let this kind of thing happen again, not in this day and age.' Another North Gauteng High Court judge granted an order that a new board of trustees be appointed, consisting of trust professionals, representatives of the beneficiaries and the former trustees.

Days later, acting national chief land claims commissioner Blessing Mphela announced that an agreement had been reached with the Matsafeni community. The stadium's land would be ceded to the municipality. Noting that the land was valued at R43 million, he claimed that in lieu of payment, the community would 'enter into a 50/50 partnership for a joint venture regarding the control and management of the stadium [in which] the community will receive a portion of the proceeds from the business operations taking place in the stadium precinct'.

Mphela's actions were in contempt of the high court rulings, and they 'showed the degree to which the corrupt and opportunistic political clique in Mbombela and Mpumalanga had friends in higher places who, like them, clearly considered themselves above the law,' McKinley observed. 'Given such arrogant disregard for the people on whose land the cash-cow stadium was being built, it should not have come as a surprise that the frustrations of the Matsafeni community boiled over.'

In the summer heat, students poured out of their classrooms, boycotted classes and protested outside the stadium precinct. They had been uncomfortable, for two years, in the metal prefabricated structures they had been provided with after their schools were demolished. They fire-bombed their classrooms. The police arrived, three students and three adults were arrested and many suffered minor injuries.

Mbombela Municipality appointed a new mayor, Lassy Chiwayo, in early 2008. He stunned politicians by announcing that he would donate his entire monthly salary to 'HIV and AIDS charities and youth leadership development programmes dedicated to helping the historically disadvantaged'. His take on the root causes of the problems in Mbombela politics was equally surprising: 'I will be frank about the rot that brought the municipality to the brink of total collapse … it was a lack of leadership and lack of true values … we all need to find our moral origins.'

In late 2008, Chiwayo and fellow anti-corruption crusader Jimmy Mohlala were instructed by the ANC's regional executive committee to immediately reinstate disgraced former Mbombela municipal manager Jacob Dladla. They blocked a motion in the municipal council by invoking procedural rules.

Hardly had the dust settled on this battle when top ANC officials, led by Mpumalanga ANC chairman D.D. Mabuza, resolved to finalise disciplinary proceedings against Mohlala and to halt the disciplinary process against Dladla. Mohlala notified colleagues that he thought people were following him; he had received 'childish' telephone threats 'warning him to mind his own business or else he would be sorry'.

On the first day of 2009, two men accosted him, robbed him of his hand-gun and fled on foot. Mohlala told the police that he did not know his attackers, but had seen them in his home town of KaNyamazane and would recognise them in a line-up. 'Not surprisingly, given the long history of police inaction and ineptitude in investigating, tracking down and arresting perpetrators of attacks on various politicians and public officials in Mpumalanga, no arrests were made,' McKinley reported.

Three days later, Mohlala was shot dead at his home in KaNyamazane and his 19-year-old son Tshepiso was injured. 'The Mbombela World Cup battle claimed its first high-profile victim – a man who had been at the forefront of uncovering its tangled web of corruption, lies and mafia-like politics,' McKinley wrote. 'This was clearly no ordinary murder but, true to form, the ANC's provincial leadership once again tried to convince the public to bury its head in the sand alongside its own.'

The day after the murder, ANC Mpumalanga spokesman Paul Mbenyane issued a statement claiming that it was 'irresponsible' to suggest that Mohlala's death was politically motivated. The police questioned two men and released them. They grilled Mohlala's widow and children in an attempt to extract a confession. Bonnie Mohlala told the *Mail & Guardian*: 'They assaulted me. They tortured us during the interrogations. They covered our faces with plastic bags before they started beating us.'

Chiwayo issued a statement claiming that Mohlala had been murdered because he had blown the whistle on corruption. 'Only national intervention will defuse the tensions and fear by helping to determine whether rogue or possibly corrupt elements within the ANC or government were responsible. If they are, we need to ruthlessly uproot them. There is no other way to win back public trust than ensuring that whistleblowers are protected.' There was no response from the leadership of the ANC or national government. It took 20 months, long after the World Cup was over, before the Mpumalanga police arrested suspects.

Mohlala had been scheduled to testify at Dladla's disciplinary hearing the week after he was murdered. According to the journalist Justin Arenstein, he planned to recommend that fraud charges be laid against Lefika Emerging Equity. This stemmed from an allegedly fraudulent letter, on a letterhead of the Mbombela Municipality, sent by Lefika to First National Bank in December 2008 as surety for an overdraft facility.

Lefika was also in trouble with the tax authorities. Its CEO Chris Gibb skipped the country in December 2008, after learning that the South African Revenue Service was investigating the issuing of an alleged fraudulent tax clearance certificate to the company in 2006 that allowed it to submit tenders for Mbombela's World Cup stadium.

Another worker dispute delayed construction of the stadium in 2009. Following a radio broadcast in which senior Mbombela politicians promised workers they would receive a R70,000 bonus when the stadium was completed, hundreds downed tools to demand a guarantee of the payment. Basil Read CEO Marius Heyns complained about 'improper political interference' and death threats to his management team. 'We just want to finish the stadium and get out,' he told Arenstein.

None of the promises politicians made to the Matsafeni community materialised. The Mbombela Municipality promised them laid-on water. Matsafeni resident Sarah Shabangu noted, 'Our water is being used for the construction of the stadium and so we have no choice but to come to these dirty holes for water.' Her neighbour Khelina Sibuyi complained: 'We use this water for drinking and for cooking and bathing ... the children get sick and have diarrhoea ... ever since they built the stadium we have been hoping for help in getting services but nothing is happening, there is no water or electricity.'

Mbombela municipal manager of technical services Dolphin Malukela said R145 million of the R262 million budgeted for the Matsafeni water project had been spent on the stadium. The municipality had asked for a R145-million conditional grant from the national department of water affairs and forestry, but they declined.

In July 2009, the council announced that a deal had been struck between the Matsafeni Trust and the Mbombela Municipality to pay R8.7 million for their 118 hectares of land on which the stadium was being built. A valuation in 2007 had pegged it at almost R43 million.

In the 2009 summer heat, students once again poured out of their metal classrooms and into the stadium precinct to protest for several days. A police car was burned, stones were thrown, and rubber bullets and buckshot were fired. Many people were injured and arrested.

In January 2010, Sammy Mpatlanyane, a deputy director at the department of culture, sports and recreation, was gunned down in the second-floor bedroom of his house in Mbombela. McKinley said the alleged motive for the assassination was the outrageous R20-million tender for Mbombela's World Cup fan park. 'Mired in controversy from the beginning because of its location on the grounds of a predominantly white and upper-class Mbombela high school, and the dearth of opportunities for informal street traders, the fan park had become yet another player in the macabre dance of corruption, greed and murder.

'A police source involved in the investigation let slip to journalists that the murder was potentially linked to Mpatlanyane's refusal to award the tender to a friend of a prominent ANC leader in the province. In any event, the tender went to Pasqa Africa, whose director Izak van der Walt was a long-time close business associate of Nonhlanhla Patience Mnisi – the wife of newly-appointed Mpumalanga Premier David Mabuza,' reported McKinley.

Chiwayo said to the *Mail & Guardian* in May 2009 that it was unfortunate that the World Cup, 'instead of bringing much-awaited hope and joy to our people, brought death and pain to some of our families, divided the province and the municipality. The biggest casualty in the process is the ANC because of the sheer greed of some of our leaders.'

As with the murder of Mohlala a year earlier, the national leadership of the ANC did not utter a word about Mpatlanyane's death, nor did Fifa's local and international leadership, who declared that the 2010 World Cup would be a 'world-class' event.

In February 2010, the *Sunday Times* published a bombshell story, headlined 'Murder Inc in Mbombela'. A 25-year-old contract killer was accusing an influential ANC leader in Mpumalanga of offering him R100,000 and a cushy government position if he poisoned government officials who were blocking tenders linked to the World Cup.

The newspaper knew the name of the 'ANC boss', implicated by more than a dozen other sources in the killings of more than a dozen senior politicians in Mpumalanga since 1998. The would-be assassin said he had been given the poison and was ready to do the job, but pulled out after a disagreement with his client about an advance fee. 'Though his three intended victims are still alive, six officials were murdered or died in suspicious circumstances in Mpumalanga last year and another one has been killed this year. Local party leaders and officials mentioned a hit list of other proposed victims and said they were living in fear.

'The *Sunday Times* has been given the full name of a Mozambican gangster known as Josh and told that he was responsible for the murder in January 2009 of Mbombela council speaker Jimmy Mohlala. Josh agreed to speak to our reporters in Mozambique, but changed his mind. ANC national spokesman Jackson Mthembu – a former speaker of the Mpumalanga legislature – said the ruling party was aware of the alleged hit list and had sent a task team to investigate those responsible for the killings of its members in the province.'

The Mpumalanga ANC said it distanced itself from the alleged hit list because the 'ANC does not kill people. It is disturbing that to date no light has been shed around the murders…'

McKinley reported that 'in the twisted sanctuary of their own home, the ANC's regional executive leadership recommended to the provincial executive the recall of one of the few ANC politicians, Mbombela mayor Lassy Chiwayo, who displayed some integrity and courage in publicly confronting the deadly and toxic politics of his organisation. Incredibly, the reason given for the recommendation was that Chiwayo publicly alleged that the former speaker of the municipality Jimmy Mohlala may have been assassinated by members of his organisation for standing up against tender irregularities relating to the Mbombela 2010 soccer stadium.'

Chiwayo stood his ground, and continued to draw the links between ANC leaders and the mayhem that characterised Mbombela's World Cup project. 'Forces within the party in the province – representing business interests rather than those of the people who voted for the ANC – were working to consolidate their position to make money from the tournament from very early on … this we see from the systematic deployment of certain people to positions like the municipal manager and the chief financial officer within the municipality,' he told the *Mail & Guardian* in May 2009.

McKinley alleges that since the late 1990s, one of the key ANC leaders at the centre of the corruption and power struggles 'was D.D. Mabuza. Not only did he survive, he prospered, reaching the pinnacle of ANC power in the province – as premier – in mid-2009. Given his history, the more intensified focus on Mbombela as the World Cup approached, and the fact that events were getting extremely messy for the senior ANC leadership, it should have come as no surprise that Mabuza's role started to be raised more directly.'

Days before the World Cup kick-off, former Mpumalanga ANC leader James Nkambule, who had been arrested and charged with defeating the ends of justice and conspiracy to commit fraud linked to his comments about the hit list, accused Mabuza of being behind most of the politically connected murders in Mbombela and Mpumalanga. 'The real crocodile, that is capable of killing, is hiding behind state resources in the premier's office – your premier, David Mabuza,' he said, addressing the media on the steps of the court. The premier denied the allegations.

McKinley reported that Mabuza and the ANC 'laughed off Nkambule's accusations, secure in the knowledge that, whatever the truth, they could continue – just as their counterparts in Fifa – to be both player and referee in a game in which they also made the rules'.

In the hope of 'partly neutralising the rotten stench that was, by now, drifting far beyond Mpumalanga', two weeks before the start of the World Cup, the municipality handed over new schools to the Matsafeni community. 'Amidst the public fanfare and hypocritical self-congratulations offered against the backdrop of Mbombela's "world class" stadium, nobody mentioned the impact of the saga on the students. The matric pass rate at the secondary school plummeted from 85 per cent in 2008 to just 44 per cent in 2009.

'If anything represents the absolutely cynical and usurious nature of South Africa's 2010 Soccer World Cup, it is how the children of the ultra-poor Matsafeni community were ignored, humiliated, beaten and patronised. As the four soccer games held at the Mbombela stadium played themselves out to crowds mostly made up of well-heeled international and domestic visitors and Mbombela's small middle-class, the Matsafeni community were right next door – in run-down houses and without any of the basic services that had long been promised.

'Besides the obvious winners and losers, the much-touted benefits supposedly accruing to informal traders and small and medium-sized businesses did not materialise. The stadium was too far away from the city to benefit most informal traders and, by all accounts from those who were allowed to sell at the fan park, the event proved to be a monetary flop.'

The end of the 2010 World Cup did not signal a halt to the murder and mayhem. 'Hardly had the last vuvuzela been blown when it became clear that the Mbombela Municipality was, again, effectively bankrupt,' McKinley wrote. 'Having spent an estimated R2 billion on the 2010 World Cup project, the municipality also used its funds for 2010 projects. It was forced to apply for a R200-million loan from the Development Bank of Southern Africa to keep afloat after the tournament. The World Cup debt legacy as a result of massive over-expenditure was passed on to residents.'

The Mpumalanga police, in conjunction with the National Prosecuting Authority, announced in October that they had arrested five suspects for Mohlala's murder. Among them were two policemen. A few days later, *City Press* journalist Sizwe sama Yende, who was investigating political murders in Mbombela, narrowly escaped a gunman who ambushed him at his home. His employers arranged 24-hour protection for him.

Days later, Nkambule, who was reportedly negotiating to have the contract killer he claimed had been hired by a senior ANC politician placed in witness protection, died under suspicious circumstances. An autopsy carried out by the province's chief medical officer concluded that his death was unnatural and suggestive of 'poison ingestion' found in his body.

'There is little doubt that, under present political circumstances, the hyper-corrosive and often personally devastating effects of corruption and murder that so blighted Mbombela's 2010 World Cup project are not about to come to an end,' McKinley warned. 'Nonetheless, as long as there are courageous and honest people, there always remains the possibility that this dragon can be slayed and that things will change for the better.'

In 2017, despite the benefit of taxpayer-funded VIP protection, Mabuza was struck down by Mpumalanga assassins' preferred deadly weapon – poison. As explained by Duduzane Zuma in a series of YouTube interviews, he was flown to Russia for treatment, on the Gupta family jet with Jacob Zuma's son Duduzane playing nursemaid. Rumour has it, and this has never been confirmed, that one of the potential victims of the poison was tipped off and switched plates at a party.

On 2 February 2017, *Business Day* columnist Natasha Marrian described Mabuza's return to work after receiving treatment in Russia: 'The Cat is back. This legendary quote was used by ANC Mpumalanga chairman David Mabuza on the day he returned to work after nearly fifty days of sick leave. He attributed his debilitating illness to poisoning, and told *Business Day* that he had let his guard down at a birthday party and suffered from a long and painful illness thereafter.'

Marrian wrote that Mabuza was eyeing the presidency of the ANC. The party's conference in December would elect a successor to Jacob Zuma and he was itching for the top position in the party after three terms as its chairman in Mpumalanga. 'A Mabuza presidency would be fascinating and terrifying,' she concluded. 'Were it to happen, it could be described as a Mussolini moment for South Africa.'

16
The path to power

D.D. Mabuza is regarded as one of the most invincible politicians in South Africa. Elected deputy chairman of the ANC in Mpumalanga in 2005, and, notwithstanding his previous poor records as MEC for education, housing, roads and transport, and agriculture and land affairs, Mabuza rose to a position on the national executive committee of his party in 2007.

He was elected ANC provincial chairman in 2008, defeating bitter rival, Mbombela mayor Lassy Chiwayo, and putting himself in line to become Mpumalanga's next premier. Members of his 'faction' in the party were elected to the other top five provincial leadership positions. Among the losers of their positions were former finance MEC Jacques Modipane and former agriculture and land affairs minister David Mkhwanazi, both of whom had been involved in the Dolphin deal.

'Mabuza clawed his way back as an apparatchik of the ANC,' Sizwe sama Yende writes in his book *Eerie Assignment*. 'The year 2008 was a turning point. The ANC in Mpumalanga was due to hold an elective conference. The venue of the showdown was the Nelspruit showgrounds. When this conference sat, the balance of forces in the ANC did not favour Thabang Makwetla to stay on for another term as chairman and premier because he was Thabo Mbeki's ally. Mbeki had just lost the ANC presidency to Zuma at a watershed conference in Polokwane. The purging of Mbeki's allies in all the provinces was in full swing.'

The outcome of the showgrounds conference 'created, widened and deepened' schisms between politicians. With his political fortunes tied to Zuma's, Mabuza became a rising and influential star in the ANC. 'Those in the know say he initially supported Mbeki but, after reading the balance of forces, jumped onto Zuma's wagon hours before the Polokwane conference started,' Sama Yende writes. 'Analysing and reading the balance of forces is Mabuza's strong point and the reason for his survival in the dog-eat-dog realm of politics. Even though his demise has been declared repeatedly because of many corruption scandals, like a cat with nine lives, his guile has kept him in the game.'

Bitter about his narrow victory over Chiwayo in 2008, ANC members in Mpumalanga complained to the party's national leaders about vote rigging. They carried their grudges for years and suggested that Mabuza hadn't stopped manipulating results since he was MEC for education and lied about the matric results. 'These kinds of allegations would haunt Mabuza – foisting upon him a responsibility to keep on defending himself,' Sama Yende writes. 'Sometimes he vehemently did so; sometimes he recoiled and became aloof.'

In Mpumalanga, government jobs or deployment – administrative or political – gave people the power to dole out tenders to others irrespective of their credentials or capability to do the work. 'In the midst of this rot, the elimination of politicians, civil servants and tenderpreneurs comes into the equation ... carried out by assassinations and poisoning in worst-case scenarios, or blacklisting from getting state jobs or tenders,' Sama Yende writes.

'I see Mpumalanga as some form of a welfare or patronage state – a tender state. As politicians fight and, disputably, kill each other, they use the public as a mere bargaining chip while they know precisely that all the strife is actually about lining their pockets. This is not a war about who can serve the public best and who therefore deserves the privilege of managing public resources, but about controlling those resources and enriching oneself.'

Fear and loathing ran deep in Mpumalanga as ANC politicians fought like cats and dogs for a share of government resources. Political battles between ruling party politicians hobbled the provincial government, but after Mabuza's rise to power the situation 'degenerated into anarchy', Sama Yende observes. 'An outsider could be forgiven for visualising a province teeming with guns and hitmen because of the spine-chilling incidents recorded. Mpumalanga is not alone in political murders, but here an ANC comrade presumably commits them against another ANC comrade.'

In May 2009, Mabuza was installed as premier of Mpumalanga. In his inauguration speech, he promised he would address the problems of poor service delivery by getting 'the right people in place'. The public, he said, should hold their officials accountable. He outlined 'five critical objectives' on which his government would focus: jobs, education, health, rural development and 'the fight against crime and corruption'. Tough action would be taken against builders who failed to deliver RDP housing and he stressed the necessity of quality health care.

Within months of taking office, his administration faced violent protests in Lydenburg, Standerton, Sabie, Kabokweni, Hazyview, Ogies, Volksrust, Balfour and many villages. The protestors demanded electricity, water, housing and a decent education for their children. Lydenburg residents accused the ANC administration of 'providing incomplete roads, rate hikes, financial mismanagement, corruption, and the sale of RDP houses'. They claimed these failures were due to the ANC's deployment of outsiders and to nepotism.

The national department of cooperative governance and traditional affairs announced that it was intervening in four municipalities that were failing to deliver services to residents. These included the capital Mbombela, where municipal manager Jacob Dladla had been suspended on full pay for suspected financial irregularities relating to the soccer World Cup. Many of Mabuza's political rivals predicted he would be unable to bring collapsing municipalities onto their feet again, and that his days as premier were numbered.

Massive water supply problems in Badplaas, Carolina and Ermelo crippled these towns. National cooperative governance minister Sicelo Shiceka appointed a task team to support the troubled municipalities. Mabuza blamed the protests on the failures of managers appointed by the Mbeki regime. His ally Raymond Makamo accused former Mpumalanga premier Mathews Phosa of 'plotting to stir up dissatisfaction and unrest'.

Municipal IQ, which collects and analyses municipal government data, recorded by mid-July 2009 that there had been 24 major service delivery protests in South Africa – more than all reported in the media in 2007 and 2008 combined. They said the media seldom covered protests in villages, so the overall number could be far higher.

The *Sowetan* published allegations that Mabuza's wife and former 'customary wife' had been involved in companies that received illegal tenders to construct buildings for the Mpumalanga government. Mabuza suspended public works department director Priscilla Nkwinika, then redeployed her as a deputy director general in the premier's office despite recommendations by the province's integrity management unit that she face criminal charges.

He refused to heed opposition parties' calls to resign, saying the involvement of his wife and former lover, Ruth Funi Silinda, in a government contract had 'nothing to do' with him. Silinda said she would sue the *Sowetan* for defamation and more than R500 million in damages to her 'reputation and dignity'. She never did sue.

The paper reported that expenditure on one of the buildings escalated from R94 million to R161 million and tender procedures had been ignored. Mabuza said he was considering charges against Nkwinika, known as 'the queen of tenders' in Mpumalanga. She filed an urgent application to have the charges quashed and the disciplinary hearing halted. She claimed Mabuza had been behind a crooked scheme to buy an office complex for the Mpumalanga government.

The buildings had been bought in 2005 and 2007 – allegedly by a company called Hardplay Investments 6 for R5.4 million. Banks had been approached to provide bonds amounting to R80 million. Nkwinika claimed that, Mabuza instructed her, when he was MEC for agriculture, to buy the buildings for R600 million under highly irregular terms. When he became premier, he insisted that she follow his orders.

Mabuza appointed a commission of inquiry into the scandal, headed by Advocate Patrick Ellis SC, who found Nkwinika's claims to be 'devoid of merit'. He recommended that she face criminal charges, but she was not prosecuted. She was either allowed to complete her contract term as deputy director-general in the premier's office and leave (her version) or found guilty and dismissed (Mabuza's spokesman's version). Internal charges of misconduct for flouting tender procedures to buy the building were brought against 13 employees of the department of public works. Political insiders said the junior officials were targeted because they 'refused to endorse questionable tender decisions'.

In Mabuza's first few months as premier, *City Press* reporter Sizwe sama Yende noted that, while he was MEC for agriculture in 2008, he had spent his department's entire budget on a single contract of R230 million, to supply tractors and other farming equipment to poor farmers. The contract was awarded, without a budget or tender, to the premier's close friend and business partner Patrick Chirwa. At the time, Mabuza served as a director on two company boards with Chirwa.

In 2010, there were allegations that Chirwa's company, Pacific Breeze Trading 474, was involved in the purchase of land near Mbombela which was sold to the city's municipality. One piece was allegedly bought for R3.1 million and sold to the municipality for R11 million – on the same day. Chirwa allegedly bought a plot in Emakhazeni for R1.6 million and sold it to the town's council for R17.4 million. His deals were financed by the provincial government.

In July 2010, Nkambule appeared in court for the fifth time in relation to fraud charges arising from the Dolphin deal. The courtroom in Nelspruit was packed with Mabuza supporters, including his spokesman Mabutho Sithole and head of security Welcome Nkuna. The former Youth League leader had, a few days earlier, laid a charge of intimidation against Mabuza, who he claimed sent him a threatening SMS on June 15. The text allegedly included the line 'I will be around till mid-July, but you won't'. Outside court after his brief appearance Nkambule accused the premier of being the author of a hit list of politicians because they opposed him or else to prevent more details about corruption from emerging. He died soon afterwards, of suspected poisoning.

A mysterious hit man, said to be Mozambican Fabiano dos Santos, known as Josh, stated in an affidavit sworn before a commissioner of oaths in Barberton that he had been hired to kill, or organise the killing of, a range of political figures in Mpumalanga, including the executive mayor of the Gert Sibande district Andries Gamede, Mbombela mayor Lassy Chiwayo, former Mbombela acting mayor Sigananda Sibonda and councillor Victor Mlimi. He admitted to poisoning Nkambule in 2002, sending him to hospital instead of killing him.

Dos Santos claimed that he had been hired by Mabuza and former safety and security MEC Steve Mabona in 2000 as a 'cleaner' – 'which means eliminating political or business opponents'. Fearing for his life after his associates were murdered, he contacted Nkambule, who arranged for him to dictate and sign the affidavit. He was driven to Mozambique after Nkambule assured him he would 'testify against my bosses once he was sure that the time was right'. Josh has never been seen or heard of again. The police have not confirmed any of his allegations.

As he struggled to grasp political control, Mabuza's critics in the ANC complained about his autocratic behaviour. The Youth League said he was meddling in their processes by trying to prevent Julius Malema from being elected chairman. Others noted that, in his capacity as Mpumalanga ANC chairman, he circumvented selection protocol to ensure that his preferred candidate became Mbombela mayor.

Calls from within the ANC mounted for Mabuza to be recalled as party chairman. A group of politicians organised a press conference to announce this demand, but it was called off after they reportedly received death threats. They wrote an anonymous letter to Zuma, accusing Mabuza of turning Mpumalanga into a 'banana province'. They asked how Mabuza had been selected as premier when more than 10 forensic reports from the integrity management unit implicated officials in the department of roads and transport of irregularities while he headed it in 2007, and no action had been taken. There had also been irregularities in the departments of education and agriculture when Mabuza was the responsible MEC.

ANC spokesman Jackson Mthembu said that the party's Mpumalanga executive committee was 'in a state of paralysis' due to the factionalism. He said the party's leadership had dispatched a task team to investigate the province's problems with service delivery.

By 2011, Mabuza had earned the nickname Hurricane, apparently from his habit of shouting at colleagues and subordinates. The media reported that his power in the province was slipping and ANC structures were discussing alternatives to replace him. Among them was Charles Makola, a popular municipal manager in the Nkangala district who had been reluctant to take high office. ANC councillors in Nkangala suspended Makola from his position a few weeks before the elections.

Mabuza's supporters won with a substantial majority in the regional party elections, virtually assuring him of a second term as premier. ANC branch members claimed that the elections had been fixed with 'fraud and money'. One said that he had been surprised to see candidates on the lists who had not been nominated by branches.

In February 2012, the auditor general noted that Mpumalanga was heading the way of Limpopo, where financial administration was so poor that national government had placed the province under administration. His report on Mpumalanga found that approximately R2.9 billion had been lost in unauthorised, wasteful or irregular expenditure in government departments under Mabuza's watch.

Despite this, Mabuza was re-elected ANC Mpumalanga chairman in April 2012. His opponents claimed that his 'lobbyists' bribed delegates to vote in his favour. His re-election was noted by political analysts as a major boost for the chances of Zuma's election for a second term as ANC chairman, and therefore president of South Africa, at the party's Mangaung conference in December.

Mabuza began cracking the whip on his officials and party members. His combative tone was reminiscent of his earlier days in politics. He arrived in a rural village in a luxury German car and described its managers as 'a disgrace to my administration' after they complained about unpaid stipends.

He focused on the department of human settlements, which in 2011 delivered only 3,980 houses instead of its budgeted 10,800. Its director general David Dube awarded R331 million in housing projects to people who were politically connected, without putting them out to tender. He bought two pieces of land in the Nkomazi and Msukaligwa municipalities for R86 million from a company that had bought them for R35 million a few months earlier.

Mabuza announced several controversial appointments to his government. He reinstated Dube as a member of the provincial legislature. He hired Jacques Modipane as the CEO of the bankrupt Mpumalanga Tourism and Parks Agency. Modipane was the former MEC of finance implicated in the multi-million-dollar promissory note scam in the 1990s, when the province's game parks were illegally offered as collateral for massive offshore loans. The appointment was made despite a warning from Paul O'Sullivan, hired by the agency to vet CEO candidates, that he had lied on his CV about an honours degree when he had no tertiary education.

Another reappointee was Kgopana Mohlasedi, who had worked with Mabuza at the department of roads and transport. He was promoted to director of the department. Richard Mnisi, who had resigned in disgrace from the department of health in 2004, was brought in from the cold. Mnisi had been implicated in wasting R19 million of the HIV/Aids budget, and purchasing R30 million in hospital equipment that had not been budgeted for or ordered.

Journalists hailed Mabuza's new tone of activism 'on behalf of the people', but they also noted that his reappointments included members of his 'bulletproof crew'. Mpumalanga citizens were sceptical. In March 2013 Mabuza allegedly fumed when only R170,000 was raised at his golf day for the Premier's Bursary Fund, an annual fundraising event attended by corporate sponsors. In June, he beat a hasty retreat from Bushbuckridge, where angry residents said he was unwelcome.

'Whether Mabuza's tough talk and stance is genuine remains to be seen,' writes Sizwe sama Yende. 'Since taking over the reins [as premier] he has developed a reputation for protecting cronies. He has also been accused of failing to take tough action against his comrades, even when they are accused of corruption.' Among the many traits that allowed Mabuza to rise to the top political position in Mpumalanga was his guile. 'He often changes his allies on a whim and he has a knack of using people. When he has reaped the benefits, he dumps them like a hot potato. Friends and allies, to him, are expendable and that may explain why he cannot lead comfortably without everyone rallying behind his back.'

In 2011, Johan Ndlovu, the ANC chief whip in the Ehlanzeni District Municipality, was shot dead near his home in Bushbuckridge. He had been a contender for the position of the town's next executive mayor after the local government elections in May. Suspects were arrested and convicted, and one of them penned an affidavit claiming that erstwhile Bushbuckridge mayor Milton Morema paid him to kill Ndlovu. The ANC sacked Morema from his position and the affidavit was withdrawn.

After Mabuza became deputy president of South Africa, former ANC deputy chairman David Dube, who had worked alongside him for more than a decade, published a bitter political memoir, *Al Capones of Mpumalanga*. 'It is my contention that we all, who claim to be good politicians, need therapy to heal the trauma that we face on a daily basis,' he wrote. 'We, in many instances, are called upon to display remarkable courage and we are not expected to reveal our hidden anxieties and share our fears that something bad might happen to our families while we are out there doing our politics.

'Fear robs you of your freedom to make the right choice. Fear made comrades not engage with David Mabuza. All they could do was to listen to what he had to tell them. In most instances, a meeting at his farmhouse was not a meeting to discuss issues. Instead, it was a gathering where comrades had to give reports, lie about others and get their operational mandates or instructions. Most of the participants were mere listeners. Their role was just to sing his praises and nod in agreement, even though they might not agree with what he had to say. Whether he was wrong or right, no one would say anything. The fear factor turned these comrades into morons or robots.'

Dube said scholars and psychologists who studied Mabuza – who himself has a postgraduate degree in educational psychology – would characterise him as 'streetwise, cunning, sly, opportunistic, ready to grab [the] limelight, exploitative in nature and a master manipulator of note. He is considered as someone whose mind is not easy to read. This is because his word is not his word and he is never to be trusted. Convenience is his speciality. He gets what he wants from you, then he moves on to the next person. His support for you is not guaranteed … it is conditional. You are in today and tomorrow you are on the highway. You will remain with the dirt but he will move on scot-free with white socks.'

'He operates like a mafia. At its core, the mafia is all about one thing – money. He is more like a boss than a leader. He is feared by many in Mpumalanga, he is also loved and hated by many too.' Dube described former Mpumalanga ANC chairman Fish Mahlalela as an 'elephant in the execution of his plans and operations' and Mabuza as a 'cheetah who acts and moves fast'. He said neither of them compromised on their positions and did not allow their prey to escape.

This is the premier Fred took to court in 2010 in search of an order that he appoint a commission of inquiry into the involvement of government officials and employees in harassment and death threats against himself, his family, employees and business.

17

Take it to the president

Fred was not only the target of the Greater Badplaas Land Claims Committee – a motley collection of politicians and fraudsters – but he was also persecuted by the Mpumalanga Tourism and Parks Agency and the Land Claims Commission. After he lost possession of Nkomazi to Dubai World and began building the Cradle of Life, the harassment did not let up. 'They wanted me and my partners off the land, away from Badplaas, so they could lay claim to the land without proving their case, and without any resistance,' Fred says. 'They were aided and abetted by the functionaries of politicians. The entire provincial state machinery was manipulated, utilised and abused in the process.'

In May 2009, Obert Mkhatshwi of the Mpumalanga department of water affairs and a colleague came to the Cradle of Life to announce that they were shutting down the project. They asked whether there had been any progress on the land claims. Fred demanded reasons for their decision and they left without achieving their aim.

Days later, another official from the department arrived with a notice stating that the project contravened activity 1(d) of regulation 386 of the National Environmental Management Act, as it had constructed facilities in a protected area. When Fred informed him that the Cradle of Life was not in a protected area, the official asked why was there a fence around the land. Fred explained that the fence kept his animals off the busy R38 road that flanked the project. The official returned a week later with another charge of contravening the Act, this time activity 1(e) of regulation 386, prohibiting lawns, playing fields or sports parks from covering an area of more than 3 hectares. Fred showed him the lawns on the Cradle of Life and proved that they did not cover more than 1.5 hectares.

In October, Mpumalanga water control officer Orex Nkosi brought a charge against the Cradle of Life for contravening the National Environmental Management Act, this time activity 1(m) of regulation 386, which prohibits the construction of infrastructure in the one-in-ten-year flood line of a river or stream. When Fred pointed out how far away the ten-year flood line was from his facilities, the official said he was contravening activity 5 of regulation 386, which refers to the removal and damaging of indigenous vegetation of more than 10 square metres within 100 metres inland of the high-water mark of the sea – which is almost 800 kilometres away.

Fred instructed Richard Spoor to send a letter to Mabuza, who had been appointed premier of Mpumalanga a few months earlier and had oversight of all the provincial government's departments. After noting Fred's interdict that had been granted against Pro Khoza, the Greater Badplaas Land Claims Committee and others to stop their harassment, Spoor wrote that it was their understanding that Mabuza was the chairman of the committee, a position to which he had been elected on 17 July 2008, as confirmed in an email sent to John Allen by Khoza on 29 July 2008.

Given his leadership position, Spoor wrote that Mabuza should be aware that Khoza and other members of the committee had recently threatened harm against Nkomazi and its employees again. The attorney said he had been instructed to bring an application for an interdict calling on the respondents to show why they should not be held in contempt of court and that Mabuza might also be cited. He asked the premier to confirm whether he was still chairman of the committee, whether he condoned its members' behaviour and what he planned to do to ensure compliance with the court order. Mabuza's office acknowledged the correspondence, but to this day they have not responded.

A few days later, Fred was contacted by the Mpumalanga department of safety and security to say they had received a complaint about him from the premier's office. He spoke to a senior official in the department, who said a complaint had been laid by Khoza. 'The police arrived at my home and said they had come to arrest me for assaulting a black man. When I demanded to see the docket, I discovered that the accused in the matter was one Frank Denel. Anyway, I was able to prove that I was in Cape Town on the day of the assault.'

In November, department of labour inspector Thomas Ngomane arrived at the Cradle of Life for a site inspection. He threatened to close it, ostensibly because not all of the contractors were on site. He left and came back the next day with a prohibition notice, stating that the contractors had not been able to provide him with their safety and health plans. Ngomane forced all the contractors to cease work. He was accompanied by two policemen who prevented the Cradle's fulltime employees from working, although the prohibition notice did not apply to them. Fred says that when he and Advocate Henk Roelofse confronted Ngomane and showed him the interdict being prepared against the Mpumalanga government to stop their unlawful persecution, the inspector became visibly nervous. He revoked the prohibition notice less than an hour after it was issued and left in a hurry.

In January 2010, Mpumalanga department of water affairs director Fanyana Mntambo threatened to issue a directive on the Cradle of Life for contraventions of section 22 of the National Water Act. The department's officials Thandi Mthembu and David Thababa came to the project a few days later to shut it down. They claimed Fred had violated the Act on two counts: by abstracting and transferring groundwater from a borehole on one property to fill dams on another and by constructing three dams fed by groundwater from a borehole without authorisation. Fred told them this was nonsensical as the property's legal water rights allowed for the abstraction of water from the Komati River and its tributaries using decades-old water infrastructure. The officials then cited his 'illegal construction of roads'. He pointed out that this was equally nonsensical as the roads had been built decades previously, and did not violate any law. 'Clearly desperate, the officials threatened to issue an unexplained directive and left,' he says.

Fred commissioned Riaan Visagie of the consultancy Eco-8 to advise if his activities at the Cradle of Life complied with environmental legislation. The report was sent to Altus Lotter, deputy director of the Mpumalanga department of environmental affairs. In April, Lotter emailed Fred to say no further steps would be taken against his project. Any officials who continued the harassment should be reported to him.

In 2010, Fred made an application in the North Gauteng High Court requesting that it order D.D. Mabuza to establish a provincial commission of inquiry into corruption in the Mpumalanga government. This was finally set down to be heard by Judge Ronel Tolmay from 26 November to 10 December 2012.

The corruption Fred set out in his affidavit extended to the highest political office in Mpumalanga so it was highly unlikely that Mabuza would appoint a commission. Fred also asked the court to grant an interdict prohibiting government officials and employees from entering any of his premises, except 'where they are authorised and entitled to do so lawfully'. He wanted them prohibited from 'acting in any way whatsoever in a vexatious, intimidatory or harassing fashion, or with malice in any manner or form'.

He asked that they be ordered to 'refrain from causing or threatening harm, injury and damages in any form or manner, including ... personal harm and injury of a bodily nature'. They must 'refrain from making any further malicious, injurious or false statements in ... any document, in any other written or electronic medium, or in the press'. He sought to prohibit the Mpumalanga Tourism and Parks Agency from any 'act contrary to the promotion of conservation and ecologically sustainable development'.

Judge Tolmay ruled on 29 November 2012 that the Mpumalanga Tourism and Parks Agency had to act in terms of their constitutional and statutory obligations to make a positive contribution towards economic development in Badplaas. Although the matter was set down for two weeks, it took only three days for the parties to consent to the interim court order: 'This application is postponed ... pending the application that was brought in the Constitutional Court.'

The application to the Constitutional Court was a parallel move by Fred. After taking advice from Accountability Now director Advocate Paul Hoffman, Fred decided to ask the president of South Africa to appoint a commission of inquiry into allegations of corruption and mismanagement by government officials and employees in Badplaas and the rest of Mpumalanga. Fred's lawyers provided Zuma with a summary of the problems faced by the Cradle of Life project, Ndwandwa Community Trust chairman Robert Nkosi and the Badplaas community since 2003. These pointed to 'serious abuse of power, maladministration and corruption ... unscrupulous political interference, unconscionable conduct and maladministration'. These actions by politicians and their employees had 'inflicted significant legal risks, financial uncertainty, social instability, safety concerns, conflict between citizens, insecurity, harm and suffering on an impoverished community and a fragile environment'.

Although the letter was acknowledged by the president's office, there was no response to the request. The lawyers had given Zuma until 8 August 2012 to appoint a commission of inquiry and his silence paved the way for Fred's next move. He would apply to the highest court in the land for an order compelling the president to appoint a commission of inquiry.

Fred had been informed that his name was on a hit list. In recent years, 21 whistleblowers had been killed in Mpumalanga, making his push for protection from the courts even more pressing. His lawyers began drafting an application to the Constitutional Court, collecting information on legislation relating to environmental affairs, nature reserves, parks and wildlife. They researched administrative, contractual and constitutional law. Their court papers comprised 4,250 pages.

In an opinion article in *Business Day* in May 2013, Hoffman explained the work that went into the application. He began by describing Badplaas as an area with 'beautiful ecotourism and game reserve potential' and Fred as a 'patriotic South African ... pursuing his vision of a pristine transfrontier world heritage site that celebrates the Cradle of Life – the oldest fossils, rock formations and systems on earth...

'Daniel's vision, some would call it a dream, is not easily attainable, even in the best of circumstances. In Mpumalanga, the best of circumstances are conspicuously absent ... the province, under the leadership of Premier David Mabuza, lurches from scandal to scandal. Political murders are not unknown. Corruption is rife. It ranges from collusive contracting on the Soccer World Cup stadium to cooldrink money for cops.

'There has been opportunistic opposition to the Cradle of Life. Daniel has had to litigate against the authorities in the province on twelve occasions in the high court. Every time he wins, but getting a corrupt public administration to do its job properly is not easily achieved via court orders. Mabuza leads a charmed life at the helm of the province. He is close to Zuma and reportedly paid for one of his more recent weddings.'

Hoffman wrote that Fred had provided Zuma with a large body of evidence of corruption in Mpumalanga. He explained in a letter requesting a commission of inquiry that the corruption was thwarting a project that could bring world fame and many tourist dollars to one of the most underdeveloped parts of the country. It would benefit the area's people by creating jobs.

'Yes, there is an element of asking turkeys to vote for Christmas in getting Zuma to have Mabuza's administration investigated,' he acknowledged. 'But there is no other legal way to break out of the cycle of litigation that has brought so many empty victories and so little progress. Needless to say, Zuma declined Daniel's request. But in a constitutional democracy under the rule of law, that is not necessarily the end of the matter. Pointing to the mountain of evidence of corruption (in much the same way as Terry Crawford-Browne did on arms deal malfeasance), Daniel turned to the Constitutional Court for an order for the appointment of a commission of inquiry.'

Fred contended that, in the face of the evidence he had assembled, it was irrational of Zuma to refuse his request to exercise his discretionary responsibility to appoint this commission. The Constitution obliged the president to reasonably, accountably and objectively consider such requests. Second-guessing a president's exercise of his discretion was no easy task, nor was ensuring that he performed his constitutional duties. These tasks were reserved for the apex court.

'In the answering papers filed by Zuma late last year, a perplexing allegation was made,' Hoffman wrote. 'He submitted, no doubt on legal advice, that the complaint by Daniel should not enjoy direct access to the highest court in the land. In effect Zuma contended that the matter should be taken away to a high court.

'Daniel had not asked for leave to be given direct access; he approached the Constitutional Court directly as of right. Imagine his surprise and consternation when, on 31 January, his attorneys received an order from the court refusing him direct access in the matter ... After first checking that the order was a genuine document, Daniel's lawyers made contact with their colleagues acting for the president to point out the patent error in the order made by the court. After desultory correspondence, the position of the president has emerged with pellucid clarity. He intends to defend the order made and contends that it is correctly made.

'If the term Stalingrad strategy is now springing to mind, it ought to be remembered that while this could possibly be condoned in a criminal matter against an individual, it is reprehensible in the conduct of state affairs ... this smacks of governing in bad faith. It is not the way constitutional democracies under the rule of law are run. It is supremely cringeworthy.'

The next round in the legal battle was described again in

Business Day, on 30 July, by professor emeritus at the University of Cape Town Wouter de Vos, under the headline 'A tale of two commissions, and the president's lawyers'. He wrote that a critical element of the rule of law was certainty about what the law was and what it required, procedurally and substantially. This required consistent conduct by those in positions of authority, a uniform interpretation of the provisions of laws and respect for precedents in cases of a similar nature.

Terry Crawford-Browne approached the Western Cape High Court in 2009 for an order that the president appoint a commission of inquiry into the arms deal. In response, the president's legal team said only the Constitutional Court could hear the matter. The campaigner reached the apex court two years later but, before an order was made, Zuma announced that he had established the Seriti Commission of Inquiry into the Arms Deal.

De Vos was puzzled. Fred had followed the legal precedent marked out by Crawford-Browne, but now the president's legal team was insisting that the appropriate forum to hear the matter was the high court. Without affording the parties a hearing, the Constitutional Court ruled in favour of the president. It found that it did not have exclusive jurisdiction in such matters, and that the high court would be the appropriate forum. The president's responsibility to appoint commissions of inquiry was not a constitutional obligation but rather a power to be exercised at his discretion.

'The inconsistent approaches of the president's legal team regarding this issue smack of opportunism, which is unfortunate for the rule of law, in particular the element that requires legal certainty,' De Vos wrote.

On 27 June 2013, the Constitutional Court handed down a judgment on Fred's recission application, clarifying the law. It held that section 84(2) of the Constitution, which gave the president the power to appoint a commission of inquiry, did not impose a *duty* on the president but a *power* that may be exercised at his discretion. 'Accordingly, the president's failure to appoint a commission of inquiry in this case did not constitute an issue that fell within the exclusive discretion of this court,' the judgment read.

In effect, it ruled that Fred could approach any high court to ask it to order the president to establish a commission, based on the evidence he presented. While he had cleared up uncertainty on where the power lay to appoint a commission, and had the appetite to take the matter immediately to the high court, another legal battle was looming. The North Gauteng High Court was about to hear his application for a provincial commission of inquiry and an interdict against the harassment and threats directed at him.

The chief justice also directed the president to file a response to the Constitutional Court application by 12 December, after which further directives might be issued by the court. Zuma filed an affidavit on deadline, three days before he opened the ANC's Mangaung conference. The timing wasn't right for him to grant a commission of inquiry into Mabuza's corruption – he was seeking a second term as the party's leader and he had been promised the Mpumalanga delegation's votes.

'Zuma – at least for now – hides behind the fact that there is already the North Gauteng High Court case and cannot, will not, consider establishing a commission until the case is concluded,' Bheki Mashile reported in *Noseweek* on 1 February 2013. 'A conveniently constructed catch-22.'

At the ANC's national elective conference in Mangaung, Zuma was elected to a second term as the party's president with the backing of the so-called Premier League, the party's most senior leaders in provinces where corruption was rife and service delivery limping – North West premier Supra Mahumapelo, Mpumalanga premier D.D. Mabuza and Free State premier Ace Magashule. A consistently large margin of around 75 per cent of the votes for the top six positions on the party's national executive committee indicated that there had been bloc voting at the conference.

Fred was treading hard on the tails of the political hyenas in Mpumalanga. He was aware of the tendency of whistleblowers to die young but failure was not an option for him. There was some relief when spring arrived in 2012. He received an email from Istithmar chief financial officer Mike Neilson, who acknowledged his passion and commitment to Nkomazi and suggested that they break out of their impasse and schedule a long-overdue meeting.

ANC Mpumalanga heavyweight David Mkhwanazi called to tell him that the Mpumalanga Tourism and Parks Agency's newly appointed CEO Jacques Modipane wanted a meeting and was eager to resolve the legal issues between them. There were faint glimmers of hope that there would be movement forwards and solutions instead of intractable legal battles that resolved nothing. Fred shelved his application for a commission of inquiry, as it seemed his relationships in Badplaas could be repaired and Nkomazi might be returned to him.

THE COMPANIES AND investors involved in Fred's project have spent around R18 million on legal costs, forensic reports and security to defend themselves against predator politicians. Their costs are mounting daily as they prepared for the North Gauteng High Court special trial from 27 July to 28 August 2020. In the 15 years that Fred battled the government in the courts to protect his investment, he attempted constantly to mediate the conflicts to restore his relationships with state officials.

Advocate Jacques Joubert was introduced to Fred by Alan Nelson SC, a respected Cape Town senior counsel who is an ardent supporter of facilitative mediation. Nelson had attended a course Joubert taught at the University of Cape Town on commercial mediation and returned to coach on the course. Joubert says Fred is 'locked in a dance of conflict' with Mabuza. 'Conflict grows a life of its own, way bigger than the original slight,' he explains. 'If the violation of dignity is not dealt with, you can easily become lost in conflict.

'Fred asked Alan for assistance with his damages claim. He had been let down by his former legal team who earned millions of rand advising, preparing and prosecuting two damages claims. They spent nearly all of his money. One day, when the money dried up, they demanded unlawful contingency agreements from him. They framed their failure to solve Fred's problems – for which they had been paid millions – as his failure, because he had run out of money.'

Nelson proposed that he and Joubert represent Fred on a contingency basis in his claims against Dubai World and the government on condition that he gave them an opportunity to persuade the defendants to settle by mediation. 'As Fred likes to say, we walked into a brick wall. We could not persuade Dubai World's attorneys or the state attorney to participate in mediation to settle the damages claims,' Joubert says.

The senior advocate abandoned the case and Joubert, a senior mediator but junior advocate, has been working with Fred ever since. 'In my experience, corrupt government officials face exposure during mediation. It is a tool to flush them out,' he says. 'Even better, it can empower and assist honest government officials to speak out against corruption.'

Mabuza and the government officials' senior legal representative Advocate André Ferreira SC advised them that there is zero risk of liability, and they will not pay any damages, Joubert says. 'Ferreira hasn't budged from this advice to his clients and when they were compelled to participate in mediation before a retired judge, he participated without his clients conceding even the possibility that they were responsible for some of Fred's damages. They refused to examine any solutions in regard to the damages claim, even without prejudice, which is the nature of mediation. To mediate on this basis is unethical.'

Some of the government employees who are defendants in the damages claim have been disciplined and found guilty of corruption in the Badplaas land scam. 'How they, and the regional Land Claims Commission, can continue denying the corruption is difficult to fathom,' Joubert says.

After the Land Claims Commission and the Mpumalanga Tourism and Parks Agency refused to participate in mediation, the conflict escalated. 'This usually means a corrupt government official is abusing his power behind the scenes,' Joubert says. 'Talk will expose that person.'

In a July 2016 proposal to the Mpumalanga government,

Joubert explained that mediation was a private, confidential and 'without prejudice' process. Parties had nothing to lose if the mediation failed and everything to gain if it was successful. Since 1994, parliament had passed 44 pieces of legislation recommending mediation and state attorneys were receiving training in the field.

'What distinguishes mediation from litigation is that it has the potential to restore relationships and create value for all the parties involved,' Joubert wrote. 'For Fred Daniel, the ongoing litigation may not bring him any closer to realising his dream to develop the Nkomazi Reserve into a source of national pride and economic opportunities for all in Mpumalanga. For the government, ongoing litigation may harm its reputation and deter potential investors from investing in Mpumalanga.'

Fred was hopeful that the mediation would help him put the conflict to rest and build fresh relationships. 'Each party was given half an hour to speak, and we were promised that the proceedings would remain confidential,' he says. 'After I spoke, Advocate André Ferreira, who represented both Mabuza and the parks agency, waved his finger at me and said that, because I had defamed his client, the mediation was no longer confidential. He said he would report me to Mabuza, and there would be consequences.'

Mediation is a confidential process. Joubert and Fred cannot disclose more of what happened at the talks, except to say that it did not settle the damages claim.

Joubert says that in all the court cases Fred has brought, most of them civil claims based on court papers, Mabuza has not testified about his alleged involvement in corruption or mismanagement. 'Mediation usually equalises the power balance, but it didn't help in Fred's case because the rot went all the way to the top of the Mpumalanga government,' he says. 'Many civil servants in Mpumalanga were not knowingly involved in corruption; they were just following orders.'

Joubert supports Fred's decision to seek a solution for his conflict and to set aside his damages trial for a later date. 'The defendants have always known how eager Fred is to resolve the conflict and get on with his life,' he says. 'He has made it known that good relationships are the key to business success. They have been reminded time and again not to fixate on the amount being claimed. But they studiously refused to consider proposals to limit their liability. They have hung themselves with their own rope.'

18
You are not alone

Fred's conflict with the Mpumalanga government is not unique as many other private tourism businesses in the province have faced similar challenges. One of them is Athol Stark, a tourism operator based in Ermelo. He was incensed when a tourism centre that he and his wife Melinda sponsored, and their 5-star conference centre, were sabotaged by the political elite in Mpumalanga.

'I know many people who fled Mpumalanga because politicians wanted to steal their businesses,' Stark says. 'The politicians recognised what they had achieved and came to hijack it. I am not going to remain silent, the only way to shut me up is … let's leave that open-ended. I have not met D.D. Mabuza but I have heard from many people that trying to deal with him is a dangerous game.'

Stark studied manpower management and industrial psychology at university, worked for a big corporate in Johannesburg and was a financial advisor before deciding that he would become his own boss. In 1990, he moved his family to Ermelo, 'a peaceful and beautiful little town, and a great place to raise children. 'Initially I spent weekends with my family travelling around Mpumalanga, meeting people, hearing about places, asking where they were and arriving there gobsmacked by the beauty. We discovered there are the most amazing heritage sites, ancient cities terraced into the mountains, abandoned old towns and the oldest rock art in Africa. There are 270 freshwater lakes in the province and battle sites of the South African War that people haven't even heard about.

'After some consideration, I established the Highveld Heritage Route. The Wine Route in the Cape and the Midlands Meander in KwaZulu-Natal were working astoundingly well and Mpumalanga had much to offer. In 1999, the Mpumalanga Parks Board invited tourism operators to a meeting to discuss a tourism development plan and strategy. I owned nothing in the industry but I had financial sector experience and thought heritage tours were going to be the next big thing, so I attended the meeting. We were told the government's plan was to divide the province into seven committees promoting the seven regional wonders of Mpumalanga.'

Stark became involved in two regions, Cosmos Country and Grass and Wetlands. He was elected chairman of the latter committee tasked with implementing provincial planning for tourism development. 'At that stage I was so innocent that I fell for the government's plans hook, line and sinker,' Stark says. 'I was enthusiastic before I really understood what was happening politically – a huge mistake.'

He realised within a year that there would be zero support for the committees from the Mpumalanga government or its tourism agency. There was no funding, no municipal or district development plans, and 'an astounding level of dismissal among senior government employees. There was also ineptitude and the level of aggression towards private sector operators was unbelievable. We realised that the provincial government was undermining us. They were not even on the same planet as us in terms of what they did and said.'

Stark and his fellow committee members continued their work. Almost two years later, the provincial plans for tourism were finalised. They were placed in a thick project file that explained, step by step, how the cooperative development of tourism would work. All they sought from the government was R11 million for signage. 'We had developed, at our own cost, marketing plans for every municipality to steer tourists towards the seven regions. I had letters of approval from the government, all the way up to the premier at the time, Ndaweni Mahlangu. I was asked by the provincial forum on tourism to take a copy of the plan to every municipality in the regions; there were seven in my region.'

He made appointments with mayors or any senior official at the municipalities who would meet him. Stark explained the project, handed over a copy of the file, and invited the officials to the launch of the tourism regions. At the Msukaligwa local municipality in Ermelo, he noticed 'something was terribly wrong. I met the director of marketing, Thokozane Nkosi, and some of his staff, explained the project and handed the file to him. After I left his office, I realised that I had forgotten to invite him to the launch. As I turned to go back, I heard him say in Zulu that this white man is crazy, followed by an almighty bang. I went inside and saw my file in his wastebasket next to his desk.'

'I get so angry when I remember these things.' He lifts his chin and stares at the ceiling for a while, his Adam's apple throbbing in his neck. 'He saw me and said sorry, the file fell off the desk. I realised then that nothing was going to come of our years of planning. We had put so much work into it, all at our own cost. We paid for our travel, our audits, everything. Apparently, R10 million was allocated for the signage, but the money disappeared, every cent of it.'

The regional tourism committees established networks of guesthouse owners, members of local organisations and other volunteers. They reported to provincial forums that liaised with the government and the Mpumalanga Tourism and Parks Agency. The province moved from seventh place to fourth in the country in terms of tourist arrivals and length of stay. But the pace of decision-making in the government was, at best, lethargic.

'We decided to continue without relying on government support,' Stark says. 'Maybe this was a mistake, and they thought it was a political problem. The attacks on our project began at a political level. We were told that we could not proceed until our projects were part of the integrated development plan at local municipal level. If they were not part of IDP planning, we were not going to secure support for implementation. We were stymied, stuffed and couldn't move forward.'

He believes the private operators' fatal mistake was that they responded by playing the political game. They asked the United Democratic Movement, the Freedom Front and the African Christian Democratic Party for their support. They organised public meetings to discuss their plans and win support. 'In Ermelo, about 600 people attended our meeting. Our message was simple: if politicians can't solve the unemployment problem, experienced business people can and should be given an opportunity to implement their plan to transform the economy.'

They registered a residents' association, Inwoners Organisasie (INWO), and persuaded councillors to join and support their vision of using tourism projects for economic development. 'I stood and was elected as an independent councillor for Ermelo on an INWO ticket and served from 2001 to 2005,' Stark says. 'We had councillors fired for wrongdoing, like stealing engine parts and swapping a tender for cleaning products and replacing it for one with TVs that were immediately stolen. We exposed wrongdoing across the province. A director at a municipality disappeared and one died of stress. We organised marches against corruption. In Ermelo, almost 3,000 people joined in. We were perceived as a threat by the politicians and the hatred levels went up pretty high.'

There was a massive boom in tourism in southern Mpumalanga. In Ermelo the number of guesthouses shot up from nine to more than 100 and there was enough business for all. Stark and his regional tourism committee organised an African Boulevard in Ermelo. They trained 127 black artists and craft workers, shut down a major street on Saturday mornings and set up stalls – at no cost to the government. People sold Emoyeni blankets, crafts woven from plastic shopping bags, duvets, paintings, wood sculpture, and more. The artists and craft workers paid nothing for the stalls and pocketed every cent they made.

'The MEC for safety and security Steve Mabona collapsed everything,' Stark says. 'He said the government did not support this piecemeal development of the tourism industry, remotely run by regions that did not match municipal demarcations. He said there should be a one-industry approach – whatever that means.

'So, we did what he asked; we reconfigured our tourism regions to follow government structures and launched Highveld Tourism and amalgamated the Cosmos Country and Grass and Wetlands regional tourism organisations. This helped to overcome the political drama. When Thabang Makwetla became premier of Mpumalanga in 2004, we received generous support. He was big on the heritage of the province. I drove him and his MECs Jabu Mahlangu and Craig Padayachee around our proposed tourism route, and he was blown away.

'We attended the national Tourism Indaba in Durban every year, sponsored by Mpumalanga Tourism and Parks Agency. After Mabuza became premier, we were told that we had to pay for our own travel and accommodation costs to the indaba. The bill for Highveld Tourism was R72,000 but we managed to raise it. Trying to deal with Mabuza was a dangerous game. If you were caught in his spotlight, chances are that you would not come out alive. Mahlangu and Padayachee put in a lot of effort before they scaled back and told us to be careful. They couldn't answer when I asked why they were so afraid.

'The big developers arrived in Mpumalanga and I became aware of Fred's project. I drove out to Badplaas to meet him. After seeing what he was accomplishing and checking out his bona fides, I got behind his plans. What was happening to him, the denial of permits and the belligerence of the parks agency officials, mirrored my experiences. We were in the same boat. Nothing we tried to do to improve relationships worked.'

Stark says politicians were deployed to local tourism associations to close them down. The Amajuba Public Association in Volksrust and Sivukile Tourism in Ermelo collapsed, as did the Secunda Guesthouse Association and Mkhondo Tourism Association in Piet Retief. 'Municipalities began insisting that their people have executive positions in the organisations. It wasn't logical, but at our first meeting with these new executive members, all they were interested in was how much their stipends would be for their attendance. They couldn't understand that these were all voluntary organisations, that we all gave our intellect and our time for free to develop the tourism industry.

'We asked them how much they wanted to be paid, expecting something like R2,000 a month for expenses. They demanded R42,000 a month, and when we refused to pay that, they stormed out and never came to another meeting. But they wrote reports about us and our work, rubbishing what we were doing. We were denounced as racist organisations.

'At that stage, we were conducting a one-year training programme for our artists and craft workers. We ran workshops teaching them how to deal with customers and manage their finances – in their own languages. We hired expert beaders, leather workers, knitting specialists and the like, all at our own cost. We hired conference venues, paid for travel costs, accommodation and meals for our craft workers.'

Stark says the political appointees to his organisation asked for their training files and they were handed over. Less than a month later, all the people participating in the African Boulevard in Ermelo were called to a meeting. They were told that the provincial government was funding the white people in tourism and asked whether they received any of that money.

'We discovered what had happened when we set up the African Boulevard after that meeting and none of our traders came. It ground to an immediate halt. The Msukaligwa Tourism Organisation changed its meetings to 10 am on Sundays, when my wife and I were usually in church. We went to the meetings. But one Sunday a new committee was elected that excluded the people who had been there at the outset. None of the new committee members had any expertise in tourism. Within months, the organisation that had created so much employment was dead.

'I called a public meeting to discuss reconstituting the Sivukile Tourism Organisation after the collapse of the Msukaligwa association and 37 people showed up. A few minutes after the meeting started, a toyi-toyiing crowd arrived. People invaded the venue carrying placards which read "Down with Stark" and other defamatory statements. We were warned that if the meeting continued, we would be assaulted. All our documents were grabbed and removed. We abandoned the meeting.

'The politicians who were deployed to the Secunda Guesthouse Association closed down its information centre. The building is still there, but it isn't giving any information to tourists looking to spend money in the area. The Amajuba Tourism Association suffered the same fate. The Pixley ka Seme Municipality destroyed museums and repurposed the information office into a changing room for security guards. In Piet Retief, all tourism activities ground to a halt.

'We realised that we had a battle on our hands, between the politicians and the private sector. But we couldn't retaliate, we were demonised and there were waves of attacks on us for being racists and greedy businessmen and women. They sabotaged us until we were a shadow of what we once were.

'We invested millions of rand into tourism and lost it all. There was no response to our letters of complaint to the Mpumalanga Tourism and Parks Agency and the MEC for economic development and tourism. But we kept going. We established the Highveld Heritage Route with assistance from the government of Switzerland, which gave us training in marketing and funded our successful trips to Switzerland, Germany and Austria.'

Stark engaged lawyers in an attempt to get government officials to desist from harassing the committee's members. He constantly wrote to officials in the government and its parks agency to address their hostility and engage their support. Like Fred's letters, his went unanswered.

A press release sent out in 2015 by Highveld Tourism, titled 'Crisis in Chrissiesmeer', highlighted the Mpumalanga government's ineptitude and lack of interest in attracting tourists to the province. 'A crisis, verging on a catastrophe, is unravelling at Chrissiesmeer where approximately 24,000 litres of effluent water are flowing into the largest freshwater lake in South Africa,' it read. 'According to inhabitants of the town, they have been reporting the flow of human waste into the lake for more than four years but were ignored until now. The Matotoland Ecotourism Association recently closed its most popular hiking and bird-watching route, which straddles the human waste that is flowing from the sewerage works across the grassland and into the lake. Grass and Wetlands regional tourism chairman Athol Stark supports the decision to close the hiking route as he is of the opinion that this spill threatens the environmental health of tourists and residents. The route will remain closed until a permanent solution can be found to this ecological crisis.'

Stark tells the story of the relentless campaign to drive him out of the tourism business through the death of a friendship. Soon after he became involved in the regional tourism committee in Ermelo and surrounding towns, he met unemployed teacher Fikile Mdlalose. 'He was affable, and we soon became home friends,' Stark says.

'At that stage, I was spending about half my income on developing the tourism industry. I didn't put any money in Fikile's pocket but I could, and did, mentor and train him in the industry. He had a good education and leadership qualities; it was going to take him very far. Fiki and I were inseparable, we criss-crossed the province to attend meetings with tourism operators. I was considering stepping down as regional tourism chairman and would have supported his nomination and election to my position.'

Stark accompanied his new friend to the opening of a tourism information centre in Secunda in 2003. Mpumalanga MEC for economic development Jabu Mahlangu gave a speech. Mdlalose was called up to cut the ribbon, and after he was done, the MEC announced that Mdlalose was going to be the next chairman of the Mpumalanga Tourism Authority.

'I was so excited. I was so pleased that a window had been opened for Fikile,' Stark says. 'Our friendship continued for a while after he stepped into his new role. But then it became sour. I went up to Middelburg to ask him what his problem was, to ask him to speak to me as an honest friend. He said that he had been instructed to devalue the role of the dominant white people in the tourism industry. He told me that it was becoming increasingly difficult to support my initiatives and he was chastised when he supported private tourism operators. He was told black people had to stand on their own feet. He said there could not be any more white heroes in South Africa, which shocked me to the core.'

The government's hostility towards private operators grew, and Stark appointed Advocate Jan Wagenaar in 2005 to write to the tourism authority, threatening to bring a claim for damages against them. His life had been threatened at several meetings and he often discovered after the gatherings ended that all his tyres had been slashed. 'About a week after Advocate Wagenaar sent the letter, at around 10 pm, I walked to the front of my house to lock up for the night. We have large windows in the front; you can see through them onto the street.

'Three shots were fired. I could hear it was a rifle, not a handgun. One bullet hit something in the yard, one ricocheted off the palisade fence. I jumped back, landed hard on my backside. I scooted back into the toilet. As I walked towards the front door, I had seen a bakkie parked on the pavement. Now I could hear it driving away.'

Stark called the police. They came, found no damage and left soon after they arrived. That night, his children slept on mattresses in the passage, where there are no windows. The next morning he inspected his garden and the pavement and found sharp-point ammunition, for a R5 rifle. 'They must have shot from inside the bakkie,' he says. 'There were no bullet casings on the pavement.

'I called a senior policeman I knew. He came to my house and took the bullet. I didn't hear from him so I tried to lay a charge a few days later. They wouldn't open a docket, said there was no evidence to back up what I was saying. I told them where they could find the bullet, but I don't think they followed up. I haven't heard from them again.'

A few weeks later, Stark's wife Melinda drove through the gates onto their property. Their dog ran towards the gate and her daughter ran after it to stop the dog before it reached the street. A silver-grey BMW pulled up, three men jumped from the car and rushed towards the girl. She turned and ran to Melinda while the dog charged at the men. They ran back to the car, which sped away.

'Soon after that my son, who was 14 years old at the time, went to the gate one evening because someone was calling. It was a man, who leaned forward and put a gun through the palisade against his head and asked where I was. He remained calm, turned his head and said, "My Dad is over there." The man removed the gun and turned to look, and my son ducked behind a tree that was broad enough to shelter him. The guy ran to a waiting car, jumped in the front passenger seat, and it roared away. Today my son is a grown man about to become a father of his first child, but when he talks about that incident there is a catch in his voice, proof of the stress it caused.

'There was a break for a while and then Fikile came to my gate one night. He called me on my cellphone, saying he wanted to come in. He told me he had come to protect me. I opened the gate and he stood on its rail so it couldn't close. He made a call and a few minutes later two bakkies pulled up, filled with about 24 men, who jumped out and poured onto my property.

'My wife grabbed the two smaller kids, raced upstairs and locked the security gate at the top of the stairs. Fikile walked towards me and said he had tried to warn me this would happen. The men had been rounded up from shebeens in town; they were coming to burn me out.

'Fiki said he could stop the men. All he needed from me was a resignation letter from the local tourism organisation. I refused and called Jabu Mahlangu to report what had happened. I asked him to get the police to my house. I went to get the hosepipe and two fire extinguishers and walked to the front door. The men had gone into the kitchen and were pouring out all the liquids they could find, tomato sauce and mayonnaise and the like. I didn't touch them, just watched.

'I called an intelligence officer at the Ermelo police station, who said he doubted what I was telling him. But the police came soon afterwards and threatened to arrest the men. They opened all the doors of the house, in case there was a fire. They got a ladder to help my wife and children scramble out through an upstairs window. Eventually the men left, walking past the police, who just watched them.

'Fikile stayed behind. I could smell the liquor on his breath, he was quite drunk and almost incoherent. He was no longer the assured chairman of the Mpumalanga Tourism Authority. I struggled to figure out what had become of him. I locked up for the night and left him to sleep on a couch in the lounge. The next morning, he got up and sat around for a while. He called someone who fetched him. He left without talking about what he had done. After that I saw Fiki from time to time at tourism meetings, but we never spoke again.'

Less than a week after the home invasion, five policemen arrived at Stark's home. They said that his name was on a hit list and they had been sent to protect him. They couldn't produce the list when he asked for it or any documentation about their deployment. He had to inform them every time he left the house and they accompanied him. 'For about six weeks the policemen followed me. They stopped and searched a car they spotted following mine. It belonged to an ANC leader in Ermelo. Then they withdrew. They gave me advice before they left: go underground and stop interacting with politicians.'

Stark didn't stop his work in the tourism industry, but he went underground for the next 14 years. He was forced to watch R870 million in funding for tourism disappear in his district without issuing a statement to the media or organising a march. He describes the municipal and provincial politicians living largely off looted taxpayers' money as a 'virus that has decimated the tourism industry in Mpumalanga'.

The harassment continued. Melinda was pulled over by a traffic officer who threatened to shoot her when she refused to leave her car and accompany him. The same officer pointed a gun at Stark's head when he pulled him over for the eleventh time to check his driver's licence. He later rose in the ranks and was appointed municipal manager at the Msukaligwa local municipality. He was fired after threatening to murder the mayor and is facing charges for the murder of a policeman in Ermelo.

'My organisation tried every avenue to get senior government officials and politicians to bring an end to the harassment, to no avail,' Stark says. 'There have been investigations by various institutions, but they all petered out with no results. We trusted the government to deal with these problems, but each time our trust was abused and turned into a weapon against us.

'We watched as strange tourism developments like market gardens, chicken farms, Zulu villages, picnic sites and community halls were developed, overcapitalised by millions of rand. Many of them fell into decay or disappeared completely. Some of them today are broken ruins with collapsed roofs and everything of value stolen or abandoned.'

Stark opened his own guesthouse in 2012 and is still volunteering his time and skills to build the tourism sector in Mpumalanga. During the 2020 lockdown due to the coronavirus pandemic, he provided accommodation for essential workers who could not get home to their families at night. He is still writing letters to politicians, seeking their cooperation in building a tourism industry that can create jobs for many poor people in Mpumalanga.

In a letter to the Mpumalanga MEC for economic development and tourism in April 2019, he described 'the desperate situation relating to tourism, tourism development, cooperation and relationship issues with the Gert Sibande District Municipality and their extremely bad track record of fostering toxic relationships with the private sector. The signing of the agreement of cooperation in June of 2016 between private sector and provincial government institutions should have heralded an end to these destructive tendencies but instead it led, unbelievably, to an increase by municipal officials in hostility, acts of sabotage, rude and disparaging behaviour and false and misleading information about tourism and the organisation we represent ... We cannot allow the destruction to continue to pull down the tourism industry and destroy the job opportunities which tourism created in this region.'

Because there was no response to their appeals, his organisation was 'left with no choice except to blow the whistle on the lack of development, lack of cooperation and the sabotage of private-sector established tourism structures in this region'. They would highlight how municipalities sabotaged and destroyed tourism structures including local tourism organisations, visitor information centres, museums, heritage sites, tourism activity – and deliberately targeted leaders of the industry.

'We would like to know what has happened over the past two decades to the tourism budgets for this district and region,' Stark wrote. 'According to our information, all tourism budgets, reported to be in the region of between R100 million and R170 million, have been repurposed for projects unknown.

'The officials orchestrating the collapse of tourism are not taking their instructions from the responsible departments of government but are taking instructions from individuals outside of government. They are not allowing development to take place on a local level, except when they can manoeuvre the finances via their own pockets. Then – and only then – are watered-down versions of any projects allowed to be developed.'

Athol and Melinda are regular visitors to Fred and Linda's home. Athol provided an affidavit for Fred's legal battle against Mabuza, the parks agency and government officials and employees. Their friendship is forged in their common vision and stubborn determination.

19

Protection and retaliation

Over time, Fred had become a thorn in the flesh of D.D. Mabuza. 'I was warned that when my name was mentioned to Mabuza, he became furious and vowed that when he was deputy president, he would ensure that the Cradle of Life was the first property to be expropriated,' he says. 'I am still haunted by the events of 2008 and 2009 when Mabuza called me and refused to discuss the land claims, but said if I did not admit to them, he could not guarantee my life.'

After he was warned in 2016 that his name was on a hit list, Fred increased the security at the Cradle of Life. He had rangers protecting his animals and the fences that were constantly vandalised; he brought in additional protection for his family. After Linda was threatened twice with harm on the roads, she was forbidden to drive. 'I had to lock myself and Jesse in the house when the staff left at 4 pm,' she says. 'I wasn't allowed to walk anywhere on my own. I had an armed guard for a while. There was no respite, no chance to recover from the last attack before the next one was unleashed.' Jesse lost a year of schooling as a result.

Fred's negotiations with Dubai World South Africa directors to purchase Nkomazi were characterised by more fits than starts. The company's employees would not cooperate with his due diligence investigation in preparation for the sale. They refused to allow him access to the reserve and cut off the water supply to the Cradle of Life. In March 2016, former Dubai World employee Linda Hartzer came to tell Fred that she had overheard her colleagues at Nkomazi plotting to burn down his lodge at the Cradle of Life. She had been dismissed and, like Fred, was refused entry onto the reserve by the guards. Hartzer obtained a protection of harassment order and had police protection when she went to collect her belongings at Nkomazi. She said a colleague who heard a senior Nkomazi manager and rangers conspiring to burn Fred's thatched-roof home was also willing to testify on his behalf.

Armed with their sworn statements, Fred approached the Carolina Magistrate's Court for a protection order against three Nkomazi employees who had been plotting to burn down his home. A few hours after his interim protection order was granted, police officers served it on the three employees and warned them that they would be arrested for contempt of court if they did not pack up and leave the reserve. They had been prohibited from being within 10 kilometres of the Cradle of Life.

Fred used the Protection of Harassment Act again in 2016, winning an order that Dubai World bring disciplinary charges against the rangers who had plotted to burn him out of Badplaas. Another Dubai World employee, its former reserve manager Manzi Spruyt, helped him win an interim protection order against Mpumalanga Tourism and Parks Agency wildlife manager Jan Muller when he conspired to block the renewal of Fred's zoological permit. A few weeks after Fred was granted the order, fires broke out at the Cradle of Life and at Spruyt's home. Days later, two shots were fired at Spruyt while she was in her home.

Fred approached the Carolina Magistrate's Court again in January 2018 for an interim protection order, this time against

Mpumalanga premier D.D. Mabuza. In a 59-page affidavit, Fred detailed the many violent and corrupt events over the previous decade that had brought him to court in search of an interim protection order against the premier. The court served Mabuza with an interim order to stop harassing and intimidating Fred. He was also instructed not to use any government department to sabotage his business. A warrant for his arrest was issued, which Fred could use if Mabuza did not abide by the order. The order was granted and served on the premier's office on the same day. Mabuza was asked to appear in court on 19 February 2018 to give reasons why the court should not issue a final protection order.

In his affidavit in support of the interim protection order, Fred said that he had been placed on a hit list. Mabuza was in a position to resolve the conflicts he faced, but the premier's actions over the past decade had been aimed to assassinate his character; block, frustrate and sabotage his business and deny him service delivery. 'Only the most powerful politician in Mpumalanga has the ability to coordinate the resources of an entire provincial government against a citizen – as happened to me.'

Mabuza had had meetings with so-called land claimants and had established the Greater Badplaas Land Claims Committee, which was 'dedicated to violence', Fred said in his affidavit. He was the chairman of the committee while being MEC for agriculture, and under his leadership the organisation 'unleashed mayhem'. Mabuza attended violent demonstrations, and incited protestors by stating that he would give them land. He did not denounce the violence or damage to property. He protected land developer Pieter Visagie, who had been charged with fraud, and authorised a payment of R3.3 million, from the department of land affairs to him.

The payment was made after Mabuza commissioned a joint task team to investigate and determine whether payments were due to Visagie. The team concluded that Visagie's company was underpaid due to a discrepancy between moveable and immovable farm assets.

'The heart of the conflict', Fred's affidavit read, 'lies in the capture of provincial institutions by Mabuza, which resulted in unlawful instructions, milking land reform funds and abusing the wildlife permit system. There is an unlawful parallel state that circumvents the constitutional state and is maintained by death threats, violence, terror, harassment and victimisation. The interests of a few powerful individuals are put before the rest of the citizens.

'Mpumalanga has been stolen and sold to the highest bidder by Mabuza, who controls it like a mafia boss. In order to cover their tracks, and avoid accountability and prosecution, the full might of the province has been deployed to go after those exposing the corruption.

'The conspiracy exposed in this application and the frequent abuse of state power against me have led to a situation where I have been forced to approach this court for assistance on a number of occasions to prohibit Mabuza's administration from continuing to harass, intimidate and prejudice me. The … risk is ongoing and so the court is asked to grant relief which would protect me against future bad faith, the malicious and intentional actions of Mabuza, and the government departments he controls with a view to harass, intimidate and prejudice me.'

Mabuza's spokesman Zibonele Mncwango told the media that the premier disputed the 'wild allegations' that he was behind a so-called campaign to drive Fred out of business and off his land. He said Mabuza would challenge the protection order.

'Mpumalanga Premier David Mabuza is an ardent supporter and have [sic] utmost respect for our judiciary and its independence. However, the abuse of our courts by Mr Fred Daniel, following his sensational, frivolous and thumbsucked allegations when he applied for the restraint order, refers. Mncwango said in a press release issued from Mabuza's office:

'The Caroline [sic] magistrate gave the order based on the lies by Mr Daniel with no notice being served on me before the unilateral interim restraint order was granted based on frivolous allegations.

'We have just learned that Mr Daniel and his partner or legal advisor (a failed ANC Presidential candidate) Mr Matthews Phosa were both in attendance at the Advocate Chambers in

Pretoria during the arbitration matter between Mr Daniel and the Mpumalanga Tourism Promotions (sic) Agency (MTPA).

'They appeared before retired Judge Geldenhuys. This matter has nothing to do with Mabuza nor land claims. If Mr Daniel with his cohorts have any evidence of any wrongdoing in particular of criminal nature, he can lay the charges directly with the police Hawks in Pretoria, the Public Protector, etc.

'The [protection] order is against Mr Mabuza in his personal capacity and not as a Premier nor against the Mpumalanga government. Mr Daniel has made frivolous allegations including defaming Mr Mabuza and has committed perjury.

Reading the political resume about Mr Mabuza in Daniel's affidavit exposes the fact that he has plagiarised an affidavit from Mr Matthews Phosa, that Mr Phosa had used in another matter against Mabuza. We are not surprised of (sic) the sensational affidavit and media frenzy because of the alleged involvement of Mr Phosa in the matter of Mr Daniel and the MTPA.

'The frivolous allegations that Mabuza threatened him and that he will deal with him once he is DP [deputy president] of the ANC is utter nonsense. Mr Mabuza has never met nor spoken to Mr Daniel who is apparently a serial accuser. According to his so-called affidavit, it is clear he has abused the courts and used the same tactics where he got restraining orders against government employees (to stop them from doing their job) and his erstwhile partners Dubai World directors, tells you more of the character we are dealing with.

'For the record, land claims are the responsibility of the National Government and not a Provincial government. Mr Mabuza have no involvement in land restitution as the decisions for or against are the responsibility of the Land Claims Commission under the Department of Rural Development and Land Reform. Further, MTPA is a government body responsible for inter alia conservation and Tourism. Apparently, Mr Daniel has for a period of time been involved in a dispute with MTPA on the important issue of conservation/game animals.

'The Premier responsibilities is inter alia to source investments into the Province and support local businesses, hence he initiated the development of a fruits and vegetable international market, working with both white and black farmers. The Premier have and continue to support tourism investments and his government works closer with these business enterprises.

'Mr Mabuza does not even know the full facts on this apparent dispute between the MTPA. The relevant respondents should have been the MTPA, MEC concerned, the Department of Finance and Economic Development and/or the Mpumalanga Provincial Government. We now understand why Mabuza's name and has (sic) personally been targeted and smeared because of Mr Phosa's involvement and personal agenda.

'Mr Daniel has instead targeted Mabuza in his personal capacity for sensational reasons so that the media frenzy can spread his lies and innuendos with the hope that Mabuza will under pressure interfere with MTPA work.

Daniel in his affidavit he does not indicate what Mabuza's interest is, in his business. Mabuza is not a businessman, nor does he have property nor live in Badplaas, where Daniel's tourism business is. Mabuza have no interest in his business and I am also sure government cannot harass any investor/business if he/she is compliant with the law especially where conservation is concerned.

'Mr Mabuza will lay perjury criminal charges with the SAPS in Johannesburg so that the matter should be investigated by the police from outside the province of Mpumalanga. We know Mr Daniel will be exposed as a liar and abuser of our court systems to defame innocent people.

'Mr Mabuza is looking forward to the hearing on 19th February 2018 at Caroline (sic) Magistrates Court. He is sure that the frivolous claims of Mr Daniel will be exposed as well as the fact that he perjured himself and abused the court. Mr Mabuza will then follow with a defamation action as he will not tolerate anyone to besmirch his good name for a personal or political agenda. Mr Daniel and his partner/attorney Phosa will not succeed to blackmail Mabuza to interfere with the work of the officials/experts from MTPA.'

The interim order against Mabuza was issued on Thursday, 2 February.

Fred had parked his car across the road from the magistrate's court when he went to seek the protection order against Mabuza. When he drove home, a front wheel of his Land Rover fell off. 'I immediately felt that I had been sabotaged,' he says. He sent the car to Nelspruit to be repaired and a mechanic told him that a special nut was missing on the wheel. Had the wheel fallen off while he was driving fast, the car could have jack-knifed. 'The mechanic said it was impossible for the nut to have fallen off; someone must have removed it.'

In a shocking twist to this legal battle, Fred's interim protection order against Mabuza was withdrawn in August. Magistrate Sarel Grabe dismissed Fred's application to have the interim protection order made permanent and labelled him a 'fabricator'. The magistrate ruled that Fred had withheld evidence during his application for the order that had been granted by his predecessor. Fred's lawyers have laid a complaint with the Magistrates Commission, but as with so many other structures they have approached for help, there has been little progress.

FRED SAYS THE corruption he unearthed was bad enough, but nothing prepared him for the retaliation. He was nearly duped in a smear campaign, probably meant to derail the looming damages claim against Mabuza and his officials. In November 2018, an elaborate plot unfolded – and quickly exploded. Had it succeeded, it would have been possible to declare Fred a serial liar who abused court processes and would have painted him as a fabricator of lies about Mabuza. It is equally likely that the intention was to kill him and his family.

Fred had been receiving strange phone calls for weeks, which were later traced to convicts in the Zonderwater Prison in Cullinan. They asked him to send money to e-wallet accounts. Fred was confused by them, but didn't consider the possibility that he was being set up.

Around lunchtime on Tuesday, 6 November 2018, Fred missed four calls from an unknown number. He answered the fifth and sixth calls but the reception was too poor to hear more than an anxious woman's voice. Fred received a text message: 'Hi can u please phone me. Its important cuz I can't hear u, I think it's the network. I'm witness Thandeka Mabuza.'

That evening, the journalist Sama Yende called to tell Fred that the same woman had phoned him. She was trying to warn Fred that his life was in imminent danger, but was struggling to reach him. Fred called her three times and finally spoke to her at 7 pm. 'She introduced herself as Thandeka Mabuza and told me that I must be careful as my life was in danger from hitmen,' Fred said in an affidavit about the plot. 'She was anxious, soft-spoken and said her uncle had sent two men to Badplaas to kill me. She knew the men…'

'Alarmed, I put the phone down and immediately took my shotgun out of the safe and warned my wife about the threat of an imminent attack on us. I made sure all our dogs were safe inside the house to prevent them from being poisoned. I checked that all the doors were locked, the windows securely closed, and that all the curtains were drawn. I turned on all the outside lights. I turned off most of the inside lights, so someone outside could not shoot us in the house and, if needed, I could see outside without being detected.

'My son asked his mother why I had taken out the shotgun. She asked me what she should tell him. I told her to tell him the truth, that bad people want to hurt us but that the police were going to make sure that we are safe. He collected his pellet gun and said he was going to sleep with it next to him. As a family, we have learnt that honesty and transparency is the only way to deal with the threats we have had to face over the years. It makes my son even more anxious when we are not honest with him, as he knows exactly what is going on.'

Fred called Sama Yende again and discovered that the journalist had received another warning, from Democratic Alliance employee Dumisile Masuku, who had also been contacted by Thandeka to warn that hitmen were on their way to Badplaas. He called the investigator Paul O'Sullivan and asked him to contact Thandeka to arrange for her to give a sworn statement.

The next caller was former premier Mathews Phosa, who had been assisting him to help the Cradle of Life achieve its potential.

'He was concerned because he had buried whistleblowers in Mpumalanga,' Fred said in his affidavit about Phosa. 'He gave me the numbers of two crime intelligence brigadiers.'

Fred listed the calls he made: 'I called my business partner John Allen to notify him of the threat ... I called Brigadier Botsotso Moukangwe, who told me he would immediately try and assist my family ... called John again and asked him to notify as many people as possible ... called Brigadier Botsotso Moukangwe again ... I called O'Sullivan and Sama Yende to help me determine if Thandeka was the person she said she was.

'I called Thandeka again to verify that her father was the oldest brother of Mr Mabuza. She confirmed this and said that she had been an orphan since 2003, living with Mr Mabuza ... called Sama Yende again to establish certain facts about Thandeka and became even more convinced and afraid that she was exactly who she said she was.

'Paul Hoffman called and said that he would contact the Zondo Commission to arrange that I give evidence there. He said they may be able to arrange witness protection for my family. Brigadier Botsotso Moukangwe called to say he had assigned Colonel de Beer to coordinate the protection of my family. Brigadier Xaba called from the Hawks in Pretoria to ask questions and offer his assistance.

'I spoke to Colonel de Beer and he said that he would send the flying squad to travel around the area with blue lights flashing to disrupt any hit. He said he would text me the phone numbers of the police officers who were on their way to patrol the area.

'Captain Vilakazi of the Badplaas police station called to offer his assistance. I asked him to send out a patrol car to ensure that the attackers were aware that we knew about their plans and they were being monitored. Only when my wife and my son saw the blue lights outside our house were they able to go to sleep.'

Jesse slept on a mattress on the floor next to his parents' bed. It would be months before they could get him to sleep in his bedroom again.

The next morning the first call came just after 6 am. It was Thandeka, saying 'she urgently needed to speak to someone she could trust. She said that her uncle had phoned her and sounded angry and suspicious. I told her that I would get O'Sullivan to call her to discuss her safety. I gave her his number.'

The next caller was Mathews Phosa, checking to see if Fred and his family had made it through the night. Colonel de Beer called, with more questions. O'Sullivan phoned to say that he had spoken to Thandeka. She called, ten minutes later, to say she was too scared to meet O'Sullivan.

'Frank Dutton, a senior investigator at the Zondo Commission, called and requested that I urgently send him evidence of state capture, so that he could see if my family [was] ... eligible for witness protection,' Fred said in his affidavit.

Fred called Thandeka and arranged to meet her at the Mbombela police station after lunch to make a sworn statement. She called two hours later and said 'that her uncle had accused her of touching his diary,' his affidavit read. 'She said she thinks that her uncle must have hidden cameras in his study and may know that she had looked at his diary.'

Fred made several more calls to senior police officers to make arrangements for Thandeka to depose a sworn statement before he left for Nelspruit, with Linda and Jesse, to meet her. 'I met Brigadier Botsotso Moukangwe, who told me that he had spoken to Thandeka and that she was on her way. After waiting a long time, we realised that she was not coming.'

Thandeka did not pick up calls for two hours. Fred called Sama Yende for advice and was given the number of Dumisile Masuku, the Democratic Alliance employee who had also been told of the assassination plot. Masuku worked at the legislature, where Thandeka had to produce her ID to gain access. Within minutes he had her ID number to pass on to O'Sullivan.

Fred called Masuku again to ask her to persuade Thandeka to meet him privately, without the police present. They agreed to meet at a restaurant. He waited with Masuku for hours at the restaurant, and decided to leave with his family before it got dark. Fred later received a call from Masuku to say Thandeka had come after he left and said she wanted to make a sworn statement 'so people would know the reason if she was killed'.

The next day Fred finally met Thandeka, at a restaurant in

Nelspruit. Masuku and a colleague were also present. 'She was anxious but very clear in what she told me and what she wanted in her statement. I assisted her to prepare a statement, most of which she typed out.'

In her statement, signed under oath, Thandeka said she was an assistant to her uncle D.D. Mabuza. She had lived with him since 2003 in Barberton and moved to his new house in Johannesburg after he became deputy president. She said she cleaned the private areas of his house, including his bedroom and study. On Monday, 5 November two men came to the house. She recognised them as 'known gangsters' from Phola Trust where she had grown up. 'I was concerned why these men were in my uncle's house and I asked what they were doing there. They said they were looking for a job. My uncle came home late at night and they slept at the house,' her statement read.

The next morning while cleaning her uncle's study, she spotted an open diary on his desk. 'I saw a very disturbing entry which read "hit list" with seven entries with telephone numbers, locations and dates. The first two entries were crossed out. The third entry had a cellphone number, a Badplaas location and 7 November written next to it. I closed the diary.'

Thandeka said after she cleaned the study, she went into the garden and found the Phola Trust men there. 'One of them was talking on his cellphone, giving directions to Badplaas, via the toll-gate from Nelspruit to Machadodorp,' her affidavit read. 'I got shocked and immediately went back to my uncle's study, opened the diary and wrote down the cellphone number listed in the third entry.'

Thandeka said she called the number but could not get through. A friend advised her to ask the Democratic Alliance (DA) or the Economic Freedom Fighters (EFF) for advice. 'I was still struggling to get through to the number and decided to drive to Mpumalanga to the DA offices in Nelspruit. I met a DA representative who assisted me. The representative looked up the number on True Caller and the name Fred Daniel came up.

'We looked up Fred Daniel in Badplaas on Google and the first entry was an article by the *City Press* dealing with a protection order. We both realised that the situation was very serious. The DA representative contacted the journalist from the *City Press* who wrote the article and told him the story. He immediately undertook to contact Mr Daniel and warn him.'

Fred said Thandeka gave him the names and ID numbers of the two hitmen. She asked what he was going to do with her affidavit. 'I said that I would like to see a judge to get an interdict,' Fred's affidavit read. 'She asked me if she could come with me because she had more evidence that she wanted to give the judge herself. I agreed, and she asked that it had to be on the next day.'

He left for Pretoria on Friday, 9 November, taking Linda and Jesse. At 9 am, he called Thandeka to check if she was on her way. 'She promised to leave immediately and meet us on the highway at the Milly's stop near Machadodorp.' He called her several more times while they drove, but she did not answer. Then her phone was switched off. 'My wife started panicking and insisted that we do not stop at Milly's and proceed to Pretoria.' He kept trying his witness's phone but it wasn't answered.

He met his advocate at the North Gauteng High Court to draft an *ex parte* notice for an urgent application supported by Thandeka's affidavit. 'We did not give prior notice of the application to the respondents because I was worried that notice would endanger Thandeka's life.'

At 4.30 pm, Fred brought the urgent application for interim relief 'to protect my family against the planned conspiracy. During all this time, my wife and son remained with me as they feared staying at home and wanted to be with me.' The judge refused to hear the application without prior notice and postponed the matter to 12 November.

That evening, Fred called Brigadier Botsotso Moukangwe and told him what had happened at court. Brigadier Xaba of the Hawks also called.

By the next morning, O'Sullivan established that one of the alleged hitmen, Ian Nyalunga, lived at Phola Trust. Fred met two officers of the Hawks in Johannesburg, who had been assigned to his case. They advised him to lay criminal charges against the suspects. 'At no stage did the Hawks officers give the impression that they were not taking the threat seriously,' his affidavit read.

'I have no doubt, with hindsight, that they must have known already that Thandeka's statement implicating Mr Mabuza was a complete fabrication ... they withheld critically important information from me. These officers, I have now discovered, work for an elite unit in the Hawks that investigates crimes against the state. I am not sure how my matter related to a crime against the state...'

At noon, O'Sullivan confirmed in an email that the head of the Hawks, General Godfrey Lebeya, had been alerted. It appeared as though the Hawks were taking the threat seriously. Fred went to the Sandton police station to lay a charge against Mabuza and the two men from Phola Trust. He received a case number.

On Monday, 12 November his advocate received a call from Mabuza's advocate telling him that the evidence had been fabricated as the deputy president had been overseas while this conspiracy was allegedly hatched. 'He threatened that he would ask the court for a punitive cost order against me if I did not immediately withdraw the application and tender costs. My counsel said he needed to see the evidence before deciding to do anything.'

There were several Hawks officers in the courtroom when Fred, his family and his legal team arrived at the Pretoria High Court at 2 pm. They were shown an affidavit made by Mabuza's special advisor General Mulangi Mphego. It stated that the deputy president did not have a niece called Thandeka and that he was in Russia on the day the woman claimed that he had hosted the alleged hitmen at his house.

Advocate Mike Hellens SC, appearing on behalf of Mabuza, asked the judge to condemn Fred's scandalous abuse of court processes and to dismiss the application. 'In an astonishing turnaround, an advocate representing Major General Sylvia Ledwaba of the Hawks demanded punitive damages because I had fabricated evidence to implicate Mr Mabuza in a conspiracy to murder me,' Fred's statement read.

'It was only then that I realised that Thandeka was not who she said she was and that I, along with Masuku of the DA and Sama Yende of the *City Press*, had been duped by an elaborate conspiracy that exposed us to arrest on charges of treason, namely that we fabricated evidence against the deputy president, which could destabilise the state.

'No one in South Africa has been more of a thorn in the flesh of Mr Mabuza over the years than the DA, Sama Yende and I. If the conspiracy had succeeded, we would have been neutralised as a threat to Mr Mabuza and he would conveniently be seen as a victim of a criminal conspiracy to discredit him.'

Masuku had not only discovered Thandeka's identity number when she visited the Mpumalanga legislature, but she also recorded her car registration number. Using that, O'Sullivan discovered the name, address and Facebook photograph of the woman who claimed she was Mabuza's niece – Nomfundo Sambo from Phola Trust, an unemployed former department of education clerk. The information reached the court just as Fred realised the Hawks officers could be there to handcuff him.

'Her sworn statement as Thandeka Mabuza is all the evidence that a prosecutor will need to prove that Sambo committed fraud, perjury and defeating the ends of justice,' his statement read. 'I trust my family will one day be able to tell her in court about the hell she put us through, especially our nine-year-old son.

'The evidence is clear that the conspiracy to discredit Sama Yende, the DA and me was sophisticated and meant to intimidate, discredit and possibly lure me to a place to kill me. The only person who would benefit from the conspiracy is Mr Mabuza. Mr Mphego, with his crime intelligence background, had the means to stage this elaborate conspiracy.

'Under the Prevention of Organised Crime Act, the Hawks are mandated to protect my family against organised crime and certainly not to protect organised crime against me. I ask that the Hawks arrest and ensure the speedy prosecution of Sambo for fraud, perjury and defeating the ends of justice. I am advised that she faces a lengthy prison sentence for what she did to my family.

'The Hawks are asked to investigate whether the plan was to lure me to a place where Sambo's fellow conspirators would have staged a robbery at the Milly's stop near Machadodorp to kill me. I ask that the Hawks investigate the role of Mr Mabuza in the conspiracy to discredit me with reference to an emerging pattern to discredit me as a witness of organised crime.'

Fred says he slowed down as they neared the Milly's stop, where 'Thandeka' had promised to meet them, but Linda had a strong instinct that they were driving into a trap. 'She said we should continue to the next petrol station, call Thandeka and ask her to meet us there. The reason she gave for wanting to meet us at Milly's was that she needed petrol.

'It was only much later that I put two and two together and remembered the phone calls from the convicts in prison. They were probably planted on my phone to connect me with crime. Had my family and I been killed that day at Milly's, the police would have concluded, after a very short investigation, that it was a criminal deal gone sour.'

Sambo was arrested in March 2019, and she appeared in the Nelspruit Regional Court on charges of fraud, forgery, defeating the ends of justice and armed robbery. She was allegedly found in possession of house robbery equipment when she was arrested. The prosecutor Advocate Henry Nxumalo said he opposed bail as Sambo was facing another pending case – armed robbery with aggravating circumstances. The Hawks discovered that R700,000 had been paid into her bank account not long after Mabuza issued a press statement in which he, among other slurs, called Fred a serial liar.

Reporting on the website News24, Kyle Cowan and Jean le Roux wrote that Mabuza had spent 15 days in Russia for 'routine' medical treatment when Fred went to court to stop the alleged plot to assassinate him. According to Mphego's affidavit filed in response to the interdict, Mabuza was in Russia from 24 October until 10 November – for 17 days. Mphego handed to the court a scanned copy of Mabuza's passport showing his entry stamp at O.R. Tambo International Airport on 10 November.

The deputy president had been receiving treatment because he was still feeling ill following an attempted poisoning. Cowan and Le Roux wrote that 'a well-placed source with direct knowledge of events, who spoke on condition of anonymity, confirmed to News24 that Mabuza was indeed in Russia for further treatment relating to the 2015 poisoning incident'.

Mabuza's spokesperson Thami Ngwenya said he was on sick leave, but he was not ill. 'At no point in our statement did we say that the deputy president is ill,' he told News24. 'We said he was on sick leave, so he was attending to his medical health.'

Fred told Cowan and Le Roux that he vowed to get to the bottom of the conspiracy. He planned to file supplementary court papers after he amended his attempted murder case opened at the Sandton police station against Mabuza and the two Phola Trust men. He had laid charges of fraud and defeating the ends of justice against Sambo.

Mabuza had appointed former crime intelligence boss Mphego as his special advisor in August 2018. The *Mail & Guardian* reported that Mphego had a 'checkered past', including links to corruption charges against Jacob Zuma. Mphego made an appearance in Redi Tlhabi's book *Khwezi*, as the man who flirted with Zuma's rape accuser Fezekile Kuzwayo while she was in police protection. According to the book, he asked Kuzwayo to sit on his lap while a photo was taken and later painted her as a 'loose woman' who had initiated sex with Zuma. He denied this.

Mphego also scuttled Zuma's corruption trial. The *Mail & Guardian* reported in 2010 that it was he who had provided Zuma with the so-called 'spy tapes' containing conversations between former Scorpions boss Leonard McCarthy and former director of public prosecutions Bulelani Ngcuka. The tapes led to NPA head Mokotedi Mpshe dropping the charges against Zuma in 2009, claiming political interference.

Mphego was head of intelligence during President Thabo Mbeki's tenure but was forced to resign in 2009 after he was accused of interfering with state witnesses in the corruption trial of the former police commissioner Jackie Selebi. A case of defeating the ends of justice against Mphego was later struck off the roll.

On 5 August 2020 Sambo pleaded guilty to fraud in the Nelspruit Regional Court, depriving Fred of an opportunity to testify in court about the trauma she inflicted on his family.

THE MOST BIZARRE smear campaign in Mpumalanga was a ping-pong affair allegedly masterminded by Mabuza against Phosa after the former premier accused him of being an apartheid spy. Journalists covering the politics of the smear in Mpumalanga were sceptical from the start that anything in this tale rang true. Fred Daniel featured in the saga.

Phosa's former house manager Jan Venter, dubbed 'a serial liar' by the media for switching allegiance several times between Phosa and Mabuza, said in an affidavit that in June 2015 he and Phosa 'fell out over a dispute between us which … has been resolved'. He called Mabuza's chief of staff Jasmin Ali seeking help to resolve the dispute. She contacted him two months later and said the premier would be phoning him in ten minutes. Mabuza allegedly called and asked for a meeting at his house in Steiltes in Nelspruit.

'I went to the meeting,' Venter said in his affidavit. 'We sat on his veranda. He told me we had a mutual problem and we could help each other. I explained the dispute I had with Dr Phosa.' Venter was facing charges of stealing R53,000 from his former employer. 'Mabuza told me that he did not get along with Dr Phosa and he would not be able to get him to listen. He told me that Dr Phosa was very powerful and I could not win.

'He offered me another option. He asked if I had read the prior day's newspaper concerning allegations that he was accused of being an apartheid spy. Mabuza then said he wanted me to falsely state that I was present while Phosa and [his business partner] Nick Elliot fabricated documents implicating him as an apartheid spy.

'I told him I would think about it, as I had to weigh up my options between lying under oath and trying to sort out my dispute with Dr Phosa. Mabuza told me I would lose the case, and that Phosa would put me in jail.

'He told me the intention of my statement was to create doubt about the allegations that he was a police spy. He said he intended to run for president one day and the allegations would kill his political career. He said everyone made mistakes and that he had been a spy for the apartheid-era government and was worried about his future.'

Venter said in his affidavit that a man arrived at Mabuza's house and introduced himself as Ian Small-Smith. Mabuza explained this was his attorney who would help with the theft charges Phosa had laid. Small-Smith told Venter to send all invoices for legal fees to him. 'From that point on, I never paid a cent towards legal fees, it was all handled by Small-Smith,' he claimed. 'I should make it clear that we have also exchanged many emails.'

The antipathy between Phosa and Mabuza soared in 2015 when Phosa alleged that his political rival had been an apartheid spy – code-named PN485 – who worked with killer Eugene de Kock and provided information about senior ANC leaders, including Zuma, basic education minister Angie Motshekga and the late Albertina Sisulu, between 1985 and 1993. Mabuza strenuously denied the allegations. Phosa gave the report – which he said he found in an envelope on his stoep – to ANC deputy secretary general Jessie Duarte and asked Luthuli House to probe the matter. He also asked Zuma for a commission of inquiry into the allegations, but, like Fred's request to the president, Phosa's was ignored.

Venter said in his affidavit that when his theft case came to trial, his lawyer planned to appoint an advocate in Nelspruit who charged R10,000 a day. 'Small-Smith said there's no way we're using him, we will use Mike Hellens. I found out that Hellens charged R53,000 a day. The charges were later withdrawn. Small-Smith told me that he got the money from Mabuza to pay Hellens.'

Venter 'made peace' with Phosa and stopped dealing with Small-Smith and Mabuza. Six months later, the attorney called and asked him to attend a meeting at an advocate's chambers in Brooklyn, Pretoria. Mabuza was there and allegedly asked Venter to testify the following day in his damages case against Phosa. The former house manager claimed that he didn't want to, but the premier 'charmed' him and got him to agree.

'Mabuza said he would buy me a car and a house and a gun and a computer and I would eat what he eats. He told me he would arrange a job for me.'

Venter and his son were booked into the Sheraton Hotel, where Mabuza was staying for the duration of the damages case in

May 2017. He testified in the Pretoria High Court for three and a half days, maintaining that he had seen Phosa and Elliot concoct the spy report. 'While the court case was going on, Mabuza paid me cash. The first day he paid me R2,000. The next day he paid me R30,000. After I finished testifying, Mabuza gave me another R20,000 in cash to go rent a vehicle from Avis, drive to Nelspruit and find a house to rent. I found a house and Mabuza paid for it.

'Mabuza used his own credit card to buy me a gun at Roses Guns in Whiteriver. He also used his credit card to buy me a laptop and an iPhone from Cash Converters in Nelspruit. A month later, Mabuza supplied me with a second-hand VW Polo that was paid for out of public funds. Small-Smith and Mabuza paid me about R4 million over the last few years.'

'In March 2017, I asked Mabuza about the house and the business he promised me. He told me that there was a man called Fred Daniel that had pissed him off. He said when he became the deputy president he was going to take all of Daniel's land away from him. He said after he takes the land away from him, he would give me one or two hectares with a house on it.'

The tone of Venter's affidavit rises in pitch. 'A few weeks ago, I woke up and realised that I would either be killed or something would happen to me for what I had done years ago. I decided I would have to come clean and tell it the way it is. Only by coming clean would I be able to carry on with my life. I called Small-Smith and told him that I planned to come clean by calling a press conference and exposing these things. Small-Smith put the phone down in anger and then he sent me an email, which I am attaching. He unilaterally cancelled our fake agreement and demanded a whole lot of invoices.

'After this, I started getting calls from private numbers and they said I would be killed. It was different people and the gist of it was to ask me why I wanted to ruin the life of the deputy president. They said if I was to carry on against the deputy president, I would be killed. I am still being threatened every night. I therefore request police investigation and protection. I will cooperate with any investigations and am prepared to attend court and give evidence.'

Small-Smith's attorneys say Venter's version of events has to be taken in the context of a litany of his emails and social media posts 'undermining the sitting president of the Republic, the NPA, various ministers, counsel and others'. Several of Venter's statements breach a court order Small-Smith obtained against him. The attorney lodged a claim for damages against Venter and laid charges against him of defeating the ends of justice, fraud and perjury.

Small-Smith denies that he is Mabuza's personal attorney, and says he has never been paid by Mabuza or any organ of state on the deputy president's behalf. He acknowledges that Mabuza introduced him to Venter and asked him to represent Phosa's former employee. He recommended counsel to Venter's existing attorney. 'Given that Venter was impoverished', Small-Smith 'rendered financial assistance' to him from his own funds but never claimed reimbursement from Mabuza, his attorneys say. He also denies attending meetings with Venter and Mabuza.

One of Small-Smith's companies employed Venter as a subcontractor for fourteen months. He was paid R40 000 a month, on submission of invoices. 'Venter also borrowed R75 000 from the company for arrears maintenance owing to his wife and children … and also borrowed money from the company for a car and tools which he never repaid. No amounts were paid to Venter by Small-Smith or Mabuza for testifying in the damages case.' The lawyers say Venter's contract with Small-Smith was terminated when 'it became apparent that he submitted false invoices to the company for hotel stays'.

Like all Mpumalanga political scandals, this one had a twist. In September 2019, Sizwe sama Yende reported: 'After spending fifteen months in the witness protection programme, self-confessed liar Jan Venter has been kicked out, leaving many questions about the allegations he made against Deputy President David Mabuza. Both the Hawks and the National Prosecuting Authority confirmed that an investigation, based on evidence Venter provided, was ongoing but declined to give details.

'Last week, Venter tried to force the NPA to return him to the witness protection programme through an urgent court application, but his attempt failed. He is now trying to testify in the Zondo Commission. It appears that the NPA kicked him out following his outburst in an email written to political parties, the media and many other people on 16 August where he revealed the address of the safe house where he lived, published cellphone numbers of senior NPA officials and accused them of being in cahoots with Mabuza to have him killed.'

20

The land turns to dust

Rampant fraud and corruption did not only affect the delivery of housing, electricity, water, education and health care in Mpumalanga – some state-owned conservation projects were destroyed. Section 24 of the Constitution states that all citizens have the right to live in a clean and safe environment and places an obligation on the government to ensure and conserve such an environment. Mpumalanga politicians ignored their constitutional duties, and looted conservation budgets for the ANC's election war chest, for their own political ambitions and to enrich themselves and an army of businessmen and legal professionals.

Forced commercialisation projects and fraudulent land claims destroyed some of Mpumalanga's largest and most magnificent conservation assets. In parks controlled by the agency, 182 rhinos were killed by poachers between 2010 and 2014. Endangered and other wild animals were slaughtered for their horns, tusks and skins and for bush meat markets. Community trusts whose land was restored to them after being stolen under apartheid were hijacked in democratic South Africa – and billions of taxpayer rand intended for their beneficiaries were stolen by corrupt politicians and businessmen.

In May 2011, Nelspruit-based environmental reporter Fiona Macleod reported in the *Mail & Guardian* that the Mpumalanga Tourism and Parks Agency, 'once one of South Africa's most respected conservation organisations', was broke. The electricity had been cut off at its Nelspruit headquarters and at Songimvelo because of outstanding bills and Telkom had cut off their communications.

'Food for emaciated buffaloes held in breeding bomas at Loskop Reserve near Middelburg is running out and there is no petrol to fetch more,' Macleod wrote. 'There is no electricity to pump water for the buffaloes. Co-management deals at five reserves shared with local communities have crumbled. At Songimvelo, under threat from local cattle barons, land claimants have not been paid income promised from last year's hunting season.'

In 2013, former public protector Thuli Madonsela investigated the awarding of tenders by the Mpumalanga department of public works for business leases in Pilgrim's Rest. Her report concluded that the process was characterised by 'gross irregularities and maladministration'. Pilgrim's Rest, a national monument established in the early 1800s, is managed by the Mpumalanga department of public works. In 2012, the department issued eviction notices to their tenants – all businesses in the tourism sector. The department issued new leases, to two people with no experience in the tourism sector, at vastly reduced rentals. The former tenants won an urgent interdict and the department of public works was ordered to submit their tender documents to the court for a review. They did not comply.

The former tenants turned to the public protector for help. Madonsela instructed the department to cancel the new leases and embark on a new tender process. She gave them 30 days to comply, but to date they have not. Pilgrim's Rest went into a steep decline after most of its tenants were evicted. It is rising to its feet again after Theta Gold Mines injected around R1 billion into the establishment of an open-pit mine near the town. The company plans to excavate an area of more than 600 kilometres for up to a hundred years.

Karyn Maughan reported in *Business Day* in January 2019 that fraud 'on an enormous scale' had been uncovered in the land reform programme. Government officials had handed out farms and millions of rand in grants to beneficiaries who did not qualify for such assistance. 'A report by the Special Investigating Unit (SIU) recommends that forty-two people, including government officials, be prosecuted for fraud and corruption linked to land scams. *Business Day* obtained the report this week through a Promotion of Access to Information application. It was handed to President Cyril Ramaphosa in March 2018.

'The government is under fire for the slow pace of land reform, which has become a major political issue. In 2018, the ANC and EFF voted in parliament to change the constitution to allow for land expropriation without compensation, arguing that it was a lack of state funds that had hampered land reform.'

The SIU probed 148 land reform projects between 2011 and 2017 and found 'major systemic weaknesses' and an alarming absence of controls and mechanisms to prevent fraud and maladministration. 'A lack of controls opened the door for so-called rent-a-crowd and other fraudulent activities on an enormous scale – with vast implications in terms of irregular and fruitless and wasteful expenditure – ultimately at the cost of taxpayers,' said Maughan.

Most of the fraudulent cases were linked to the Land Redistribution for Agricultural Development Programme which gave grants to beneficiaries to cover the costs of buying agricultural land. 'Crucially, beneficiaries were expected to stay and work on the farms they were given grants to purchase, as a way of partially paying back the money they had received,' Maughan wrote. 'But, according to the SIU, this is not what happened in a quarter of the land reform projects it investigated.'

In an analysis of the fraudulent projects, the SIU detailed how, in many instances, thousands of alleged beneficiaries 'were not even aware of the project and had never been to the farm, had never lived or worked on a farm and did not qualify for grants.

In one instance, many of the 57 people listed as the beneficiaries of a Newcastle land reform project lived 200 kilometres away in Pietermaritzburg. Several were related to a department official involved in the project.

'The Land Redistribution for Agricultural Development Programme has been suspended and replaced by the Proactive Land Acquisition Strategy sub programme, which – instead of using grants to enable black people to own land – entailed the government taking ownership of the land and leasing it to beneficiaries, with the eventual goal that they would purchase it,' Maughan reported. 'But the SIU has warned that the systemic weaknesses it has identified, including vagueness on critical issues in land reform policy and failure to follow proper procedure, still need to be addressed.'

As a result of the evidence of fraud and corruption the SIU gathered, 24 farms valued at more than R382 million had been forfeited to the state. The Asset Forfeiture Unit won court orders to freeze all activity on seven other farms, valued at R82 million, pending the outcome of applications for their permanent forfeiture.

'There has been little progress so far in prosecuting the perpetrators,' Maughan wrote. 'National Prosecuting Authority spokesman Luvuyo Mfaku said he had been advised by the prosecutor leading the state's Anti-Corruption Task Team that the majority of the alleged reform corruption cases were still under investigation, but there were a limited number on the court roll. The SIU also recommended that the Department of Land Reform take disciplinary action against the thirty-seven officials for misconduct. The department has yet to confirm if this has happened.'

THE CORRUPTION IN the land reform programme also had a deleterious impact on public conservation land. One example of environmental destruction in the Badplaas area of Mpumalanga is the Songimvelo Game Reserve . *Business Day* reporter Theto Mahlakoana went to the reserve in September 2018. 'On the rolling hills of the grassy Barberton mountains and its deep valleys is the largest provincial game reserve in Mpumalanga. The 47,000-hectare Songimvelo Nature Reserve has the highest recorded plant diversity in the province (with more than 1,400 species identified), four of the big five and 73 other mammals.

'It hosted former president Nelson Mandela in March 1992. Once an attractive tourist destination and key economic contributor to the province, the reserve is now degraded, with dilapidated infrastructure putting a stop to visits by tourists or locals.'

The Songimvelo Community Property Association's claim for the restitution of land in the reserve was gazetted in 2012. 'However, the land has not been transferred to its rightful owners and only one title deed has been issued for one of the twenty-seven farms on the land – to Msauli village nestled in a valley below the Ngwenya mountains.' The village had been transferred to the 2,500 households which claimed Songimvelo, but the 101 houses identified for tourist accommodation had been abandoned and lay empty.

Douglas Nkosi of the Community Property Association, who is suspected of helping destroy Fred's fences in 2008 and who allegedly led a team of land invaders into Songimvelo, said that he had had big dreams of economic empowerment and improved quality of life, 'but those dreams have all faded away'. With no government support to finalise their claim and to develop Msauli village, the association ran out of options. He said he was angry at the Mpumalanga Tourism and Parks Agency for 'abandoning' the reserve.

Community Property Association member July Mazibuko lamented: 'Politicians want the land for themselves. We are in desperate need of this development ... about 80 per cent of people in our communities are unemployed and it hurts to watch this big asset unused.'

The reserve, which had employed hundreds of people, had only 14 employees in 2018. The field rangers, drivers and other employees spent most of their working days languishing under trees. The condition of the animals on the reserve was unknown as the field rangers' movements were limited because only one faulty truck was operational.

In its 2016/17 annual report the Mpumalanga Tourism and Parks Agency said 'contested land claims' were negatively affecting its ability to realise the full potential of the conservation and tourism capacity in protected areas. But it stated later in the report that it had the legislative mandate and right to use, manage, preserve and develop game reserves – although Songimvelo received none of those services.

In January 2019, police officers destroyed a dagga plantation on Songimvelo and another conservation asset managed by the parks agency. They found dagga with an estimated street value of R21.9 million planted in Barberton Nature Reserve.

'It is quite shocking that Songimvelo means "we conserve",' Fred says. 'Decades of conservation efforts there have been reversed.'

IN A FEBRUARY 2020 investigation for Oxpeckers Investigative Environmental Journalism, reporter Michelle Nel discovered another hijacked community trust in Mpumalanga that was failing to distribute the fruits of land restitution to their beneficiaries. 'Details of the land claim settlement for MalaMala, one of South Africa's most exclusive and expensive game reserves, are unlikely ever to be made public after a deal was reached outside of court proceedings in 2013,' she began.

'The settlement was the largest in the country's history and saw the government pay R1.1 billion – almost R300 million more than the asking price – to the private owners of the reserve. A total of 960 claimants who had been removed from the land to make way for the reserve were listed as beneficiaries of the deal. The claimants opted not to resettle on the land, situated on the western border of the world-famous Kruger National Park, but chose instead to enter a partnership with MalaMala's ecotourism business and to benefit from jobs, profit sharing and rentals.

'MalaMala has since paid millions of rand into community accounts as a result of the deal. However, only an elite group of 250 people are benefiting from these payments, and among those who have still not received a cent are many who have died and about 500 elderly people who are surviving on government pensions.'

Angry beneficiaries claimed that the association had been 'captured' by its former treasurer Derrick Mthabine and his family, in collusion with government officials. Mthabine declined to comment. Richard Ngomane, a community elder with a doctorate in leadership from the University of Pretoria, told Oxpeckers: 'When MalaMala started paying monthly into the account of the community property association, a few individuals became greedy and devised means to oust the officially elected executive committee and replace it with an interim committee elected in secret. To our surprise, this was endorsed by the provincial department of land affairs and rural development and our lawyer.'

Claimants evicted from the association wrote to the department of rural development and land reform and President Cyril Ramaphosa. The land affairs portfolio committee was sent to investigate and reported to parliament in 2018, and again in February 2019.

The disgruntled group took the Community Property Association and the department to court in May 2017. North Gauteng High Court Judge N.V. Khumalo ordered that there be a forensic investigation into the association, that all financial statements of the MalaMala deal be made public, that its beneficiary list be verified and that the interim committee be replaced at an elective annual general meeting to be held within 60 days.

Yet, another high court judgment was ignored in Mpumalanga. Michelle Nel sought comment from the department of rural development and land reform and received no response. Her questions to the judiciary asking if action would be taken for contempt of court were also ignored.

When communities lodged claims in 2002 on 21 farms in the Sabi Sands game reserve, of which MalaMala is a part, the department decided to make them 'more streamlined and winnable. Instead of dealing with multiple landowners in the Sabi Sands game reserve, the department decided to go after the nine farms belonging to one landowner – Michael Rattray of MalaMala.'

Research on the claimants found that they became tenant labourers when private landowners moved onto the farms in the 1940s. Emeritus professor Peter Delius of the University of the Witwatersrand told Oxpeckers: 'Our research team argued very specifically in the original land claim that the group of claimants was not a true community. They had lived in settlements that overlapped farm boundaries.'

During apartheid, the claimants were evicted from the farms and settled in Bushbuckridge, which had an unemployment rate of 80 per cent. Between November 2014 and December 2017, the N'wandlamarhi Community Property Association received R36.2 million in lease payments from MalaMala. From 2014, it received R5.5 million in tourism levies – every guest at the exclusive reserve pays a levy of R125 to uplift the community. In 2017, MalaMala paid out a dividend of R40 million.

The association's lawyer Louise du Plessis, who had represented all of the original 960 beneficiaries but who now only supported the group of 250, said that the beneficiaries who were not receiving dividends should be compensated from land claims on the rest of the Sabi Sands farms. 'There are claims on other farms. Yet we [the group of 250] must now accept other people foisted on us by the Land Claims Commissioner.'

Delius, who verified the original MalaMala claims, said the outcome was a mess. 'To settle this claim out of court was mad,' he told Nel. 'The worst possible outcome is to favour one group over the other claimants. The matter needs to go back to court, and the funds should be frozen until then. MalaMala is a critical example of state capture. There should be no political interference in land claims. The MalaMala restitution should be stopped in its tracks and sent back to the Land Claims Court.'

21

Time to say goodbye

Fred wants to nourish the ancient bonds in the natural environment that bind humans to all life on earth. He aspires to teach people that they are travelling through time with all living things, sharing limited space and resources. He is keen to contribute to a healing project aimed at restoring the dignity of people, the land and their collective future.

Peace and justice are his foremost concern. He requires a stable business environment to provide opportunities for people to lift themselves out of poverty, liberated from exploitation and the abuse of authority. 'People are losing their crucial connections to nature, land and each other,' he says. 'The country's beauty, health, stability, resources and wellbeing are seeping away as it is exploited and squandered for short-term gains'.

'No businessman wants conflict with his government, but academics show how South Africa's civil service was systematically repurposed away from service delivery to benefit an elite through systematic, illegal and unethical activities and practices. A shadow state secretly and strategically co-ordinated such actions, using deployees located in significant centres of power. A distinct pattern and clear modus operandi have emerged, with mountains of evidence showing how corrupt politicians gained control of the constitutional state.

'In a modern industrialised economy like South Africa, there will always be conflict and problems. They can't be ignored or avoided, but there's a good chance they can be turned into opportunities. The first step is to correctly identify the cause – as the saying goes, a problem identified is a problem solved. The facts established should be taken to a decision maker, and if there is a will to find a solution, it can be resolved.

'Through my hard experience and the insight gained from experts, I now understand that corrupt civil servants will never support mediation and transparency. They benefit from keeping the conflict alive. They are able to litigate on a luxurious scale, with an endless supply of taxpayers' money diverted from service delivery. This causes intractable conflicts; it shatters the social contract between the government and its citizens.'

Fred appointed experts, forensic investigators and lawyers to help identify the problem that bedevilled his initiatives to protect biological diversity and develop tourism in Mpumalanga. He brought in John Allen, a communications and property expert, to engage with the civil servants mandated to protect the environment and grow tourist numbers. With his director Simon Huba, he had investors lined up and a business plan that would have provided skilled employment for his poor neighbours. It was derailed when Huba was allegedly kidnapped, locked in a safe and tortured by the police. Although he did not press charges, there is evidence of his injuries.

'I am still haunted by the events of 2008 and 2009, when there was a concerted effort to force me off the land using fake land claims and violent demonstrations, when D.D. Mabuza phoned to tell me that I must admit the land claims otherwise he couldn't guarantee my safety,' Fred says. 'It was traumatic to experience attacks in broad daylight while the police failed to protect us. After hours the lawlessness surged, tourists were held up and car windows were smashed. I had to employ armed guards to risk their lives while protecting my business and Mabuza just pulls up, climbs into the back of a bakkie, raises a loudhailer and tells a mob they can go home, he will ensure that they will get my land.

'My life was almost ruined by the plot Nomfundo Sambo dragged me into in November 2018. Had it not been for the DA employee who wrote down the registration number of her white Golf, I would have been arrested for trying to frame the deputy president for attempted murder. Captain Mathipi, who was assigned to the case, was at the restaurant where I met her when we thought she was Thandeka Mabuza. He accompanied her to the post office to confirm and sign her statement. He also made copies of her statement.

'Mathipi provided me with proof that a R700,000 payment was deposited into her account. When she was questioned, she told the police she had won the money at the Witbank casino. They investigated her claim and proved that she lied. Then Mathipi was removed from the case and I wasn't informed about her next court appearance. I wanted to give evidence to show the magistrate how serious the matter was. Sambo was granted R2,000 bail. Mathipi does not take my calls. The new investigator has never contacted me.'

In early 2019, there was a second attempt to discredit him. Gustav de Waal, who was facing criminal charges for attempting to use the shelf company Ifasa to raise funds from the government to buy Nkomazi, was central in this scheme. 'I had last heard from him in 2011 and he emerged back in my life with a bang. De Waal created a R370-million fake Eskom invoice against the Cradle of Life. It was sent to the master of the court with an application to appoint a liquidator of their choice to sequestrate me. Had they succeeded, my standing as a juristic person would have been removed and I would not have been allowed to proceed with the damages case.

'At a judicial case management meeting in May 2019, [which] arranged to ask for protection for my section 34 rights to be heard in a court of law, within a reasonable time and at a reasonable cost, Advocate André Ferreira SC told Deputy Judge President Aubrey Ledwaba that I had been sequestrated, that I should not be given a special hearing for my damages claim as I have no standing in law.'

Fred's attorney, Phillip Lessing, argued that although there had been an attempted sequestration, the provisional order was set aside by the high court and the matter was moot. Advocate Jacques Joubert told Judge Ledwaba that Fred was not obsessed with the damages claim, but had split the merits and damages issues so that the trial could focus on the merits alone. The damages could be adjudicated later. It was more important for his client to restore his reputation as an entrepreneur, Joubert said. If the trial succeeded in that respect, whether the court awarded R1 billion or R1 in damages, Fred would be satisfied. Judge Ledwaba allocated a special hearing and a trial date, starting on 27 July 2020.

The trial did not begin on schedule in the North Gauteng High Court after advocates representing Mabuza and some of the other 24 claimants objected to several issues, including Fred's standing as a plaintiff and the witnesses on his list. Mike Hellens SC, who had successfully delayed former president Jacob Zuma's corruption trial for more than a decade, is insisting that a new date be set for a 60-day hearing. Fred remains steadfast and refuses to be intimidated by their attempt to draw out the matter. A new date for the trial has not yet been established.

Fred's neighbour and partner Don Shirley, who runs a world-renowned dive site at Komati Springs, sat him down for a talk in January 2019. Says Fred, 'He told me that he knew failure was not an option for me but there comes a time when a man must give up. If I walked away, it would not be because I failed but because I was getting nowhere. He said he would not blame me if I turned my back on the project.'

'I consulted Paul O'Sullivan, he wrote a report on my situation and referred me to the Nelspruit psychiatrist Dr Brauteseth. Both experts advised that my best option was to sell up and get out of the firing line. After more than a decade of trying to resolve the disputes, I realised that the government had a front-row view of the harassment, making it too risky to do business in Mpumalanga. Dr Brauteseth booked me off from work and instructed me to get my family to safety and pull my life together.'

Leaving Mpumalanga, walking away from a project two

decades in the making, came on Fred's terms. His detractors had finally succeeded in driving him off his land, out of Badplaas and Mpumalanga. The only way the Cradle of Life could be sold was to carve it up into smaller pieces of land and offer it to more than one seller. 'This will undo the 20 years of conservation work to which I had dedicated the best part of my life.'

Fred says ANC councillor Pro Khoza, who had launched the Greater Badplaas Land Claims Committee with Mabuza, called and complained that he had left without saying goodbye. 'I laughed and asked if he was phoning because he felt guilty that so many investments and jobs were destroyed or because he was trying to find out where I was so he could continue with his harassment. I said I hadn't said goodbye because we will meet at the hearing on 27 July [2020] and we will have an opportunity to say our farewells in court. He laughed nervously and said he will phone me again so we could discuss the case.'

Fred did not leave Badplaas with enormous wealth: that had never been the plan. He amassed fond memories and a wealth of knowledge from great scientists and entrepreneurs like Sol and Butch Kerzner. 'So many people who supported the project taught me things no corrupt official can ever take away from me. I learnt from John Allen how, even in a very toxic environment, you can track down the truth and get people to open up through communication.

'Shirley helped me understand when it was time to move on. Dr Mathews Phosa inspired me, although in the end he could not help me realise the potential of the project because the problems were all political. Professor Wouter van Hoven and his postgraduate students shared their knowledge of wildlife and gave me the tools, and their management recommendations based on solid research to implement Professor Aldo Leopold's land ethic principle devised in 1949: a thing is right when it tends to preserve the integrity, stability and beauty of the biotic community.

'Professor Carl Anhaeusser of the Economic Geology Research Institute in the School of Geosciences at Wits University and many other scientists from around the world inspired me to appreciate the immense geological treasures and cultural wonders they found on their field trips. They helped me understand which sites were priceless and needed protection. Their advice guided my land acquisitions and planning to ensure that nature comes first. I am forever grateful for the integrity, trust and expert advice given to me that allowed us to achieve miracles.

'Former Mpumalanga premier Thabang Makwetla visited Nkomazi, and instead of staying for an hour as he planned, he was on the reserve for an entire day and marvelled at the project. He tried his best to help me and admitted that he failed because he never understood what informed the conflict. Johan Kruger of MultiVision sat with me for thousands of hours to capture my vision and create awe-inspiring presentations for a website where the world can see how the Cradle of Life team healed the earth to take back our future.

'Unfortunately, corruption prevented us from developing the project into a source of local, provincial, national and international pride. Mabuza stepped in to deal with me and unleashed a string of violent events and unlawful acts. I could diarise the month my permits were supposed to be renewed and predict that there would be a new drive to close down my business.'

'My life has been characterised by catastrophic environmental degradation and mass extinction, just as my school teacher Mr Hand predicted,' Fred says with a heavy sigh. Over the past four decades, all mammal, bird, fish and reptile populations have declined by 60 per cent. The world's foremost experts warn that this ecological emergency threatens the existence of many more species. The symptoms of irresponsible human activity are clear to see – rising temperatures, melting icecaps, rising sea levels, firestorms, floods and more.

'We live in a web of life that took billions of years to create,' Fred says. 'Humans depend on nature for their wellbeing, and ignore the signs that it is falling apart. It's like flying in an aeroplane with rivets that are popping free, one after another. You may travel a distance in that plane, but it's guaranteed that one of those rivets will be the last one keeping it in the air. Nature is buckling under the pressure of humans. We will reach a point, suddenly, when our damage will be irreversible. Nature is not a nice-to-have; it is the earth's life-support system and we are losing the race to keep it intact.'

Fred says he drew a line in the sand after he and Linda decided to leave Badplaas. They packed in a rush, there was no time for goodbyes, no farewell parties and no regrets. 'The conflict, over which we had no control, would disappear from our lives when we left. Our staff were shocked and traumatised and many wanted to go with us. Some of them cried and Linda and Jesse wept with them.

'We knew that the rest of our lives lay ahead, that our success lay within us. We were going to start again, build new ideas from scratch and out of nothing, which is what I do best. The years of instability held Jesse back. Despite home schooling, he lost two years of education. He is a brave child and will catch up with what corruption has stolen from him.'

The Daniel family has not been back to Badplaas since they left Mpumalanga in May 2019.

As the world went into lockdown in January 2020, scientists said the connection between environmental stress and human health was made apparent by the Covid-19 pandemic. The virus was transmitted to humans at a time when they were encroaching on nature at levels never seen before. In cities, the virus was detected on particles of pollution.

As factories and industries came to a grinding halt, pollution cleared. People in Punjab and Nairobi took photos of soaring mountains that had been hidden from view by smog. Around the world, people woke up to clear blue skies, clean waterways and wildlife in suburban streets. 'This proves that we can stem and reverse environmental degradation,' Fred says. 'The virus forced humans to pause and nature was given a chance to breathe and start the slow process of rejuvenating itself.

'The question remains: if corruption continues to corrode human morals and ethics, and our compromised behaviour is the main cause of environmental degradation, will this crisis be a turning point? When we save ourselves, the planet will rebound and we see that our wellbeing is linked to its wellbeing. Every creature plays a role in the web of life to maintain the balance we need for our survival.'

Index

013News 117

A
Above Average Trading Corporation 45 CC 135
ABSA Corporate 55
Accountability Now 173
Adnamics 9
African Boulevard 186, 188
African National Congress (ANC) 4, 13–18, 25–28, 31, 52, 73, 92, 105–114, 117, 146, 149, 151–152, 154–158, 159–191, 164–168, 178, 193, 201, 214, 221, 231
Agri Badplaas 68, 71–72
Al Capones of Mpumalanga (David Dube) 167
Ali, Jasmin 213
Allen, John 84, 118–120, 123, 136, 170, 205, 228, 231
Amajuba Public Association 187
Amajuba Tourism Association 189
ANC Youth League 26, 27, 92, 111, 164
Anhaeusser, Carl 231
Anti-Corruption Task Team 222
Arenstein, Justin 21, 22, 25, 27–30, 62–65, 67, 71–72, 109, 144, 146, 152–153
Art of War, The (Sun Tzu) 112
Asset Forfeiture Unit 222
Austria 189

B
Badplaas Development Forum 55
Badplaas ix–xi, 2, 24, 33–36, 43, 44, 49, 50–57, 59, 61–69, 71–75, 84, 85, 91, 92–96, 99, 101–102, 105, 117–123, 126, 130, 133–139, 150, 162, 169, 173, 174, 178, 179, 187, 198, 204, 207, 222, 231, 233
Badplaas Police Station 119, 123, 139, 205
Bahamas 44
BakaNkosi-Ginindza Community 100
Balfour 161
Baloyi, Paul 75
Bam, J.P. 97, 138
Baqwa family 24
Barberton Greenstone Belt 36
Barberton ix, 2, 44, 33, 35, 44, 112, 113, 119, 164, 207
Barberton Makhonjwa Transfrontier Park 40

Barberton Mountainlands 35, 36, 37, 38, 53
Barberton Mountainlands Nature Reserve 40
Barberton Nature Reserve 40, 224
Barberton police station 112
Basil Read 145, 148, 153
Bermuda 23
Bin Sulayem, Ahmed 126, 128
Blue Nightingale 147
Blyde River Canyon 22, 23, 24, 35
Boekenhoutrand 33, 35, 37, 38, 49, 51, 61, 100, 102
Bohlabela regional committee 111
Bouygues Travaux Publics 148
Brauteseth, L.T. 5–6, 228
Bryanston 9
Burgess, Chris 73
Bushbuckridge 167, 226
Business Day 34, 158, 174, 176, 219, 222
Business Venture Investments 1145 127

C

Cape Town 10, 44, 125–126, 145, 171, 176, 178
Carolina 162
Carolina Magistrate's Court 2, 72, 82, 85, 198
Carson, Rachel 7–8
Cash Converters 215
Caxton 74–75
Centre for Wildlife Management, Pretoria University 34
Chirwa, Patrick 114–115
Chiwayo, Lassy 163
Chrissiesmeer 189
Christian Democratic Party 186
Christianson, Astrid 133
City Press 2, 62, 63, 66, 111, 114, 157, 163, 207–208, 209
Cliffe Dekker Hofmeyr Attorneys 126
Cobbett, Billy 16
Coetzer, Johan 117

Commercial Crime Unit 67
Community Property Association 96, 223, 225
Constitutional Court 173–177
Cosmos Country 184, 187
Cowan, Kyle 211–212
Cradle of Life 36, 40, 71, 77–79, 82, 83, 86, 119, 120, 121, 128, 131, 169–174, 197–198, 204, 229, 231, 232
Crawford-Browne, Terry 175–176
Cronje, Sam 26

D

Daily Maverick 5
Daniel, Jesse 2–3, 127, 197–198, 205, 206, 208, 233
Daniel, Linda 2, 3, 14, 45, 56, 66, 127, 140, 195, 197, 206, 208, 211
David Mabuza Foundation 112
De Beer, Colonel 205–206
De Waal, Gustav 133–136, 139, 229
De Wet, Koos 80
Delius, Peter 51, 100–102, 226
Delphis 22
Denel, Frank 171
Department of Agriculture and Land Affairs 39, 49, 50, 51, 52, 53, 59, 68, 69, 92, 96, 115, 149, 165
Department of Cooperative Governance and Traditional Affairs 161
Department of Culture, Sports and Recreation 154
Department of Education 16, 165, 210
Department of Environmental Affairs 24, 172
Department of Finance and Economic Development 202
Department of Health 166
Department of Housing 16, 113
Department of Human Settlements 116

Department of Land Affairs 64, 67, 68, 93–94, 99, 100, 149, 199, 225
Department of Land Reform 222
Department of Public Works 162–163, 220
Department of Roads and Transport 165, 166
Department of Rural Development and Land Reform 201, 225
Department of Safety and Security 171
Department of Water Affairs and Forestry 153, 169, 171
Development Bank of Southern Africa 75, 127, 157
Dhlomo Dhlomo Community 96
Didiza, Thoko 65–67, 69, 98
Dladla, Jacob 144–149, 151, 152, 161
Dlamini-Zuma, Nkosazana 108
Dolphin Group 22–31, 33, 130, 159, 163
Doornhoek 63, 91
Dos Santos, Fabiano 'Josh' 164
Doyershoek 53
Dreyer, Willem 132–134, 137
Du Plessis, Louise 226
Duarte, Jessie 214
Dubai 23, 125–126
Dubai World 125–132, 134–140, 169, 179, 198, 201
Dubai World Africa 126–128
Dubai World Africa Conservation 127
Dube, David 166–168
Dutton, Frank 206

E
Ebersohn, Piet 122
Ecolife 140
Economic Geology Research Institute, School of Sciences, Wits University 231
Eerie Assignment (Sizwe sama Yende) 2, 159
Ehlanzeni District Municipality 167

eHlanzeni regional committee 111
Elliot, Nick 213, 215
Ellis, Patrick 163
Elukwatini 31
Elukwatini Guardian 120
Emakhazeni 163
Engelschedraai 62, 65, 91
Ermelo 162, 183, 185–187, 188, 190, 193–194
Ermelo police station 192
Ernst & Young 66–68, 72, 91, 93
Eskom 10, 229

F
Fairview Investment Trust 9
Farmer's Weekly 63, 72–75
Fenetic Investments 25, 28
Ferreira, André 4, 179–180, 229
Financial Mail 125, 127
First National Bank 152
Fluorspar Valley Mine 9
Forever Resort 136

G
Gamede, Andries 164
Gazankulu 15
Gebrekidan, Selam 16, 106–108
Germany 189
Gert Sibande District Municipality 164, 194
Gibb, Chris 152
Gilfillan, Durkje 23
Gobodo Inc. 29
God's Window 35
Goedehoop 102
Govender, Nelson 4
Govender, Prega 68
Government Gazette 50, 59, 99, 101
Grand Valley Estates 35, 39, 43, 47, 49, 53–56, 63, 74, 78, 128, 131
Grass and Wetlands 184, 187, 190
Gray, Alan 22, 25–27, 29
Great Cats in Crisis South Africa 82
Great Nkomazi River Valley 35
Greater Badplaas Land Claims

Committee 117, 120, 122, 123, 137, 170, 199, 231
Greater Barberton Mountainlands Conservancy 40
Greenpeace 10
Griffiths, Derrick 64, 67–68, 71–73, 91
Grobler, Hennie 110
Groenvallei 61
Grootkop 91
Guardian yase Mpumalanga 133
Guernsey 23
Gwanya, Tozi 64, 68, 72, 92, 147

H
Hanks, John 22
Harper, Paddy 110
Hawks 139, 201, 205, 208–211, 216
Hay, Michelle 51, 100–102
Hazyview 161
Healing of the Earth 35
Heath, Willem x, 129–130
Hellens, Mike 5, 209, 214, 230
Henry Nxumalo Grant xi
Heuer, Kenneth 82–84
Heyns, Marius 153
Highveld Heritage Route 184, 189
Highveld Tourism 187, 189
Hlathi, Leonard 113
Hlmuhlumu Mountains 35
Hoffman, Paul 173–175, 205
Huba, Simon 126, 228

I
Idasa 26
Imperial Bank 73, 75
Inkaleni Land Owners Association 126
integrity management unit 115, 162, 165
Investment for Agricultural Sustainability in Africa (Ifasa) 135–139, 140, 227
Inwoners Organisasie (INWO) 186
Istithmar 126, 178

J
Japan 9
Jatropha biodiesel project 133–134
Jenkins, Paul 74
Johannesburg Magistrate's Court 8
Josh *see Dos Santos, Fabiano*
Joubert, Jacques 178–180, 230

K
Kabokweni 161
KaNgwane homeland 14, 16, 22, 34, 102
KaNyamazane 151–152
Kees Zyn Doorns 708 JT 96–97
Kennet, Tony 53–54, 65
Kenya 9, 22–23
Kerzner Group 45–46
Kerzner International 44–47, 75, 77, 125, 126
Kerzner, Butch 45, 46, 97, 125, 231
Kerzner, Sol 44, 229
Khanye, Victor 14
Khoza, P.M. 112–113, 117
Khoza, Pro 119–124, 170–171, 231
Khumalo, Livion 118–119
Khumalo, N.V. 223
Khwezi (Redi Tlhabi) 212
Komati River 33, 35, 40, 57, 78, 127, 129, 172, 230
Komati Springs 40, 57, 230
Kriel, Jan 109–110
Kruger National Park 35, 40, 126, 224
Kruger, Johan 230
Krugersdorp 82
Kuzwayo, Fezekile 212
Kwaliweni claimant community 101–102
KwaZulu-Natal 35, 184

L
Labour Court 29, 145
Land Claims Commission 43, 46, 49, 61, 62, 63, 65, 66, 67, 68, 69, 71, 72, 91–101, 123, 124, 125, 127, 128, 133–135, 137, 138, 169, 179, 201

Land Claims Court 2, 50, 97, 98, 99, 101, 127, 134, 226
Land Redistribution for Agricultural Development Programme 221–222
Languedoc 61
Le Roux, Jean 211–212
Lebeya, Godfrey 209
Lebowa 15, 27
Ledwaba, Aubrey 4, 18, 209, 229–230
Ledwaba, Sylvia 209
Lefika Emerging Equity 144–146, 148, 149, 152
Leopold, Aldo 231
Lessing, Phillip 230
Life Form Taxidermy 84
Lloyd, Charles 79, 82
Lodge, Tom 15
London 10, 22, 24
Loskop Dam 22–24, 220
Lotter, Altus 172
Louw, Chris 72–75
Lowveld Valuators 56
Lowvelder, The 118, 123
Luthuli House 214
Lydenburg 83, 161

M

Mabena, Jacob 28
Maboa, Harry 97
Mabona, Steve 15, 18, 27–28, 164, 187
Mabuza family 101
Mabuza, Thandeka 204–211, 229
Machadodorp 119, 121, 207, 208, 210
Macleod, Fiona 220
Madonsela, Thuli 220
Maduna, Patrick 23
Magashule, Ace 177
Mahlakoana, Theto 222
Mahlalela, Fish 107, 168
Mahlangu, Jabu 187, 190, 192
Mahlangu, Johannes 27, 29
Mahlangu, Ndaweni 17, 88, 109, 185

Mahumapelo, Supra 177
Mail & Guardian 5, 10, 22, 64, 65, 71, 73, 109, 110, 111, 112, 113, 152, 154, 156, 212, 220
Maine, Bruce 131–132
Majolo Trust 121
Makamo, Raymond 162
Makhaya, Nkosana 68
Makhonjwa Mountains 35, 40
Makinde, Shukrat 85
Makola, Charles 165
Makwetla, Thabang 159, 187, 232
Makwetu, Kimi 13–14
MalaMala 224–226
Malolotja Nature Reserve 40
Malomane, Ronnie 110–111
Malukela, Dolphin 153
Mandela, Nelson 13, 114, 223
Manuel, Trevor 25
Manyeleti Game Reserve 24
Maphanga, Sonnyboy 96
Markinor 26
Masai Mara Game Reserve 22
Maseko Community 100
Mashego-Dlamini, K.C. 144, 147–148
Mashile, Bheki 133–134, 177
Masilela, January 28
Masina family 100
Masuku, Dumisile 204, 206–207, 209, 210
Mathekga, Ralph 109
Mathipi, Captain 229
Matotoland Ecotourism Association 190
Matsafeni 144–151, 153, 156–157
Matsafeni Trust 144, 146–148, 153
Maughan, Karyn 221–222
Mauritius 44
Mavundla, Moses 150
Mbatha, Linda 66–69
Mbeki, Thabo 16, 29, 30–31, 64, 71, 160, 162, 212
Mbete, Baleka 17–18
Mboa, Harry 92

Mbombela Municipality 143–158, 159, 161, 163–164, 206
McCain Foods 94
McCarthy, Leonard 212
McKinley, Dale x, 36, 52, 143–144, 148, 150, 152, 154–158
Mdlalose, Fikile 190
Mdluli, Phineas 149
Merchant Bank 55
Merten, Marianne 5
Mfaku, Luvuyo 222
Mgwenya College of Education 109
Mhangwani, Peter 97, 99
Mhaule, Reginah 109
Mhlabane, Jabu 109
Middel, Jappie 72
Midlands Meander 184
Millennium Trust xi
Milly's 208, 210–211
Mkhatshwi, Obert 169
Mkhondo Tourism Association 187
Mkhwanazi, David 22, 23–26, 28, 31, 159, 178
Mlimi, Victor 164
Mnisi, Chief 121
Mnisi, Nonhlanhla Patience 154
Mnisi, Richard 166
Mntambo, Fanyana 171
Modipane, Jacques 25–27, 31, 88, 159, 166, 178
Modise, Joe 28
Mogale, Differ 144–148
Mohlala, Bonnie 152
Mohlala, Jimmy 144, 148–149, 151–152, 154–155
Mohlala, Tshepiso 152
Mohlasedi, Kgopana 166
Moldenhauer Commission 17
Mopotu, Jean 28
Morema, Milton 167
Mosidi, Solly 129
Motaung, Bobby 145, 149
Motheo Construction 16
Motshekga, Angie 214
Moukangwe, Botsotso 205–206, 208

Mozambique 26, 35, 155, 164
Mpatlanyane, Sammy 154
Mphego, Mulangi 209–212
Mphela, Blessing 150
Mpshe, Mokotedi 212
Mpumalanga Community Survey 114
Mpumalanga Department of Agriculture and Land Affairs 39, 49, 92, 135
Mpumalanga Department of Environmental Affairs 172
Mpumalanga Department of Home Affairs 34
Mpumalanga Department of Land Affairs 34
Mpumalanga Department of Public Works 220
Mpumalanga Department of Safety and Security 171
Mpumalanga Department of Water Affairs 169, 172
Mpumalanga Land Claims Commission 66, 69, 72, 96, 98, 99, 100, 125, 127, 138
Mpumalanga Parks Board 21–23, 25, 27, 29, 35, 37, 38, 40, 43–46, 61, 66, 77, 184
Mpumalanga regional Land Claims Commission 67
Mpumalanga Rural Housing Project 16
Mpumalanga Tourism and Parks Agency 31, 77, 80, 81, 83, 84, 85, 87, 117, 118, 124, 125, 128, 132, 140, 141, 166, 169, 173, 178, 179, 185, 187, 189, 190, 193, 198, 201, 220, 223, 224
Mpungose, Khayalihle 150
Msauli 45–47, 223
Msukaligwa local municipality 14, 166, 185, 193
Msukaligwa Tourism Organisation 188
Mthabine, Derrick 225
Mthembi-Mahanyele, Sankie 16
Mthembu Jackson 17, 155, 165

Mthembu, Thandi 171
Mthethomusha Nature Reserve 40
Mufamadi, Lucas 123, 134
Mulaudzi, Hangwani 139
Muller, Alice 14
Muller, Jan 47, 79, 80, 83–84, 87, 88, 89, 131, 198
MultiVision 232
Municipal IQ 162

N

N'wandlamarhi Community Property Association 226
Nairobi 23, 231
Namaqualand 9
Namibian, The 134
National Assembly 13, 17, 105, 107, 109
National Environmental Management Act 170
National Party 16, 24
National Prosecuting Authority 2, 29, 157, 216, 222
National Treasury 148
National Water Act 171
Natives Land Commission 51
Ncongwane, Josia 96
Ndabeni, Charles 80, 85, 86, 88
Ndamase, Ndayeni 79
Ndlovu, Johan 167
Ndlovu, Thandi 16
Nduli, Terry 147
Ndwandwa 64–66, 69, 72, 75, 91–99, 118, 123–124, 133–139, 150, 173
Ndwandwa Community Trust 66, 72, 91–95, 99, 118, 124, 134, 136–139
Neilson, Mike 178
Nel, Michelle 224–226
Nelson, Alan 178
Nelspruit Regional Court 27, 79, 139, 211, 212
Nelspruit *see Mbombela*
Netshiozwi, T.G. 85
New York 10

New York Times 16, 106, 107, 108, 109, 113
Newcastle 222
Ngcuka, Bulelani 29, 212
Ngomane, Richard 225
Ngomane, Thomas 171
Ngwenya Mountains 223
Ngwenya, Thami 22
Nhlabathi family 100
Nkambule, James 25, 26–31, 156, 157, 163–164
Nkomazi local municipality 111
Nkomazi Wilderness Reserve iv, 6, 36–39, 45–47, 49, 53–55, 60–61, 77–78, 80–81, 92, 97, 118, 128, 180–181, 216
Nkosi, Douglas 118, 119, 122, 223
Nkosi, Mangiai J. 91, 93, 118, 124, 134, 136, 137, 138, 139
Nkosi, Mfana 146
Nkosi, Orex 170
Nkosi, Robert 91, 93, 94, 95, 99, 133, 136, 137, 138, 173
Nkosi, Thokozane 185
Nkosi, Ziyanda 106
Nkuna, Welcome 113, 162
Nkwinika, Priscilla 162, 163
North Gauteng High Court 2, 3, 74, 86, 94, 124, 135, 138, 146, 150, 177, 178, 208, 225, 230
Noseweek 177
Nqana, Nceba 46, 55, 59, 61–65, 67, 68, 69, 73, 96
Nsibande, Justice 144, 146
Nxumalo, Henry 211
Nyalunga, Ian 208
Nyoni, Peter 112
Nyundu, Mxolisi 11

O

O.R. Tambo International Airport 211
O'Sullivan, Paul x, 69–70, 86–89, 95–96, 139, 166, 204–206, 208–210, 230

Odendaal, Ferdinand 139
Ogies 161
Okavango Bio Energy 133
One&Only 44, 47, 75, 77, 97, 125, 127
Onishi, Norimitsu 16, 106–108
Onverwacht 62, 91
Orange River 9
Oxpeckers Investigative Environmental Journalism 224–226

P
Pacific Breeze Trading 474 163
Padayachee, Craig 187
Paperbark 127, 135
Paranie Nature Reserve 40
Peace Parks Foundation 40
Phakamani Security Services 26
Phambili Construction 27
Phola Trust 109, 207, 208, 209, 210, 212
Phosa, Mathews 15–18, 26–31, 33, 109, 162, 200–201, 202, 203, 204, 213–215, 231
Pienaar, Gert 139
Piet Retief 187, 189
Pietermaritzburg 222
Pilanesburg National Park 45
Pilgrim's Rest 24, 35, 45, 220
Pixley ka Seme Municipality 189
Platinum Sport 145, 146
Polokwane conference 106, 160
Premier's Bursary Fund 167
Pretoria High Court 209, 215
Prevention of Organised Crime Act 210
Prime Investment Holdings 134
Problem Animal Fund 86, 87
Promotion of Access to Information Act (PAIA) 98, 221
Protected Areas Act 78
Punjab 233

R
Radebe, Jeff 129

Ramaphosa, Cyril 29, 30, 31, 108, 109, 114
Randburg 2, 45
Rattray, Michael 223
Regenstreich, Moshe 25, 28
Reserve Bank 25
Restitution of Land Rights Act 49, 61, 98, 101, 128
Revelas, Elna 29
Rhino and Lion Park 82, 84
Rhodes University 8
Richtersveld 9
Right2Know x
Roesch family 97–98
Rootman, Pieter 27, 28
Roses Guns 215
Rous 102
Roux, Albert 56–57
Russia 158, 209, 211

S
Sabi Sands farms 226
Sabi Sands Game Reserve 126, 225
Sabie 35, 161
Sambo, Nomfundo 210–212, 229
Scorpions 28, 29, 109, 110, 210
Seboka, Tumi 136, 137
Secunda 190
Secunda Guesthouse Association 187, 189
Sedibe, Collen 113
Selebi, Jackie 212
Seriti Commission 176
Sexwale, Tokyo 29, 30
Shabangu, Sabelo 146
Shabangu, Sarah 146, 153
Shamwari Game Reserve 131
Sheraton Hotel 214
Shirley, Don 230, 231
Sibande, Gert 111, 164, 194
Sibiya, Abe 45–46, 64, 73, 118
Sibiya, Vusi 147
Sibonda, Sigananda 164
Sibuyi, Khelina 153
Silent Spring (Rachel Carson) 7

Silinda, Ruth Funi 162
Sisulu, Albertina 214
Sithole, Faith 110
Sithole, Mabutho 30, 164
Sithole, Nelisiwe 115
Sivukile Tourism Organisation 187, 188
Sizwangendaba 115
Skhosana, Steve 91–92
Skimmelfontein 61
Small-Smith, Ian 4, 214–215
Soccer World Cup 30, 125, 130, 156, 161, 174
Somalanga 26
Songimvelo Community Property Association 118, 122
Songimvelo Game Reserve 22, 26, 40, 45, 46, 118, 127, 220, 222
South African Defence Force 8, 28
South African Police Services 123
South African Revenue Service 152
South African War 184
Sowetan 115, 162
Special Investigating Unit 2, 25, 221
Spoor, Richard 49–53, 56, 59, 61–63, 66, 72–73, 78–79, 82, 85–86, 92–93, 96–98, 123, 146, 149
Standerton 161
Stark, Athol 183
Stark, Melinda 191, 192, 193, 195
Steiltes 213
Sterkspruit 54, 56, 61, 101, 103, 131
Stolzburg 49, 51, 53, 54, 102, 131
Sun City 45
Sun Hotel Group 44
Sun International 44
Sunday Times 68, 154, 155
Sunday Tribune 138
Swanepoel Boerdery Trust 56
Swanepoel, L.M.P. 53–54, 57
Swaziland 35, 40, 51
Switzerland 189

T

Thababa, David 171
Theeboom 49, 51, 100, 101, 102

Theta Gold Mines 220
Tiba, Delani 45
Tlhabi, Redi 212
Tolmay, Ronel 172–173
Tourism Indaba 187
Transnet 126
Transvaal Game Parks 21
Travelport 40, 119

U

Umkhonto weSizwe (MK) 8, 16, 111
United Arab Emirates 125
United Democratic Movement 186
University of Cape Town 176, 178
University of Pretoria 34, 225
University of South Africa 109
University of the Witwatersrand 51, 100, 226, 231

V

V&A Waterfront 125, 126
V8 Cattle Ranch 60
Vaalkop 63
Vaderland, Die 73
Van der Walt, Izak 154
Van der Westhuizen, Egbert 110
Van Hoven, Wouter 34, 140, 231
Van Niekerk, Anna Sophia 101
Van Niekerk, Hester Maria 101
Van Niekerk, Ockert Tobias 101
Van Schalkwyk, Nico 131
Venice 10
Venter, Ansie 82
Venter, J.G. 136
Venter, Jan 213–216
Vergelegen 100
Vermeulen, Johannes 120–121
Vilakazi, Captain 205
Visagie, Pieter 53–56, 60, 65, 67, 69, 72, 73, 75, 91–96, 123, 133, 137, 139, 199
Visagie, Riaan 172
Volksrust 161, 187
Vriesland 102
Vygeboom 54, 55, 59, 60, 61, 63, 67, 95

W
Welgelegen 49, 51
Wensing, Dick 35, 38, 61, 80–81
Western Cape High Court 176
White Mischief 22
White River 53, 84
Wilderness Game Farm 97
Wilson, James 126–127, 128–130, 132
Wine Route 184
Winkelhaak 61
Wits Journalism Department xi

X
Xaba, Nyameka 205, 208

Y
Yende, Sizwe sama 2, 111–112, 114–115, 157, 159, 160–161, 163, 167, 204, 205, 206, 209, 210, 216
Young Communist League 118

Z
Zambia 9
Zenani, Nana 67
Zitha, Mangisi 26
Zondo Commission of Inquiry into Allegations of State Capture 2, 14, 204, 205, 216
Zondo, Raymond 5
Zuma, Duduzane 158
Zuma, Jacob x, 4–5, 28, 106, 107, 108, 158, 165, 166, 173, 174–175, 176, 177, 212, 214

We thank the following for their support in publishing this book:

Arthur Goldstuck
Ashwin Moyene
Ben Williams
Beverley Naidoo
Carolyn Raphaely
Catriona Jarvis
Corinne Rosmarin
Denis Hirson
Dianne Stewart
Gill Bolton
Glen Impey
Graeme Friedman
Helen Douglas
James Bissett
Karin Pampallis

Kevin Ritchie & Associates
Louis Gaigher
Maeve King
Mamma Jacqui
Mary Burton
Michelina Giacovazzi
Moira Levy
Roger Southall
Rona V van Niekerk
Ryan Childs
Sebastian Seedorf
Steven Dubin
Sue Grant-Marshall
Trisha Cornelius